HEADING HOME:
OFFENDER REINTEGRATION
INTO THE FAMILY

THESE PAPERS INITIALLY WERE PRESENTED AT THE
ANNUAL RESEARCH CONFERENCE OF THE INTERNATIONAL
COMMUNITY CORRECTIONS ASSOCIATION, HELD SEPTEMBER
23-26, 2001 IN PHILADELPHIA, PENNSYLVANIA, AND HAVE
BEEN UPDATED FOR THIS VOLUME.

VIVIAN L. GADSDEN
DIRECTOR, NATIONAL CENTER ON FATHERS AND FAMILIES
UNIVERSITY OF PENNSYLVANIA, PHILADELPHIA, PENNSYLVANIA
EDITOR

Mission
The American Correctional Association provides a professional organization for all individuals and groups, both public and private, that share a common goal of improving the justice system.

American Correctional Association Staff
Charles Kehoe, President
James A. Gondles, Jr., CAE, Executive Director
Gabriella M. Daley, Director, Communications and Publications
Harry Wilhelm, Marketing Manager
Alice Heiserman, Manager of Publications and Research
Michael Kelly, Associate Editor
Dana M. Murray, Graphics and Production Manager
Michael Selby, Graphics and Production Associate

ICCA Executive Director: Peter Kinziger
ICCA President: Donald Evans

Cover design by Michael Selby

Copyright 2003 by the American Correctional Association. All rights reserved. The reproduction, distribution, or inclusion in other publications of materials in this book is prohibited without prior written permission from the American Correctional Association. No part of this book may be reproduced by any electronic means, including information storage and retrieval systems, without permission in writing from the publisher.

Printed in the United States of America by Graphic Communications, Inc., Upper Marlboro, MD.

ISBN 1-56991-165-7

This publication may be ordered from:
American Correctional Association
4380 Forbes Boulevard
Lanham, MD 20706-4322
1-800-222-5646

For information on publications and videos available from ACA, contact our worldwide web home page at: http://www.aca.org

Contact the ICCA home page at: http://www.ICCAWEB.org

Library of Congress Cataloging-in-Publication Data

    Heading home : offender reintegration into the family / Vivian L. Gadsden, editor.

    p. cm.

    "Most of the chapters in this volume were presented as papers in a special research strand of the annual meeting of the International Community Corrections Association in the Fall of 2001"–Pref.

    Includes bibliographical references and index.

Contents: Introduction / Vivian L. Gadsden – Parent education for incarcerated parents: understanding "what works" / Glen F. Palm – Linking father involvement and parental incarceration: concepts and contexts for considering "what works" – Families, prisoners and community reentry: a look at issues and programs / Creasie Finney Hairston – What works: children of incarcerated offenders / Denise Johnston – What works in the treatment of family violence in correctional populations: issues and directions / Lynn Stewart and Natalie Gabora-Roth – Afterword / Vivian L. Gadsden.

    ISBN 1-56991-165-7

1. Prisoners—United States—Family relationships—Congresses. 2. Prisoners' families—Government policy—United States—Congresses. 3. Prisoners' families—Services for—United States—Congresses. 4. Prisoners—Rehabilitation—United States—Congresses. 5. Community-based corrections—United States—Congresses. 6. Recidivism—United States—Prevention—Congresses. I. Title: Offender reintegration into the family—What Works. II. Gadsden, Vivian L. III. International Community Corrections Association. Research Conference (2001 : Philadelphia, Pa.)

HV8886.U6.H43 2003

365'.6—dc21

                                                                                        2002043873

TABLE OF CONTENTS

Foreword
    James A. Gondles, Jr., CAE vii

Preface
    Peter Kinziger ix

Chapter 1

Corrections, Families, and Communities: Coping With Incarceration, Absence, Reentry, and Reintegration
    Vivian L. Gadsden 1

Chapter 2

Families, Prisoners, and Community Reentry: A Look at Issues and Programs
    Creasie Finney Hairston, Ph.D. 13

Chapter 3

Linking Father Involvement and Parental Incarceration: Concepts and Contexts for Considering "What Works"
    Vivian L. Gadsden
    R. Karl Rethemeyer 39

Chapter 4

Parent Education for Incarcerated Parents: Understanding "What Works"
    Glen F. Palm 89

Chapter 5
What Works: Children of Incarcerated Offenders
> Denise Johnston 123

Chapter 6
What Works in the Treatment of Family Violence in Correctional Populations: Issues and Directions
> Lynn Stewart
> Natalie Gabora-Roth 155

Chapter 7
The Viability of Mentoring as a Correctional Strategy: A Look at "What Works"
> Betsy A. Matthews 205

Chapter 8
What Works in Faith-based Programming
> Chris Carr
> Dwight Cuff
> David Molzahn 241

Afterword
> Vivian L. Gadsden 269

Index 275

About the Authors 291

FOREWORD

There is a perception among much of the public that when a crime is committed and the offender is caught and locked up, we can say, "job well done," and that is the end of the story. Well, those in corrections know that is not the end of the story. In fact, it is just the beginning. The vast majority of offenders are released eventually. Sadly, by some estimates, more than 60 percent of these individuals will break the law again and be arrested. The problem of recidivism is enormous, and too often our best efforts are frustrated by its impact. Crime prevention is a major responsibility of criminal justice, and correctional practitioners can prevent crime by working to find ways to reduce reoffending. Treatment programs to help offenders transition back into their communities and families when they are released are powerful weapons for fighting recidivism.

Heading Home: Offender Reintegration into the Family is the latest book in the "What Works" series from the American Correctional Association (ACA) and the International Community Corrections Association (ICCA). This collection of essays introduces readers to innovative practices throughout the United States and Canada that consider the offender's family, particularly the children, as an integral part of the offender's treatment program. The book looks at such topics as parenting education, father involvement, family violence, faith-based programming, and mentoring from a perspective that sees incarceration as not just affecting the offender, but also having an impact on families and entire communities.

Adjusting to life after incarceration can be a huge challenge for the offender and the family. Preserving or reestablishing family bonds can help make that adjustment smoother and mean the difference between recidivism or successful reentry. In addition to this book, ACA is in the early stages of developing a parenting education curriculum for offenders. We hope this book will go a long way toward making corrections more effective.

James A. Gondles, Jr., CAE
Executive Director
American Correctional Association

Preface

Who could have predicted just ten-short-years ago that the successful reentry of offenders would begin to focus on family support systems, mentoring, children of offenders, parenting, faith and community-based support systems, and the reduction of family violence. Still, that is where we find ourselves today. The examination of "what works" has led us to understand that the road to successful reentry resides with creating and maintaining an environment that will support an offender returning to the community after incarceration. Successful reentry is more complicated than fixing the offender. Family, community and other supports are as necessary as the treatment programs offered to change criminal behavior. Who would have thought this ten years earlier?

In the past, community corrections practitioners came together and discussed the state of their profession. Invariably the discussion would turn to the question of why community corrections did not receive the same financial support that prisons and jails enjoyed. Prisons were expensive and did not work. Community corrections programs were relatively inexpensive and they worked. Why then didn't the community side of corrections earn the same support as its institutional cousins?

Most people working in the field understood the benefits of reintegrating an offender into the community after a period of incarceration. Who could argue that an offender being released from prison or jail would not benefit from the support of a halfway house or day treatment center? Didn't every offender need time to find employment and affordable housing? Didn't all offenders need to develop new community ties and to save money to support them to live independently? Didn't offenders need assistance finding community treatment services to help them deal with their addictions and criminal lifestyles? After all, what were the alternatives?

As a society, could we expect offenders reentering our communities to succeed without benefit of food, housing, employment, treatment, relationships, and support while under the watchful eye of a justice system waiting for them to make a mistake? Wouldn't most pro-social individuals, under the same circumstance, struggle to succeed without benefit of a structured support system? The alternatives then suggest that without the benefit of good community correctional programs, the offender will fail. The result would manifest itself in the form of higher crime, more victimization, and greater costs to society.

Ten years earlier it was reasoned that policymakers needed to be informed of the facts. Once the facts were known, additional funding would be made available for community corrections. To practitioners, the facts were clear. Community corrections worked. It reduced recidivism. It changed offender behavior. It gave an offender a new start in life. Besides, it was less expensive than incarceration and more successful than straight probation or parole.

To influence policymakers, evidence was needed to demonstrate that community corrections worked. Community corrections advocates did not have the evidence. What was obvious to practitioners was not obvious in the literature. The evidence that practitioners thought was there was not. Or, if it did exist, it was not in the format useful to make arguments for the expansion of community corrections.

In the early 1990s, the International Community Corrections Association (ICCA) brought practitioners together to explore the state of evidence-based research. As a group, we knew little about applied research. It was assumed that someone, somewhere had been conducting the studies needed to prove the value of community corrections. There was a feeling that while there might have been some research out there to support community corrections, there was probably a need to engage universities to do more work in the area. There was an erroneous perception that new research could be easily and quickly commissioned.

Needless to say, we were badly mistaken. Evidence to practitioners and evidence to researchers are worlds apart. Just as practitioners feel that their work with offenders is not understood, it became obvious that practitioners did not understand the complexities of academic studies. The kind of evidence practitioners need takes time to collect and money to support.

It was at these initial meetings where we began to learn that, in fact, there was a substantial body of research supportive of effective interventions. However, this body of research looked much different than most people realized. It did not say that community corrections worked. It did not show that halfway houses or day treatment or probation worked. Instead, it broke down human service practices into smaller components. We were soon to learn that some things work for some offenders some of the time, some things work for most offenders most of the time, and some things just do not work in spite of our professional opinions.

At this point, the ICCA began its explorations of "what works." The first "What Works" Research Conference was held in Philadelphia, in 1993. Nine years later, ICCA returned to Philadelphia still exploring "what works" but with an agenda that could not have been imagined a decade earlier.

What have we learned and what more is to be learned?

In general, we have learned more than we had bargained for. We now understand why punishment and incarceration do not work. We have gained an understanding of why supervision alone does not work. We have learned what offender treatment really is and what treatment is not. We learned that many of the current practices that were thought to work on offenders in fact, do not work and why they do not work.

At times, the learning has been difficult and hard to accept. A Pandora's box of sorts has emerged from the study of "what works." By opening the box, practitioners are confronted with having to work with offenders differently than they had in the past. Offender treatment became more complicated and clinical. The learning and the demands upon correctional providers increased dramatically.

A science of effective interventions and offender's assessments are now a necessary prerequisite to operating programs that deliver "treatment effect." The science of effective interventions also tells us that the treatment of offenders is a task beyond the scope of the correctional professional alone. Correctional professionals, while critically important, cannot assume full responsibility for the successful reintegration of offenders into communities. They can drive treatment, help to reestablish community and family ties, support the offender for the short term and perhaps provide relapse protections, but they cannot assume the roles of the family and community.

The chapters found in this volume are examples of how far we have come in terms of understanding "what works" but how far away we are from implementing effective reintegration systems for offenders in our communities. After reading the following chapters, it should become obvious that the successful reintegration of offenders into the community will be greatly enhanced by connecting the offender with family, community, and mentors. Could it be that the "what works" literature is telling us that it takes a whole community to reintegrate an offender?

Who could have imagined just ten-short-years ago that the successful reentry of offenders would begin to focus on family support systems, mentoring, children of offenders, parenting, faith and community-based support systems? In many ways, the treatment of offenders has become more complicated, but in many ways, it is beginning to make sense.

I hope that you learn from the many contributions found in this volume as I have. I want to thank the authors for their work and dedication to the publication as well as for their ongoing efforts in bringing to light the issues presented in their papers. Finally, I want to thank Dr. Vivian Gadsden for chairing the conference and editing the publication. It has been my pleasure working with her. Her work and dedication are greatly appreciated.

>Peter Kinziger
>Executive Director
>International Community Corrections Association

CORRECTIONS, FAMILIES, AND COMMUNITIES: COPING WITH INCARCERATION, ABSENCE, REENTRY AND REINTEGRATION

1

Vivian L. Gadsden
Associate Professor, Graduate School of Education
University of Pennsylvania
Philadelphia, Pennsylvania

The heightened attention given to incarceration and its effects within the past decade comes at a critical time in the larger discussion of children, families, and communities and in the ongoing debates around poverty, equity, and access to opportunity that expose disproportionate numbers of children and families to hardship. Long examined primarily within criminal justice and corrections literatures, incarceration and the attendant issues of recidivism and reentry have been integrated into discourses among researchers, practitioners, and policymakers concerned with the well-being and welfare of children and families—from social services, to education, to public policy.

Like their colleagues in corrections who have struggled with little support for countless years, this expanding body of child, family, and community specialists is acutely aware of the fact that the incarceration of a single human being does not have an isolated impact. The road to the reintegration of offenders—many of whom were family and community members prior to incarceration—may be a singularly difficult transition, requiring an understanding of tensions within home and community settings pre- and postincarceration. It is a transition that involves the offender, family, and community and necessitates the consent and will of all three to set and negotiate their roles, expectations, and behavioral parameters.

The focus of this volume—incarceration, reentry, and reintegration within families and communities—is intended to address the need for an interdisciplinary and cross-domain effort that seriously examines problems faced not only by offenders and ex-offenders but also by the children, families, and communities that they leave behind and into whose lives they seek to re-enter. The chapters are written by researchers and other specialists representing diverse disciplinary, research, and practice backgrounds in corrections, families, parenting, and public policy. Each provides critical perspectives and analyses on the complexities of prison-to-home transitions and the ways in which the problems of absence, poverty, economics, employment limitations, poor schooling, and race intersect to complicate the process of reentry and reduce the quality of the transition. This is particularly true in minority communities that have experienced the most severe erosion of social and human capital resulting from incarceration and that have restricted resources to facilitate the transition.

The Issues and Context for the Volume

Data on the number of incarcerated adults and the percentage of those who are parents paint a compelling and troubling picture. During the past decade alone, there has been a substantial increase in the number of parents in state and federal prisons: from 452,500 to 737,400 an increase of 63 percent; the number of affected children has risen from 936,500 to 1,531,500 an increase of 69 percent. Recent data estimate the incarceration rate in the United States at about 7 percent, second only to Russia (Western and McLanahan, 2000; U.S. Department of Justice, 1999). More than 5 million adults in the United States are under the supervision of the criminal justice system; more than 1.9 million of these adults are in prisons or jails (Beck, 2000). Nearly 59 percent of women in federal prisons and 65 percent of women in state prisons are mothers of children under eighteen years of age. Well over 90 percent of incarcerated adults are men, and more than 63 percent of men in federal prisons and nearly 55 percent of men in state prisons are fathers of children under eighteen years of age (Mumola, 2000). More than two-thirds of inmates will be re-arrested within three years of their release.

With every re-arrest, questions about the problems that lead to recidivism are raised. Are such re-arrests the result of narrow views about, inadequate attention to, and/or poor policies on reintegration? Some argue that they are, in large part, the residual effect of limited understanding of the dimensions of the problems faced by ex-offenders and their families, poorly conceptualized transitional approaches, incomplete or inept analyses of unintended consequences of policies and laws, and differential laws at state levels; such laws often fail to consider the long-term implications for communities and frequently appear more punitive for the poor and minority (Travis, 2001; Myers, 2001; Spriggs, 2001).

Issues of reintegration are as much about reinforcing communities as eliminating recidivism. High rates of parental incarceration deplete communities of the human resources that are needed to sustain family and community support systems. When a community is deprived of a member through incarceration, the capacity of the community to support its families and children fully is diminished. Thus, as Travis (2001) notes, recidivism is not the best measure of punishment policies; rather, he suggests, we should look at incarceration as a process with the measure of its effectiveness being reintegration: That is, how successful is the returnee's adjustment and reconnection to work, family, and peers?

John Hagan and Juleigh Coleman (2001) offer a poignant example of why the problems of incarceration are entrenched, and the process of incarceration and reintegration so tenuous. They note, for example, that the recent American "war on drugs" has dramatically and negatively affected African-American inner-city neighborhoods and families. Increased imprisonment has meant an absence of fathers that has left many families economically imperiled, and the removal of mothers has placed many children in the care of relatives or persons biologically unrelated to them. As these young men and women return to their neighborhoods and families, the settings they are reentering are not the ones they left behind. In the aftermath of the drug war, many within these communities see more signs of revenge than of reconstruction.

In short, inner-city African-American communities have experienced a loss of civic goods and services provided by public organizations. These institutions, such as police, schools, and welfare, now serve less as vehicles of social integration than as instruments of surveillance, suspicion, and exclusion. The larger consequence of such harsh legal and social policies is the formation of "negative social capital," leaving a situation in which, say Hagan and Coleman, "the derelict public sector of America's urban core is patently unfit to fulfill the integrative mission bestowed upon it."

Content of this Volume

Most of the chapters in this volume were presented as papers in a special research strand of the annual meeting of the International Community Corrections Association in the Fall of 2001. The papers were intended to examine approaches that recognize and address the complexities associated with the absence and reentry of incarcerated parents—fathers and mothers—in the lives of children and families. Taken together, the chapters offer a portrait of the vast range of issues that should be considered in supporting incarcerated adults, many of whom are parents and family members, who have experienced hardship and are seeking guidance. The authors connect the worlds of research, practice, and policy and attend to problems facing a population which, over the past three decades, has increased rapidly, placing increasing numerous children and families at risk.

Individually, the chapters provide a critical lens onto the specific issues and problems faced by different subgroups within the larger population of prisoners: those who are fathers, those whose families face uncertainty upon the prisoner's return, those who have been perpetrators of abuse or who have been the victims themselves of abuse, those who turn to faith-based institutions and programs, those who aim to enhance their parenting, and those who are the children of the incarcerated. The chapters cut across a range of issues and venues, both those that, relatively speaking, have been at the forefront of discussions—for example, parenting, domestic abuse and violence, and community reentry—to those that have only recently received attention. Those in the latter category include the following: perspectives of and impact on children, faith-based programming, father involvement, and mentoring. In addressing these diverse interests and topics, the chapters weave a story of complexity and hardship in a society and a system that have not been able to reconcile the punitive role of incarceration with the threat to child, family, and community welfare when a family member is incarcerated.

Throughout the volume, the authors refer to the different roles that prisoners hold within the different settings of their lives—home, work, and community. Four of the seven chapters address family development, parenting, and child well-being issues directly, recognizing that children and families are among those most directly affected by the criminal act of a prisoner and of the process of incarceration. For example, in the second chapter, "Families, Prisoners, and Community Reentry: A Look at Issues and Programs," Creasie Finney Hairston of the University of Illinois-Chicago provides a comprehensive examination of competing demands of correctional systems, policymakers, and social institutions and their differing expectations. She describes the realities of separation, distance, and erosion of relationships experienced during incarceration and exacted upon ex-offenders and their family upon their return. Finney Hairston describes a system and a society that have been attentive in theoretical terms to the problems facing the families of prisoners and to issues of reentry more broadly considered. She then offers a strong commentary on how the system has typically failed, on a practical level, to respond to these problems. In an incisive analysis of issues related to family structure, family relationships, and the conceptualization and process of reentry, Finney Hairston describes the "push and pull' with which family members and the offender grapple and the negotiations within families that are required. She explores the possibilities inherent in maintaining family ties during imprisonment, the strains placed upon these ties during imprisonment, and the problems emanating from the ties upon release—as prisoners and families must consider what it will mean for the prisoner to return home. She offers examples from family and fathering programs that have struggled with the issues of supporting prisoners returning home and helping families and ex-offenders craft approaches to cope with the changes in their lives.

Many of the themes of neglect and denial in research, policy, and practice discussions raised in the second chapter are expanded upon in relationship to fathers in the third chapter, "Linking Father Involvement and Parental Incarceration: Concepts and Contexts for Considering "What Works?," by R. Karl Rethemeyer of the State University of New York-Albany and this author. We draw upon the emerging body of work on fathers and families to highlight the significance of the topic within the burgeoning area of corrections. Noting that work on parenting and incarceration has focused mostly on mothers—and recognizing that such attention has been largely inadequate—we provide a set of concepts, contexts, and issues to consider in constructing a framework in which problems facing fathers—as parents, children of parents, and community members—might be located, studied, and addressed while also bringing attention to the problems facing mothers. Research that connects fathers and incarceration is in the early stages, holds the potential to address the dearth of research on mothers, and may help lift constraints on policy and funding initiatives that assist incarcerated parents in demonstrating positive, engaging, and responsible behaviors toward their children, families, and communities.

Given the disproportionate number of men in the prison system, the high number of men in the prison system who are fathers, and policy demands around child support within welfare legislation, we believe that the matter of responsible fathering will have increasing importance in the larger field of corrections. With this in mind, we conclude the chapter by examining the intersections and parallels between the two areas—responsible fathering and corrections—by focusing on the *Fathers and Families: Core Learnings* as a critical practice-based framework for investigating and integrating the issues of incarceration and reentry and determining, as we learn more, what works. These core learnings are lessons and hypotheses drawn from the work and commentaries of practitioners.

Glen Palm of St. Cloud University builds upon both these chapters but diverges in notably appropriate ways to focus on the specific issues around parenting education for incarcerated parents. Palm focuses on understanding what works by providing a sound analysis of the literature on parent education and its applications to current and emerging work on incarcerated parents. Palm encourages the reader to be an active participant in unraveling the interrelationships between and among parenting, education, and incarceration and in determining the feasible features of parenting education for daily practice with incarcerated parents. He calls upon his own experience as a researcher-practitioner, data from interventions and empirical studies, and issues from the field to examine three perspectives: (1) theories and conceptual frameworks that explain how parent education works; (2) research on the outcomes and effectiveness of different parent education programs; and (3) effective program practices and critical learnings from practitioners. This third perspective is particularly compelling as he uses the *Fathers and Families Core Learnings* as a framework to unpack issues related to the conditions, needs, and potential of parenting education to help incarcerated parents and to increase opportunities for reflective practice. He addresses thorny questions about whom should deliver parent education services—parent education professionals or parent peer educators—and outlines the qualities that parent educators need. He concludes by providing a thoughtful discussion of future directions and reflections in which the issues of culture and family may be examined.

The fifth chapter, "What Works: Children of Prisoners," by Denise Johnston of The Center for Children of Incarcerated Parents, provides the context for and challenge to the prior chapters. As Johnston notes, understanding what works for children of prisoners acknowledges and responds to questions about the effects of parental incarceration. Providing an engaging summary of what she describes as the three eras of research on incarcerated parents and their children, Johnston identifies a range of issues related to conceptual barriers to research on children of incarcerated parents. She makes clear the significance of looking at these children in relationship to their parents' pre-incarceration lives—that is, the problems around poverty, crime, neglect, race, and hardship—and parent absence due to incarceration—a situation she would suggest exacerbates existing plights faced by a disproportionate number of children. Perhaps one of the most critical dimensions is the discussion of assumptions made about the effects of incarceration on children and families and the tendency to accept such assumptions without empirical examination or verification. She concludes by providing a window onto studies that have been conducted by The Center for Children of Incarcerated Parents that provide provocative findings on racial demographics, family configurations, and related issues, along with recommendations for research in the field.

In the sixth chapter, "What Works in the Treatment of Family Violence in Correctional Populations: Issues and Directions," Lynn Stewart and Natalie Gabora-Roth, both from the Family Violence Prevention Programs of the Correctional Service Canada, offer a critical examination of one of the most intense issues in considering incarceration and family reentry: in other words, family violence, most often of men toward women. Drawing on their work in Canada, on literature in the United States and Canada, and from their own professional experience, Stewart and Gabora-Roth note that the treatment outcomes in programs applying treatment models is not convincing. In response, they argue for the establishment of a family violence program model for offenders based on effective corrections criteria rather than on political or ideological grounds. They examine the risk, need, and responsivity principles of Andrews and Bonta (1998) and offer a well-articulated, insightful analysis of the practicality, limitations, and potential of these principles and current empirical and evaluation studies in providing a solid analysis of whether and how the criminal justice system addresses the problem of family violence. In addition, they address the significant problem of evaluating programs that aim to address family violence among offenders, focusing on the strengths and limitations of current efforts.

Chapter 7, "The Viability of Mentoring as a Correctional Strategy: A Look at What Works," by Betsy Matthews of Eastern Kentucky University, promotes the idea of a broadened perspective on how to support incarcerated adults and adolescents. Noting that mentoring is touted in both public and private discussions about youth, Matthews moves the reader through a range of scenarios and possibilities in which support would be expected for an incarcerated adult but would be difficult to obtain. Her chapter reminds us that the role of mentoring (and in more recent discussions, surrogate families) are as much a necessity for adults whose histories or current actions make them vulnerable as it is for adolescents and children. She also reminds us, however, that the task of providing such support is complicated, despite the picture of mentoring as a facile task in which a bond is created between the mentor and mentee. In fact, Matthews suggests, the potential for such a bond is thwarted, in part, by the contexts of the mentoring such as in correctional facilities and transition programs where respect and mutual trust—concepts at the center of mentoring—are difficult to achieve.

In Chapter 8, Chris Carr, Dwight Cuff, and David Molzahn, all from the Chaplaincy Division of the Correctional Service Canada, provide the reader with an opportunity to reflect on the humanity of correctional support and prison-to-home transitions. Entitled "What Works in Faith-Based Programming," the chapter carries the reader through the processes of questioning the basic tenets of faith-based programming by raising the question: What is faith? The authors' query in this reference challenges the use of the term, "faith-based," as a catchall, sectarian label aimed at respecting all faiths while limiting inferences about any one denomination or religious sect and order. As they note, the literature on faith-based programming for the incarcerated is modest, at best, mostly because it has not been examined as an empirical issue. Yet, inmates report faith and religious transformations. Carr, Cuff, and Molzahn engage in a bit of self-reflection themselves by bringing their own work in the field into the text of the chapter. Their focus on community ministries and on Aboriginal healing lodges is particularly forceful in the insights they provide practitioners who are considering what a prison ministry would entail and for those working with oppressed indigenous populations.

Casting the Discourse

The chapters in this volume focus on the human and developmental domains of incarceration and the differential effects that incarceration has on the children, families, and communities affected by the imprisonment of an adult and the return of the adult to the family and community once he or she has served a term. In addressing the fundamental question in corrections of "What Works?," the authors engage the reader in considering the ways that incarceration reshapes families and communities and the prisoners—a reshaping that often makes it difficult for the offender to return and that requires a range of approaches and techniques to initiate, sustain, and achieve success in reintegration.

The analytical and descriptive accounts that the authors provide denote both how much we know and how much more we need to learn. They point to the ways in which different segments of the criminal justice/corrections/restorative justice communities have attempted to respond to an expanding field and the problems that accompany that expansion. In this way, the chapters represent a core of work intended to identify pathways leading to an integrated knowledge base that will be useful to researchers, practitioners, and policymakers. They also highlight the possibilities and limitations of an evolving field that is attempting to integrate and be integrated into relevant arenas—social service, education, and public policy—while maintaining its own identity and mission—to serve and address the problems of the incarcerated and those who are affected by their crimes and their absence due to incarceration.

The chapters in this volume also consider the issues that make incarceration a complex and harshly examined matter not only for the prisoner but also for children, families, and communities who experience the prisoner's loss and potential contributions. In other words, the chapters in this volume make visible the effects of incarceration—how they are felt upon arrest, once the adult is incarcerated, and when the adult is released—creating a set of experiences, expectations, and demands upon families and communities, both of which may be unprepared or unwilling to cope with the absence of the prisoner or to assume the responsibilities of guiding his or her transition or reintegration back home.

This volume is being released at a critical juncture in the revisioning of the field of corrections more broadly and specifically community corrections—a field that has the potential to intersect with a range of areas and issues confronting families who are often among those with the fewest resources. The significance of this point in our history is evident in each chapter. In the Afterword to this volume, Elijah Anderson and this author revisit these intersections, the interconnectedness of the issues addressed by the authors, and the potential that the issues hold for understanding and supporting children, families, and communities affected by incarceration and reentry; institutions grappling with ways to support prisoners and their children and families; and approaches that inform us about the needs and challenges and help us gauge and monitor the measure of impact.

Vivian L. Gadsden
University of Pennsylvania
August 2002

References

Andrews, D. and J. Bonta. 1998. *The Psychology of Criminal Conduct, 2nd Edition.* Cincinnati, Ohio: Anderson Publishing Co.

Beck, A. J. 2000. Prisoners in 1999. *Bureau of Justice Statistics Bulletin.* Washington, D.C.: U.S. Department of Justice, Bureau of Justice Statistics, NCJ 183476.

Hagan, J. and J. P. Coleman. 2001. Returning Captives of the American War on Drugs: Issues of Community and Family Re-entry. Paper presented at the Fathers and Families Roundtable Series on *Constructing and Coping with Incarceration and Family Re-entry: Perspectives from the Field*, National Center on Fathers and Families, University of Pennsylvania.

Mumola, C. 2000, August. Incarcerated Parents and their Children. Bureau of Justice Statistics, Special Report. Washington, DC: U. S. Department of Justice, NCJ 182335.

Myers, S. 2001. Keynote Address. Fathers and Families Roundtable Series on *Constructing and Coping with Incarceration and Family Re-Entry: Perspectives from the Field*, National Center on Fathers and Families, University of Pennsylvania.

Spriggs, W. 2001. Keynote Commentary. Fathers and Families Roundtable Series on *Constructing and Coping with Incarceration and Family Re-Entry: Perspectives from the Field*, National Center on Fathers and Families, University of Pennsylvania.

Travis, J. 2001. Heretical Propositions for Improving Re-Entry. Keynote Address. Fathers and Families Roundtable Series on *Constructing and Coping with Incarceration and Family Re-Entry: Perspectives from the Field*, National Center on Fathers and Families, University of Pennsylvania.

U.S. Department of Justice, Bureau of Justice Statistics. 1999. National Prisoner Statistics Data Series NPS-1. Washington, D.C.: U.S. Department of Justice.

Western, B. and S. McClanahan. 2000. June. Fathers Behind Bars: The Impact of Incarceration on Family Formation. Working Paper 00-08-FF. Princeton, New Jersey: Bendheim-Thoman Center for Research on Child Wellbeing, Princeton University.

Families, Prisoners, and Community Reentry: A Look at Issues and Programs

2

Creasie Finney Hairston, Ph.D.
Professor and Dean, Jane Addams College of Social Work
University of Illinois
Chicago, Illinois

Traditionally, the children and families of individuals involved in the correctional system have not been a population of concern for public policy makers, criminal justice administrators, or social service providers. Few policies or programs have been designed to address their needs and conditions, and research to broaden understanding of their circumstances, the problems they face, and the ways they address those problems has been limited. Although historically prisoners' ties to families and communities have been recognized as important on a theoretical and philosophical level, little attention has been given to the implications of those ties for public concerns and policy directives.

Several factors during the 1990s, including a large and rapidly increasing correctional population, a substantial increase in the number of women prisoners, disproportionate numbers of men and women of color involved in the criminal justice system, and welfare reform, have elevated prisoners' families to a new level of visibility in the social discourse about crime and justice (For example, *see* Gilliard and Beck, 1998; Hirsch, 2000; Illinois Criminal Justice Authority, 1997). The anticipated release of hundreds of thousands of men and women from prison annually and concerns about their recidivism and its impact on the general community have made their connections with families and friends, or lack thereof, a pressing social issue.

This chapter examines the family aspects of prisoners' community reentry and reintegration and the factors that inhibit or support successful reintegration. Individual/family situations, correctional administrative practices, and public policies are discussed and family program models and services are presented. Throughout the chapter, particular attention is given to the relationship of the different areas to recidivism and to what we know, do not know, or need to consider in determining what works in family-oriented policies and programs. The social and behavioral sciences literature, reports of professional practice, and the author's research and practice experience in the area of families and the correctional system provide the basis for the ideas presented here. Most of the material, particularly as it relates to public policy, is based on experiences in the United States and/or Canada, although information from other countries is used, as appropriate. For the most part, the focus is on returning adult prisoners, although some information has been drawn from studies of juvenile populations.

Family Ties and Recidivism Prevention

The problem of recidivism dominates most discussions of community reentry and is a major reason for the emerging interest in the family consequences and dynamics of incarceration. There is evidence that families affect the ways in which prisoners adjust to imprisonment and their postrelease success. Hairston's (1991b) review of research, conducted in different geographical locations with different correctional populations and during different eras, shows one consistent finding: that male prisoners who maintain strong family ties during imprisonment have higher rates of postrelease success than those who do not. She also found that men who assume family roles and responsibilities following incarceration have lower levels of recidivism than those who do not.

Dowden and Andrews' (1999) review of studies of women offenders found family process variables to be significant in explaining women's success rates, and Wright and Cullen (2001) found family support to be an important matter in the prediction of delinquency behavior. Some social scientists (for example, Wright and Wright, 1992) have taken the family connection a step further by positing that programs which include families in the treatment process within and after imprisonment can be instrumental in improving inmate-family-community relationships.

Some authors caution policy makers and program planners not to limit their discussions of families to the positive role that families have in preventing recidivism. They indicate that unrealistic expectations should not be placed on families. Whereas families offer practical and emotional supports to newly released prisoners, some family relationships and living environments actually exacerbate ex-convicts' problems or even lead them back into criminal activity (Quinn and Holman, 1991; Travis, Solomon, and Waul, 2001). Others reason that recidivism should not be the only measure of postrelease success and that family reunification, positive family functioning, abstinence from substance use and participation in the work force are all equally valuable goals of community reintegration (Hairston, Wills, and Wall, 1997; Travis, Solomon, and Waul, 2001).

This need for the inclusion of more indicators of success is shared by diverse constituencies including advocates concerned about the well-being of prisoners' children and corrections personnel who have the major responsibility for monitoring the community behavior of convicted individuals. Among the items which employees of a probation department in Scotland considered as evidence of effective supervision were reducing reoffending, changing attitudes, increasing victim empathy, and tending to the probationers' needs (McNeil, 2000). Child welfare professionals consider the ability of parents to reestablish households and assume responsibility for the care and protection of their children as a measure of postrelease success. Since incarceration can, and often does, lead to the permanent, legal severance of parent-child relationships (Genty, 1998), parent-child reunification following incarceration cannot be taken lightly.

Still, others indicate that families should be viewed not only in terms of the resources that they provide for prisoners but also in terms of families' needs. These individuals reason that families may need help themselves, given the special challenges of incarceration and criminal justice involvement and the poverty, racism, substance use, violence, and other challenges that mark the daily lives of the families and communities most affected by incarceration and reentry (Hairston, 1989b).

Family Structure and Family Relationships

The reintegration of families following incarceration is not an isolated event or process that can easily be disentangled or considered separate from family structure and commitments. The idea of what constitutes "family" differs considerably from one person to another and from historical notions of the American family. Most prisoners are not married (U.S. Department of Justice, 1993), and the idea of a spouse who is anxiously awaiting the return home of an imprisoned mate is more fiction and fantasy than fact. Among the minority of individuals who are in committed marital relationships at the time of arrest, family disintegration and marital termination during imprisonment are rather common. In a study of long-term prisoners, Hairston (1989a) found that three-fourths of the men who were married at the time of their arrest were divorced at the time of the study. Sharp and Mendoza (1998) report similar findings regarding marital breakups in their study of individuals incarcerated on drug charges.

Many prisoners, not unlike many other individuals, have had more than one intimate partner or committed relationship that resulted in parenthood. High percentages of incarcerated mothers and fathers with more than one child report that their different children have different fathers or mothers (Hairston, 1991a, 1995). Some parents had none or only one of their children living with them at the time of their arrest. Many women had relinquished the daily care of their children to other relatives prior to imprisonment. In some cases, child abuse or neglect charges have been brought against them. Surveys typically find that about 10 percent of mothers report their children are in foster care (Bloom and Steinhart, 1993; Hairston, 1991a; Mumola, 2000). This number may be considerably higher in states with kinship care provisions that allow relatives to provide care as part of the formal foster care system. A study under the author's supervision and currently underway at the University of Illinois at Chicago is illustrative. Of the 100 mothers of adolescent daughters interviewed at the Cook County, Illinois jail, 20 percent indicated that one or more of their children was under the custody of the state child welfare department; 42 percent indicated that one or more of their children had been under the state's custody at some time in the past.

The key individual who commonly emerges as "family" in research with prisoners is the prisoner's mother. She is the individual prisoners mention most often as their primary source of support, most frequent visitor, or the person with whom they communicate regularly (Hairston,

1995). Female prisoners name their own mothers most often as their children's caregiver (Bloom and Steinhart, 1993; Hairston, 1991b; Mumola, 2000). Although males indicate that their children's mothers, rather than grandmothers, are the children's primary caregivers, these mothers are not, for the most part, individuals with whom the males have enduring bonds or commitment (Jeffries, Menghraj, and Hairston, 2001). Nurse (2001) found, for example, that many of the returning young fathers she interviewed had been in prison longer than they had been in a preprison relationship with their children's mothers. While the men had affection for their children, they did not refer to their children's mothers as family or even consider them as such.

African-American family literature and research indicate that as a cultural tradition, family is much broader than the nuclear group of husband, wife, and children or even the family of origin, in other words, parents and siblings (Martin and Martin, 1995). Family includes aunts, uncles, and cousins along with a number of fictive kin who act and are treated as if they are family members. This more inclusive concept of family can be expected to be found among imprisoned African-American men and women as well.

The more inclusive concept of family found in the African-American family literature, revealed in research studies of prisoners and their families and observed by this author, presents major challenges for family-oriented reentry planning. It is clear that much more thought than has usually been the case will be required to even understand family structure and dynamics, let alone implement policies and design programs that foster family reintegration. These complex and changing family situations and arrangements suggest that serious attempts to involve families in any meaningful way in positive reintegration efforts will have to move beyond textbook descriptions of the nuclear family. Current policies and practices regarding families must also be reexamined to determine the extent to which they are based on assessments that reflect realistic pictures of family arrangements and cultural traditions.

Maintaining Family Ties During Imprisonment

Women and men who are prisoners express the desire to reunite with their children and families following imprisonment. At the same time, they are concerned about their ability to maintain family ties during incarceration. The hope and expectation associated with going home is counterbalanced by the fear that they will be, or have been, replaced and someone else will assume, or has already assumed, the family roles they once held or visualize as holding in the future. If contact with their families and children during imprisonment is a measure of family stability or the strength of family relationships, these fears are not unfounded.

The maintenance of family ties during imprisonment is very difficult. Most imprisoned mothers and fathers never see their children or see them infrequently. The 1997 survey of inmates in state and federal correctional facilities indicated that 57 percent of fathers and 54 percent of mothers in state prisons had never had a visit with their children since admission; 33 percent of fathers and 22 percent of mothers did not have monthly contact via telephone, mail, or visits (Mumola, 2000).

There are many barriers to family reunification and a prisoner's assumption of family roles and responsibilities following imprisonment. Prison policies and practices provide opportunities for communication between prisoners and families but at very high psychological, social, and financial costs.

Over 60 percent of parents in state prison are being held more than 100 miles from their homes (Mumola, 2000), usually in locations that have limited or no public transportation. Some corrections departments place prisoners in facilities that are far away from their homes as a matter of policy (Jeffries, Menghraj, and Hairston, 2001); some send prisoners to correctional facilities in other states to serve their sentences (Canadian Families and Corrections Network, 1998). Visiting restrictions limit the time, frequency, and duration of visits as well as the individuals who can escort visiting children or give them permission to visit. Some prisons allow children visitors only if the child's custodial parent accompanies him or her on a visit; others permit a child to visit only if the family can produce a birth certificate verifying that the imprisoned parent is the "real" father or mother (Hairston, 1998).

The conditions of visiting are less than hospitable at many facilities. Practices regarding acceptable identification, clothing, and searches vary from one prison to another and sometimes from one visit to another, creating humiliation, confusion, and frustration for adults and children visitors alike. Among the problems noted in the Florida legislature's report of prison visiting in that state were long waits sometimes in facilities without toilets and running water, the lack of nutritious foods in visiting room vending machines, and the absence of activities for children (Taylor, 1999).

Communication via telephones and the mail is likewise fraught with problems. Telephone calls are made collect to prisoners' families and at their expense. Telephone calls from prison to home are very expensive and cost as much as twenty times the amount the same call would have cost if placed from a residential telephone. These exorbitant telephone rates are a direct result of lucrative, profit-sharing contracts which departments of corrections negotiate with private telephone companies. Communication by mail is not financially expensive but carries a social stigma as letters from prison are marked with a large external, penitentiary identification stamp and disclaimer. Contemporary means of communication such as e-mail and fax are not available to prisoners and prisoners with poor reading and writing skills may find it difficult to communicate via letters.

Correctional administrative policies and practices that affect the maintenance of relationships between incarcerated individuals and their families and friends generally, and between parents and their children specifically, are rarely subjected to external scrutiny. When they are, charges of impropriety or sensitivity are easily dismissed as correctional administrators usually defend questionable practices on the basis of security needs and safety precautions. The Florida legislative report mentioned earlier is an exception to business as usual. Some state legislatures and public service commissions have also begun to investigate prison telephone systems and contracts.

The stance that public officials have generally taken in regard to prison family issues is not unusual. Historically, what went on in prisons was viewed as largely irrelevant to anything going on in the community, and it was well-understood that prison life and living conditions and operations could be left pretty much to the discretion of those who were responsible for running the institutions.

Efforts to reduce the incidence of repeat crime and deal with a number of other social conditions have demonstrated, however, that this reasoning is naive and unsound. The high percentage of returning prisoners with AIDS, tuberculosis, and hepatitis, and the effect this could have on the health of the general public have certainly made health practices and care in prison a public health concern. Similarly, research on substance abuse treatment with both juvenile and adult prisoners has demonstrated the need for treatment during and after imprisonment if persons with drug addictions are to be successful in maintaining a drug-free lifestyle following imprisonment (Hiller, Knight, and Simpson, 1999; Nelson and Trone, 2001).

Returning Home

In general, the communities to which prisoners return are not ones that are highly supportive of family reintegration. In addition, public policies do not support the resumption or assumption of a place in the family. Many former prisoners live in communities that have few social services or employment resources. Often these same communities are high crime areas and/or hot drug spots and, therefore, have crime-fighting and/or war-on-drug strategies that decrease the likelihood of family reunification and enhance, rather than decrease, the probability of arrest and/or recidivism. Among these strategies are police surveillance and monitoring, housing occupancy and job prohibitions, voting disenfranchisement, and welfare/child welfare reform stipulations.

There is a paucity of research on the transition from prison to community living and limited empirical documentation of the impact of reentry on families and the factors that influence positive family and individual outcomes following imprisonment. Paralleling the limited research is a paucity of programs focused on helping families deal with a family member's incarceration and that member's return to community living. Our general understanding of common human needs and family development as well as our experiences with families reuniting after separation for other more socially acceptable reasons, in other words, immigration, job relocation, or military deployment provide some indicators, however, of the issues that families separated by incarceration face. Successful handling of these issues enable family members to function effectively as a family unit, carry out their family roles, responsibilities, and obligations, and to support each other in achieving prosocial goals, including recidivism prevention.

Meeting Practical Needs

The ability to provide food, shelter, and clothing for family members is a fundamental concern for families reuniting following the imprisonment of a family member. Given the high levels of poverty among families most impacted by imprisonment, a returning prisoner creates additional stresses in a family's ability to provide these basic resources. This is the case more often than not. Most men and women leaving prison do not have the financial resources to establish their own homes. They instead go to homes of relatives or close friends that they consider as family. Welcoming home a former prisoner, however, puts many families at risk of losing their own homes.

Public housing and subsidized housing rules prohibit individuals convicted of certain crimes, namely drugs, from residing in that type of housing (Brown, 2000; Housing Agencies . . ., 2001). Rental agreements and leases in private housing often restrict the number of tenants to those who are actually on the rental agreement or lease. If the returning prisoner was not living in the unit at the time of his arrest, it is unlikely that he is listed on the lease. Many rental applications ask questions about a potential tenant's arrest and conviction history, ostensibly to screen out tenants with a criminal background. In those cases, it is unlikely that the new "tenant" will be eagerly added to the household list, and it is more likely that the tenants will be asked to move themselves.

Depending on the type of crime committed and the publicity surrounding it, family members who own or are buying their homes may not be in a better position to provide housing to their returning relative. Few individuals who have managed to purchase homes would welcome having their address displayed in newspapers and on public websites as the home of a registered sex offender. All states in the United States maintain sex offender registries; many disseminate this information to the general public using newspapers and public websites (Travis, 2000). Such an identification and singling out puts them at risk of social isolation, hostility, verbal abuse, and demonstrations by neighbors who seek to drive the offender out of their neighborhood.

Families who are caring for relatives' children under formal arrangements with child welfare departments are in jeopardy of having the children removed from their homes if they allow a criminal to occupy the premises. Federal law requires a criminal background check of all the individuals who will occupy a home, in order for foster parents to be licensed (Brown, 2000). An occupant's criminal history, including that of the child's parent, could lead to loss of the foster home license and removal of the child to the home of unrelated individuals.

The need to "hide" the returning family member for one reason or another may be compounded by the fact that there really is not any room for him or her. The high cost of housing in most urban areas precludes individuals with low or modest incomes from maintaining a guest room with an extra bed. The returning prisoner's "room" is likely to be a chair or sofa.

Since home usually means a place to eat as well as sleep, reentry also means that the family member providing a home absorbs the additional costs of an extra mouth to feed. Moreover, he or she, and sometimes other family members, may be expected to provide funds for transportation, clothing, and other personal items as the returning member has no income and no means of obtaining such items.

Under these conditions, welcome home is very short-lived. To extend this welcome, many former prisoners, if not most, move around from the home of one relative or friend to another. Others are homeless, using homeless shelters at night and the streets during the day as their home (Larivee, 2001). Although they have a "permanent" address for official reporting purposes, they are actually vagabonds with no real place to call home. When they refer to home, it is often where their mothers live, not necessarily where they themselves live or the address they use.

Reentry has an immediate financial impact on families' daily survival that is directly related to many families' poverty-level subsistence and to public policies, many of which were designed ostensibly to wage a war on drugs. Planning for release seldom takes either the immediate or long-term impact of these policies into consideration and relies instead on the thought that families or communities will somehow subsume or be able to assume these financial challenges. Assuring that a prisoner has an address to which he can report upon leaving prison or which a parole officer can visit will definitely not be enough in any serious effort to craft successful reentry programs that work in reducing recidivism.

Men and women leaving prison need immediate paid employment to reunify and reintegrate successfully with their families. In the absence of employment, other forms of temporary assistance, such as welfare benefits, food stamps, and Medicaid, are essential. Unfortunately, the war on drugs has placed these benefits beyond the reach of former prisoners, especially those with drug convictions (Brown, 2000; Hirsch, 2000).

Families expect adults who are physically and mentally able, at a minimum, to take care of their own subsistence needs, if not the needs of their children, other children living in the household, and other family members. Poor families do not have the financial resources to absorb the costs of maintaining an additional household member beyond a few days. After this, returning prisoners must be able to move out and set up their own households or contribute financially, indirectly or directly, to the household in which they reside.

Returning prisoners are often "between a rock and a hard place" in terms of securing and maintaining jobs that allow them to take care of themselves and their children and families. Many do not have the type of training, work experiences, or social networks that are needed to secure and hold legal jobs. Prison-based jobs have seldom prepared them for jobs in the public or private sector, and private companies running prison-based industries are not required to provide community employment for the returning prisoners who are their former "employees."

Community-based training programs are few and far between. The postincarceration community-based training programs offered by the Safer Foundation in Illinois and Project RIO in Texas, as described by Nelson and Trone (2001), are exceptions rather than the rule. When training is provided, stipends wherein individuals might be able to sustain themselves during training are rarely offered, and full-time, stable employment at or above minimum wage is seldom guaranteed.

Handling Correctional Supervision

One of the major challenges that faces families who reunite after imprisonment and that distinguish this type of reunion from other family reunions is the direct and indirect intrusion of agents of social control in family life. Monitoring and surveillance by parole officers and other law enforcement agents extends beyond the ex-prisoner to others with whom she or he is connected or resides. This monitoring of prisoners' comings, goings, and daily activities can be expected to increase with more formalized reentry programs that coordinate the work of police, the courts, parole and probation officers, and social service providers. The impact on children and families will be exacerbated in situations where the former prisoner actually resides, for reasons noted above, in several different locations or moves around from place to place when her or his welcome wears out. Whereas the extra monitoring is viewed by officials as a means of assuring success, the short and long-term impact may indeed be counterproductive to policy and family goals. The outcome of extra watching may have the effect of casting a wider net with the end result being more rearrests and reincarceration resulting from technical violations, as has been observed in intensive supervision programs (Jernigan and Kronick, 1992).

External monitoring and the resulting internal monitoring roles that families assume produce stressful situations for everyone involved (Fishman, 1986; Nurse 2001). Some families take it upon themselves to act as guards, thereby triggering negative reactions by the former prisoner who is sick and tired of being guarded; others assume that they themselves are being watched and guarded and begin to act accordingly. Sometimes, family members use the prisoner's status to achieve personal objectives. An example of the latter is when a family member or intimate partner threatens to call the police or parole officer and have a person sent back to jail when there are interpersonal problems or family conflict or the individual misbehaves. Some family members just give up as the scrutiny, in light of everything else that may be going on, is just too much for them to handle.

Many families are not prepared to handle the correctional supervision and monitoring aspects envisioned for community reentry and reintegration programs. Without changes in the prevailing approach for handling prisoners' reentry and the justice system's communication with families, few families will understand what the criminal justice system expects from the returning prisoner or from his or her family. A lack of understanding of this nature prevails and can be expected to continue despite widespread incarceration in specific neighborhoods and even among some families. This understanding is not present even when family members themselves have been incarcerated, or there has been repeated incarceration of the returning family member. The rules are different from one type of program to another and practices of different officers or caseworkers in the same or similar programs vary from one individual to another. Families are seldom given written information about policies and procedures and have limited opportunities to ask meaningful questions of, or engage in discussion with, anyone in authority who appears to know what is going on or to be able to make decisions.

Families' limited access to information is not confined to the postincarceration phase but rather is evident at each stage of criminal justice processing. Family advocacy organizations have identified families' limited access to information as a key barrier to family well-being. The Family and Corrections Networks of both Canada and the United States have adopted policy recommendations calling for correctional authorities to provide families with basic information at each stage of criminal justice processing (Canadian Families and Corrections Network, 1995; Hairston, 1989b).

Families are not in the best position to support reentry goals or the prisoners' compliance if they do not know and understand the nature and type of reentry monitoring that will take place. Families need to know what to expect from authorities in terms of random telephone calls, unannounced late night visits, drug tests, and regularity of office visits. They also need to know what authorities expect from them and the implications thereof as well as the types of programs and services that will be available to assist when problems or concerns arise.

In the absence of adequate preparation for this new aspect of family functioning, positive outcomes for everyone are easily thwarted. Family-oriented booklets explaining the parole process, procedures, and expectations similar to the one that the South Carolina Department of Probation, Parole, and Pardon Services (2000, August) provides to parolees, and the prisoners' family handbooks, developed by Hairston and Taylor (1991), provide examples of resources which help families manage correctional supervision.

Emotional and Social Issues

Families who are reuniting must deal with myriad emotional and social issues and adjust to changing roles and relationships brought about by the reentry of a family member who has not been a part of the household for an extended period. The special strains and stresses that occur when military families separate and then reunite after extended periods of separation are well-documented in the military research literature, as are recommendations for programs and services to prevent or alleviate this stress. Burke and Moskos (1996) found that reunifying families must adjust to changing family roles because when husbands are absent, wives assume more independent, decision-making roles. More recent studies of women in the military report on the multiple changes that families undergo to accommodate mothers' absence and how those changes affect mothers and children during and after their separation (Pierce and Buck, 1998).

Studies of returning prisoners conducted by Fishman (1986) and Nurse (2001) describe problems in male-female relationships when husbands and boyfriends return home after being in prison that are similar to those experienced by military couples. Intimate relationships change during and after imprisonment, and individuals once central in each other's lives begin to occupy very peripheral positions. Problems involving children are also exacerbated when a parent who has been in prison returns home and attempts to resume a parenting role. Some caregivers are reluctant to return children to their parents. The caregivers become attached to the children, do not want them to be hurt again when the parents leave again as has been the case before, and/or just think the parent is not capable or fit to care for the child. Former spouses or partners similarly restrict contact between parents and children for reasons having to do with what they perceive to be the in the child's best interest, but also for reasons that may be solely in the adults' interest or disinterest (Jeffries, Menghraj, and Hairston, 2001).

Families, Prisoners, and Community Reentry: A Look at Issues

Families separated by incarceration must deal not only with normal separation and return issues but also with the negative aspects of crime and punishment. These include the conditions of dependency, deprivation, and extreme control under which the former prisoner has been living, the social stigma attached to the label of ex-convict in the broader society, perceptions of the crime that was committed, and the former prisoner's remorse for and acceptance, or nonacceptance, of responsibility for the crime committed.

The conditions of prison, and the requirements for living in prison, hardly constitute what is needed for even minimum, adequate functioning in the community and one's home. Engaging in many, if not most, of the behaviors required to comply with prison rules or to outsmart one's peers in prison would certainly not be constructive in community living situations. After many years living in a prison environment, former prisoners just may not know how to live and function in a family environment with different norms and expectations.

Imprisonment is also damaging to the social identity of the individual and family. Only among a small circle of friends is an individual likely to be able to take pride in having committed a certain crime. Having served time in prison, in and of itself, shows that the person was not that smart, since he or she cannot boast about having gotten away with whatever was done. Imprisonment is not a normal or normalizing event, even for those whose lives are directly impacted. A case in point is African-American families and communities wherein one out of every three young men is involved in the criminal justice system and 30 percent of adult males can expect to spend some time in prison during their lives (Mauer, 1999).

Families accept the former prisoner and accept the fact that she or he has been in prison, but no matter how common, incarceration is not a source of pride or cause for celebration. It is not the goal that one sets for self, for one's children, or for other family members and loved ones. There is a broad societal stigma that is attached to being a convict or ex-convict and that stigma is accompanied by disenfranchisement, denial of benefits, job terminations, and public ridicule and harassment that extend beyond the individual to his or her kin. The assumptions that are made about the kind of person an ex-convict is extends to his or her children. "Like father, like son" is taken as a given with predictions, among social scientists and the general public alike, that the children of prisoners are on their way to jail themselves.

Reentry to the household can, therefore, set the stage for family conflict and turmoil directly related to the crime that led to incarceration and/or to the crime or lifestyle the returning family member was leading prior to imprisonment. These are touchy situations that few families are prepared to handle in a way that can lead to healing as opposed to further dissension and sometimes violent confrontations. Some family members have never had or taken an opportunity to talk about the crime that led to imprisonment and know little more than what appeared in newspapers. Sometimes, the crime was committed against another family member or close friend, and communication and relationships among family members have been strained or unproductive. In some instances, the criminal activity has never been acknowledged. It is the elephant in the room that everybody sees, but chooses to ignore. Other family members may have benefited from the criminal activity or silence. There may also be resentment and strong feelings about things that have taken place during the prisoner's absence that make family relationships very vulnerable during the reentry period.

In situations wherein drug abuse is an issue, the lifestyle that preceded incarceration often included child neglect or abandonment, stealing from other family members, disregard and disrespect for family and societal rules, and abdication of most family roles. The promise to do better this time is probably the latest in a series of promises that have little, if any, credibility. While family members question the returning prisoner's credibility and truthfulness, the former convict questions their loyalty to, and faith in, him or her.

Families that are functioning well or poorly will have a difficult time absorbing returning family members when old issues have not been talked about, let alone resolved. Whereas sometimes it is best to let "sleeping dogs lie" or to take the position that some things are better left unsaid, it is not wise or even possible to let "bygones be bygones" in some situations. These attachments, or lack thereof, could easily affect the family's future and ability to function as a family and hasten the returning prisoner's road to relapse and recidivism pretty quickly.

Family-oriented Programs and Services: What Works

Family-centered, community-based programs for former prisoners and their families are not a standard component of the established, traditional network of social or correctional service programs. Consequently, program and evaluation information is not readily available in the scholarly and professional literature.

There are a variety of programs and services that have been designed to assist families whose lives are impacted by incarceration. Among the prison-based programs that are provided during incarceration are overnight family visits, parent education for prisoners, marital therapy for prisoners and their spouses, visiting centers located at the site of or near prisons, and children's visiting centers or areas in prison. Community-based programs include those that operate to maintain family ties during imprisonment and, to a lesser extent, those that provide postincarceration services. The former include:

- support groups and counseling for children's caregivers, children, and prisoners' spouses/partners
- transportation services for prison visiting
- overnight lodging programs for prison visitors
- support groups for couples
- programs providing legal assistance for resolving parent custody or child support issues
- information and referral programs

More recent developments for the postincarceration or family reentry period include family-centered programs that look at families as systems and have program interventions that address individual and family needs. Given their holistic and more comprehensive approach, they require professionally trained staff, full-time staffing arrangements, office facilities, and an administrative and resource structure to support program maintenance and development.

Although there is a diversity of services and program models, there are major difficulties in determining what works. First of all, it is difficult to determine what exists. Many programs are short-lived, as they do not have a stable base of funding and/or have funding that is not adequate to meet basic operating expenses. Many programs are run by volunteers and small grass roots organizations that have neither the time nor resources to engage in activities beyond service delivery and fundraising. Few programs document and disseminate their program models and program experiences. Hardly any conduct evaluations or disseminate findings when evaluations are conducted. Experimental studies that provide a scientific approach to tying program outcomes to program activity are rare indeed.

Documentation of program activities and outcomes has been hindered by the lack of substantial funding to support this type effort. The family and corrections field is not an area to which foundations or governmental agencies have allocated monies for purposes of determining the state of the field. For many years, the Family and Corrections Network directory of programs, Boudouris' (1996) compilation of parent education programs in prisons, and Hairston's (1996) descriptions of prison-based program objectives and strategies provided the only listings and summaries of programs and program types. An overview of the field, or some aspect thereof, could be obtained by reviewing these documents. None of these reports, however, provided an assessment of the strengths or weaknesses of the different programs or program models. They, in addition, did not identify program outcomes or relate program activity to conceptual models or program results.

Only since the late 1990s has there been a major coordinated, funded effort to determine and assess the type and nature of family-oriented correctional programs. The Vera Institute of Justice study, funded by the Bureau of Justice Assistance and the Charles Mott Foundation (Jeffries, Menghraj, and Hairston, 2001), examined prison and community-based parenting programs for incarcerated and formerly incarcerated fathers. The University of Illinois' study of programs serving children and families of prisoners (Bates, 2001), funded in part by the Annie E. Casey Foundation, reviewed community-based programs for children and families affected by incarceration and compared them with family needs as identified in the literature and through focus groups with different constituencies.

The consistent finding of both the Bates (2001) and Jeffries, Menghraj, and Hairston (2001) studies is that there is an absence of evaluative data on which to base conclusions about program effectiveness. Both studies provide ample evidence of program need and document barriers to family maintenance during imprisonment and postrelease success including family reunification and the prevention of recidivism. Each study also identifies program elements that speak to family needs as identified by program designers, program staff, prisoners and their family members, the developing body of research on prisoners and their families, and practice literature on families dealing with crises, separation, reunification, and other difficult problems.

As a consequence of the limited efforts to assess the field, the diversity of programs and services, and the general absence of evaluative data, it is very difficult to be able to say what works in family programming. We certainly do not know which of these programs or services are effective in reducing recidivism. The programs do not generally collect data on recidivism and recidivism prevention is not the primary or an explicit goal of many of the programs.

Promising Program Models and Approaches

Although we do not know what works in reintegrating former prisoners with their families, we do have theories and conceptual frameworks to guide the development and testing of reintegration programs for families. There are also program models and service approaches that have been found to be of modest success in helping families deal with many of the same types of problems that confront returning prisoners and their families. While reintegration programs must take into consideration the special problems associated with crime and incarceration, at the same time they can draw from the experiences of other family-strengthening programs.

Restorative justice models have been discussed as promising approaches for reintegrating returning prisoners with their families and communities (Travis, 2000). Restorative justice has a certain appeal because of its focus on healing and its involvement of individuals impacted by the crime in problem resolution. We view an ex-convict's taking ownership of and responsibility for the crime that he or she committed and recognizing the harm that it caused the victim and others as an important step in reentry. Advocates of restorative justice view the participation of the family, victim, and community in problem-resolution as an effective means of addressing the issues related to the crime that has been committed and the stigma associated with incarceration.

Restorative justice approaches have not been used often in adult corrections and in postincarceration programs. Similarly, while the principles underlying them are embraced by both criminal justice and social services professionals, there is limited evidence of their effectiveness in improving family functioning, reuniting families, or reducing recidivism. We do not know if they are effective or not in these latter areas as studies have not been done with those objectives in mind.

Restorative justice practices have been used primarily in cases of nonviolent crime involving juvenile offenders. They are also typically used at the front end of the justice system, rather than as a postincarceration approach. Assessments of outcomes have focused primarily on whether the individual accused of crime followed through with the orders resulting from the family conferences/mediation and whether offenders and victims were satisfied with the process and thought it was fair.

Most of the published work on restorative justice programs also focuses on its use with juveniles. Studies of various models of restorative justice including family group conferences and victim mediation report that victims, families, and offenders find the process fair and that they are satisfied with the outcomes of conferences (Braithwaite, 1998; Doolan, 1999; McCold and Wachtel, 2000). The percentage of satisfaction increases with the degree to which the practice is fully restorative, and offenders generally report higher levels of satisfaction with outcomes than victims (McCold and Wachtel, 2000). Information on outcome data related to crime prevention is limited.

A strength of restorative justice approaches is the focus on the delinquent act/crime and the development of a consensus arrangement related to repairing the damage the act has caused in a manner that can be embraced by the victim and offender and their families and communities. A major criticism of the use of these models, however, is the narrow focus on the delinquent act/crime. Braithwaite (1998) notes that family conferencing and other uses of restorative models focus narrowly on the offense and ignore other problems such as family violence, unemployment, and drug abuse. Since these other problems are crucial factors in family functioning and recidivism prevention, it is clear that restorative practices, as we understand them now, could be only one of several important components for consideration in designing a family-focused reintegration program.

The family support, strengths and resiliency, and social assets literature provides theoretical concepts and explanations that move beyond families' problems and stresses to interventions that build on family strengths even in the midst of major difficulties. Social work models for working with families from diverse racial backgrounds and experiences and the focus on the dynamics of family interactions and cultural traditions and practices underlying those interactions also provide useful conceptual models for defining principles to guide reentry programs and services. In recognizing family strengths, as well as areas in need of change or development, they offer a foundation for designing effective and compassionate prisoner reentry programs that are responsive to family needs and community concerns.

Two family-oriented postincarceration programs that show promise for achieving broad family and community reentry goals to address postrelease problems are presented here as models for further development, testing, and evaluation. The program designs are based on a sound theoretical understanding of family processes and build on family strengths while helping families work on areas in need of development.

They also address major problem areas specific to incarceration and criminal histories and behavior. Both also involve correctional and social services personnel in partnerships to support family growth and well-being and compliance with societal norms and correctional system mandates.

Family Support Services, a collaborative effort of the University of Texas at Austin School of Social Work and the Texas Department of Criminal Justice (although no longer in operation because of funding problems), provides a family-oriented community reintegration services model for further consideration (*see* Johnson, Selber, and Lauderdale, 1998) for a detailed description of the program. Using a family supports and family-strengthening perspective, the program model concentrates on offenders and their families, provides a network of community services, and focuses on the aspects of behavior and the social environment that could be changed. Intervention is aimed at helping the entire family and community cope with the multiple challenges of criminal behavior, rather than just on the future recidivism of the offender. The program design is based on an analysis of the needs and concerns of former prisoners and on theoretical and empirical understanding of ways to address those needs within the context of a family and community setting.

Service components include comprehensive case management; psychosocial assessments for offenders and their families; individual/family service plans; support groups for children, prisoners, and couples; referral to community agencies; and advocacy to assure service provision. Research and evaluation are also an integral part of the program design as is staffing provided by professionally trained social workers and student interns. A particular strength of this program is the provision of a continuum of services that begins during incarceration and continues following release from prison.

Family Support Service's university connection supported a strong research component which informed development of the program model as the project evolved. The inclusion of research from the point of project initiation also allowed the project to document program processes and outcomes and to provide process and outcome information about what works. Evaluations of the support group for children indicated that participants showed improved class behavior, school attendance, and grades. A quasi-experimental study of recidivism showed no statistical difference between those who participated in the program and those who did not. There was, however, a 10 percent lower recidivism rate for those who completed the program as defined by their service plans and those who did not, and two-thirds of those who completed the program remained free after four years.

Similar to the Texas program, La Bodega de la Familia in New York City uses a comprehensive case management approach in its work with returning prisoners and their families (*see* Shapiro and Schwartz, 2001 for a detailed description of the program). Family strengthening and social supports are also core features of this program, as is the emphasis on respecting and honoring cultural traditions. Formal partnership with the state parole department and connections with other community service providers and the capacity to provide a continuum of family-oriented services prior to and after prison release are integral program components. The program model has been extensively documented, but evaluation data regarding recidivism, family functioning, and individual and family well-being have not been disseminated as a part of that documentation.

The Work Place, a responsible fatherhood program based in Memphis, Tennessee, offers a third, family-oriented program approach for addressing community reentry and reintegration. Employment is the central feature of The Work Place program. The program model, designed to serve returning prisoners who are fathers, features a four-week, prerelease job training program to be provided at correctional facilities. The prerelease program recognizes returning prisoners' need for immediate employment and the inability of many poor families to provide financial support to family members engaged in extended, unpaid training efforts. The prison-based program is similar to the four-week training program which The Work Place provides for low-income fathers residing in the community. (*See* Jeffries, Menghraj, and Hairston, 2001 for a description of the program.) Prisoners who complete prerelease training enroll in a community-based, family-oriented, job support program upon their release. The community-based program provides full-time, stable employment with Memphis area employees. During the first few weeks of employment, the new employee is on The Work Place payroll and continues to participate in job support sessions provided at The Work Place offices.

Many components of this program model stand out as distinguishing features. First, there is a continuum of services from prison to community and a guarantee of full-time employment on release for those who successfully complete training. Second, in addition to job preparation and job placement, the training program provides training on responsible parenting roles including providing emotional and financial support for children and training on the impact of criminal justice system involvement of prisoners and their families and children. Third, the Memphis area employers with whom the agency contracts to provide workers have agreed to hire employees in spite of their criminal backgrounds.

Changes in the funding stream for responsible fatherhood programs—the source of funding for the job training component—have kept The Work Place from implementing the prison-to-community continuum as planned. The program model, nevertheless, offers, a promising approach for addressing family issues, criminal justice system involvement, and employment in a holistic way. The organization's experiences with the use of the same program design as a responsible fatherhood, community-based program for low-income fathers point to success in addressing employment concerns, as all of the men who complete the training program do secure and maintain full-time jobs, and most maintain them. In addition, the organization has increased both the number of contracts it has with Memphis area employers and its contract budget each year of program operations. The Work Place has not publicly disseminated program data, however, that compares outcomes among different groups of participants or that provides an assessment of recidivism or family outcomes.

Summary and Conclusions

We have a beginning understanding of the family aspects of incarceration and of the issues that families face when a former prisoner returns home. There is evidence that family ties during and after imprisonment are interdependent and that both must be considered in community reentry programming and decision making. Maintaining family ties during imprisonment and reunifying households, however, are very difficult. Prisoners' and families' personal issues, correctional administrative practices, and public policies limit personal choices and options and pose major challenges to successful family functioning and recidivism prevention.

We know that several different programs and services have been developed to assist families who are involved with the correctional system. Most are not a part of traditional correctional or social services networks. Few focus on the postincarceration period, and most have not documented program activities or produced evaluation reports to guide further program development.

There are promising program models and service approaches derived from sound theory, conceptual models, and empirical research that have been used to assist families and help communities deal with the aftermath of crime and the criminal justice policies that have been enacted in response to crime. These models focus on family strengths, correctional supervision, responsibility for and ownership of criminal behavior, basic human needs, and cultural differences. In the context of major policy changes, they offer promise for enhancing the postrelease success of the hundreds of thousands of prisoners who will return home in the next several years. At this time, however, we do not really know what works in improving family functioning during reentry or in involving families in the prevention of recidivism.

References

Bates, R. 2001. *Improving Outcomes for Children and Families of Incarcerated Parents*. Chicago: University of Illinois at Chicago, Jane Addams College of Social Work, Jane Addams Center for Social Policy and Research.

Bloom, B.and D. Steinhart.1993. *Why Punish The Children? A Reappraisal of the Children of Incarcerated Mothers in America*. San Francisco: National Council on Crime and Delinquency.

Boudouris, J. 1996. *Parents in Prison: Addressing the Needs of Families*. Lanham, Maryland: American Correctional Association.

Braithwaite, J. 1998. Linking Crime Prevention to Restorative Justice. Paper presented at The First North American Conference on Conferencing, Minneapolis, Minnesota.

Brown, R. 2000. Helping Low Income Mothers with Criminal Records Achieve Self-Sufficiency. *Welfare Information Network News Issue Notes.* 4: 13.

Burke, S. and C. Moskos. 1996. Family Readiness: Applying What We Know and Highlighting What We Need to Know. *Military Family Issues: The Research Digest.* 11, 1-7.

Canadian Families and Corrections Network. 1995. *Policy Recommendations on Families of Adult Offenders*. Kingston, Ontario, Canada: Canadian Families and Corrections Network.

———. 1998, April. Connecticut Sending Inmates Out of State. *Corrections Compendium*. 23(4).

Doolan, M. 1999. The Family Group Conference–10 Years On. Paper presented at the Building Strong Partnerships for Restorative Practices Conference, Burlington, Vermont.

Dowden, C. and D. A. Andrews. 1999. What Works for Female Offenders: A Meta-analytic Review. *Crime and Delinquency*. 45(4).

Fishman, L. 1986. Repeating the Cycle of Hard Living and Crime: Wives' Accommodations to Husbands' Parole Performance. *Federal Probation*. L1: 44-54.

Ganow, M. 2001, May. New Challenges for States in Financing Child Support. *Welfare Information Network Issue Notes*. 5(7).

Genty, P. H. 1998. Permanency Planning in the Context of Parental Incarceration: Legal Issues and Recommendations. *Child Welfare*. LXXVII5: 543-559.

Gilliard, D. and A. Beck. 1998. *Prisoners in 1997*. Washington, D.C.: U.S. Department of Justice, Bureau of Justice Statistics.

Hairston, C. F. 1989a. Men in Prison: Family Characteristics and Parenting Views. *Journal of Offender Counseling, Services and Rehabilitation*. 14: 3-30.

———, ed. 1989b. *Voices and Visions: Proceedings of the First North American Conference on Families and Corrections*. Waynesboro, Virginia: Family and Corrections Network.

———. 1991a. Mothers in Jail: Parent-Child Separation and Jail Visitation. *Affilia*. 62: 9-27.

———. 1991b. Family Ties During Imprisonment: Important to Whom and for What? *Journal of Sociology and Social Welfare*. XVIII1: 87-104.

———. 1995. Fathers in Prison. In D. Johnston and K. Gables, eds. *Children of Incarcerated Parents*. Lexington, Massachusetts: Lexington Books.

———. 1996. Family Programs in State Prisons. In C. McNeese and A. R. Roberts, eds. *Policy and Practice in the Justice System*. Chicago: Nelson-Hall Inc.

———. 1998. The Forgotten Parent: Understanding the Forces that Influence Incarcerated Fathers' Relationships with Their Children. *Child Welfare*. LXXVII5: 617-638.

Hairston, C. F. and C. L. Taylor. 1991. *Visiting with Families and Friends*. Indianapolis, Indiana: Indiana University School of Social Work.

Hairston, C. F., S. Wills, and N. Wall. 1997. *Children, Families, and Correctional Supervision: Current Policies and New Directions*. Chicago: University of Illinois at Chicago, Jane Addams College of Social Work.

Hiller, M., K. Knight, and D. Simpson. 1999. Prison-based Substance Abuse Treatment, Residential Aftercare and Recidivism. *Addiction*. 94(6): 833-43.

Hirsch, A. E. 2000. The Impact of Welfare Reform on Women with Drug Convictions. Pennsylvania: A Case Study. *Women, Girls, and Criminal Justice*. 13: 33-34.

Housing Agencies Have Latitude to Kick Out Drug Abuse. 2001. *Criminal Justice Funding Report.* June 6, 2001.

Illinois Criminal Justice Authority. 1997. *Trends and Issues 1997.* Chicago: Illinois Criminal Justice Authority.

Jeffries, J., S. Menghraj, and C. F Hairston. 2001. *Serving Incarcerated and Ex-offender Fathers and Their Families.* New York: Vera Institute of Justice.

Jernigan, D. E. and R. F. Kronick. 1992. Intensive Parole: The More You Watch, the More You Catch. *Journal of Offender Rehabilitation.* 173(4): 65-76.

Johnson, T., K. Selber, and M. Lauderdale. 1998. Developing Quality Services for Offenders and Families: An Innovative Partnership. *Child Welfare.* LXXVII5: 595-615.

Larivee, J. 2001, June. Returning Inmates: Closing the Public Safety Gap. *Corrections Compendium.* 26(6).

Martin, E. and J. Martin. 1995. *Social Work and the Black Experience.* Washington, D.C.: NASW Press.

Mauer, M. 1999. *Race to Incarcerate.* New York: The New Press.

May, C. 1999. *Explaining Reconviction Following a Community Sentence.* Home Office Research Study 192. United Kingdom: Home Office.

McCold, P. and T. Wachtel. 2000. Restorative Justice Theory Validation. Paper presented at the Fourth International Conference on Restorative Justice for Juveniles, Tubingen, Germany.

Mc Neil, F. 2000. Defining Effective Probation: Frontline Perspectives. *The Howard Journal.* 39(4).

Mumola, C. 2000, August. *Incarcerated Parents and Their Children.* Washington, D.C.: U.S. Department of Justice, Bureau of Justice Statistics.

Nelson, M. and J. Trone. 2001, May/June. Why Planning for Release Matters. *Offender Programs Report.* 51: 1-2, 10-13.

Nurse, A. 2001. Coming Home to Strangers: Newly Paroled Juvenile Fathers and Their Children. Paper presented at the Conference on the Effects of Incarceration on Children and Families, Chicago, Illinois, Northwestern University.

Pierce, P. and C. Buck. 1998, January. Wartime Separation of Mothers and Children: Lessons from Operations Desert Shield and Desert Storm. *Military Family Issues: The Research Digest.* 22: 1-17.

Quinn, J. F. and J. E. Holman. 1991. Intrafamilial Conflict among Felons under Community Supervision: An Examination of the Co-habitants of Electronically Monitored Offenders. *Journal of Offender Rehabilitation.* 16(3/4): 177-193.

Sharp, S. and S. Marcus-Mendoza. 1998. Gender Differences in the Impact of Incarceration on Children and Spouses of Drug Offenders. Paper presented at the annual meeting of the Academy of Criminal Justice Sciences, Albuquerque, New Mexico.

Shapiro, C. and M. Schwartz. 2001. Coming Home: Building on Family Connections. *Corrections Management Quarterly.* 53: 52-61.

South Carolina Department of Probation, Parole, and Pardon Services. 2000, August. *South Carolina Offender Handbook.* Columbia, South Carolina: South Carolina Department of Probation, Parole, and Pardon Services.

Taylor, V. 1999. Florida Law Requires Prisons to Improve Visiting Conditions. *Corrections Journal.* 3(21): 3-4.

TCI Offers Cheaper Collect Calls through Billed Party Preference Service. 1999, Spring. *Vermont-CURE News.* 11: 11.

Travis, J. 2000, May. But They All Come Back: Rethinking Prisoner Re-entry. *Sentencing and Corrections: Issues for the 21st Century.* Washington, D.C.: U.S. Department of Justice, National Institute of Justice.

Travis, J., A. Solomon, and M. Waul. 2001. *From Prison To Home: The Dimensions and Consequences of Prisoner Re-Entry.* Washington, D.C.: The Urban Institute.

U.S. Department of Justice, Bureau of Justice Statistics. 1993. *Survey of State Prison Inmates, 1991.* Washington, D.C.: U.S. Department of Justice, Bureau of Justice Statistics.

Wright J. P. and F. T. Cullen. 2001. Parental Efficacy and Delinquent Behavior: Do Control and Support Matter? *Criminology.* 39(3): 677-698.

Wright, K. and K. Wright. 1992, September. Does Getting Married Reduce the Likelihood of Criminality? *Federal Probation.* 61(3): 50-56.

Linking Father Involvement and Parental Incarceration: Concepts and Contexts for Considering "What Works"

3

Vivian L. Gadsden
   Associate Professor, Graduate School of Education
   University of Pennsylvania
   Philadelphia, Pennsylvania

R. Karl Rethemeyer
   Assistant Professor of Public Administration
   State University of New York—Albany
   Albany, New York

Since the mid-1990s, research and practice on fathers and families has expanded dramatically. Increasingly we are coming to understand the breadth and scope of the issues that influence fathers' engagement with their children, particularly low-income fathers. We also have begun to examine the effects of father absence on children and families; the different forms of father-child and father-family interactions; the nature of father identity formation; and the role of communities in supporting positive father presence. However, within the larger discussion on fathers and fathering, father absence due to incarceration has not received much attention. This is true, despite findings (for example, Mumola, 2000) that suggest that a disproportionate number of men in prisons are fathers.

In this chapter, we provide an analysis of the conceptual background and practical contexts that form the basis of much of the discussion on father incarceration—as a pretext to addressing the question: "What works?" We focus on incarceration of fathers as a research and practice issue, both affected by and affecting policy decisions which, in turn, have an impact on the children, the families, and the communities in which they live. The chapter is divided into five sections. In the first, we respond to the question: Why focus on fathers and incarceration? In the second, we provide a brief overview of parent incarceration and its impact on children and child well-being. In the third, we describe some of the perennial issues in research on fathers and families—that is, issues and problems highlighted in the literature and by practitioners themselves. In the fourth, we draw parallels between research and practice related to fatherhood and research and practice related to incarceration to explore the range of options for integrating the two areas of work. In this section, we use the *Fathers and Families Core Learnings*, described later in this chapter, as a context to reframe inquiry, practice, and policy and as a way to highlight the relevance of rigorous work on incarcerated fathers. In the final section, we offer closing considerations.

Focusing on Incarcerated Fathers

Father absence—for example, its nature and consequences for children and families—is a persistent theme in the research literature on fatherhood and family structure, and in practice and policy. Despite considerable research, however, the kinds and forms of father absence and the nuanced demographic and social factors that differentiate how diverse populations negotiate aspects of father absence to promote family functioning and family preservation are still a matter of limited discussion and exploration. For example, most discussions in research on father absence restrict their focus to absence resulting from separation, divorce, or premarital parenthood. Fathers whose absence is complicated by their confinement in penal institutions, military service, or private sector jobs that require prolonged separation (for example, sea-based oil drilling) are rarely studied as a noteworthy subset of the larger population of fathers. In short, these types of father absences are typically interpreted as intervening variables in father involvement, rather than as independent variables or unique areas of study.

In focusing on father incarceration as a research issue, we seek to identify the effects of various types of father absence to understand the broad dimensions of the resulting risks to child and family welfare, such as the placement of children into foster care and intergenerational poverty. These effects are likely to be found in a range of internalizing and externalizing risk factors such as emotional trauma, emotional distress, poor school performance, and juvenile criminal activity (Hagan and Dinovitzer, 1999; Johnson, 1995; Johnston, 1995). Moreover, father absence resulting from incarceration is likely to engender a specific set of risk factors for children, particularly those who are impoverished or living in unsafe environments, and for families and communities seeking to create positive settings for children's psychosocial and cognitive development.

Father incarceration is also a significant practice issue. In most areas of social services and social welfare, incarceration as a causal risk factor has been considered to be indistinguishable from related risk factors such as poverty, other types of father absence, and community decay. Practitioners note that many—though far from all—of the men in these programs have been incarcerated, have had "brushes" with the law, or are at-risk for incarceration as a result of a number of demographic features: for example, their age, race, social class, lack of education, and limited employability, among other characteristics (Kane, Gadsden, and Armorer, 1996).

These features increase the likelihood that young, poor, minority men will face arrest, and possibly incarceration, irrespective of the type and scale of offense. Researchers such as Clear and Rose (1999), Hagan and his colleagues (1996), and Hairston (1998, this volume) note that many such arrests of low-income, African-American and other minority men will be for nonviolent crimes typically related to the possession of illegal drugs. They have also found that the relative impact of these men's incarceration on low-income communities will be greater, more sustained, and more devastating in terms of negative effects on children and families than in higher-income communities. The sheer number of nonminority men who are arrested in low-income African-American and Latino communities will be greater than the number of such men in higher income communities, even when the infraction or offense is of comparable seriousness. In terms of the numbers of arrests and incidents of incarceration alone, the "damage" to a low-income, minority community is more severe and potentially intractable.

Father Involvement and Parental Incarceration: Conceptual Issues

Although absent fathers are not found exclusively among poor or minority men, an inordinate amount of attention has been focused on these men, in large part because of the plight of their children, the reliance of their children's mothers on public assistance, and the growing invisibility of the men themselves in the neighborhoods and homes where their children and families reside. Hence, many of the men who constitute the "young fathers" served by child, family, and father-focused programs and who have been the subject of recent national fatherhood efforts and studies are also likely to have their involvement with their children interrupted by incarceration. The neighborhoods in which they live are rendered more vulnerable, and residents are more likely to accommodate their daily lives to the piercing disruptions of multiple and frequent incarcerations. Children observe the evolution and pattern of behaviors that result in a specific kind of social and institutional response; in turn, these children, along with their families and communities, run the risk of becoming inured to the absence of their fathers.

Practitioner reports support the conclusions of research. Fathering practitioners often highlight the social alienation and vulnerability they observe among the fathers they serve, and the ways in which the high probability of being incarcerated and/or past experience of incarceration combine to militate against positive father involvement. The identities such men form, and the personal expectations that evolve from these identities, factor into the ways in which they interpret and respond to their paternal roles. For example, many young fathers cite the "lure" of the streets as a pretext to incarceration and remark on the transformative nature of fathering, which they say often serves to reduce the appeal of the activities likely to lure them away from their families and responsible fathering (Gadsden, Wortham, Wojcik, Ray, and Pinderhughes, 2001).

In such cases, the possibility of incarceration is seen as both a threat to familial engagement and a reality of life in high-crime neighborhoods. As we discuss in the body of this paper, there is an urgent need to increase the quality and quantity of research and practice on incarcerated parents, and on incarcerated fathers in particular. Input from young fathers and the practitioners who serve them reinforces analyses suggesting that, just as family and community cultures are defined by the behaviors and social practices of individuals over time and intergenerationally, so too do families and communities suffer the secondary effects of incarceration—both in the structural indicators of family and economic life and in the individual's sense of personal control and access to opportunity.

Thus, to cope with community and family problems in the presence of poverty—which is itself correlated with being young and a member of a racial or ethnic minority—requires a focus on incarceration and its effects on community, family, and children. In poor neighborhoods, incarceration determines the *demographics* of the community, creating an ebb and flow of young men and young fathers as criminal justice policies change and adapt to shifting political and social trends. The presence or absence of young men in these communities is connected to a series of secondary flows—of children, money, expertise, and social resources. The work of those who devote themselves to improving the lives of impoverished children and strengthening communities cannot be fruitfully directed without understanding the complex dynamics of incarceration and fatherhood.

Lastly, father incarceration is increasingly a policy issue—in both the traditional areas of corrections and justice and in the fields of health and human services. In part, this new status stems from the growing realization in different disciplines that incarceration stands at the intersection of competing yet intertwined policy values. The interaction of imprisonment, child support, and risk of intergenerational transmission of criminal conduct offers a case in point. Incarceration satisfies the societal need to separate and rehabilitate its "deviant" members. Yet, those who are incarcerated—whether men or women—cannot be understood as simply playing the role of "criminal" or "deviant." They often fulfill the role of "mother," "father," "caregiver," or "support system," as well. Incarceration isolates more than the individual; it also separates that person's child and life-partners from a source of economic, emotional, and social support. A lower bound measure of this lost support is the estimated $122 million in child support payments owed by incarcerated fathers to their families (Cavanaugh and Pollack, 1998).

When familial social support systems fail, government steps in to fill the gap. Yet, over the past five years, welfare reform has stipulated that fathers and mothers must take *more* responsibility for their children and household expenses and pending revisions to welfare reform (for example, Temporary Assistance for Needy Families) work requirements threaten to intensify this trend. However, when a father is incarcerated, government's responsibility for his children and family tend to rise. To address this issue, welfare reform legislation (that is, the Personal Responsibility and Work Opportunity Reconciliation Act known as PRWORA) reinforced existing efforts to collect unpaid child support from incarcerated parents. As a result, most fathers exit prison not only homeless, jobless, and socially isolated, but also with substantial child support arrearages.

Within the justice literature, it is also known that men exiting prison are likely to stay "outside the walls" of the prison if they are linked to a family, have employment, and experience success early in their postincarceration experience (Travis, Solomon, and Waul, 2001; Lynch and Sabol, 2001). Large child support debts have been shown to impair both family linkages (where disputes around support and shame regarding the inability to provide for children may undermine reintegration) and employment (where the rewards of employment are siphoned off through the payment of support arrearages).

The justice literature also highlights the risks to children who lack a father. Similar to reports from fathering programs and from research reports on the effects of absent fathers, more than one-half of all incarcerated men report having had little or no contact with their own fathers (Child Welfare League of America, 1999). As the prison population has exploded, so has the number of children with a father in prison—increasing from 872,800 in 1991 to 1,372,700 in 1999 (a 57.2 percent increase). Thus, incarceration may be helping to create the next generation of children at risk for entry into the criminal justice system. Incarceration reduces one type of societal risk by separating "the criminal" from society. But, it also creates other, indirect risks by separating child from father and, through the mechanism of child support arrearages, negatively affecting successful family reintegration. In short, our criminal justice and welfare policies conflict with one another.

What is the impetus to focus on incarcerated fathers? As this short synopsis illustrates, substantial overlap exists between the values pursued by social services policies and criminal justice policies, but these connections only recently have begun to be explored. However, the realization that these policies do interconnect has created a "space" within the policy debate to consider reform. Perhaps the greatest impetus lies in addressing the dearth of systematic studies and lack of comprehensive data on incarcerated fathers or their children and families. The data we do have are incomplete at best and mainly anecdotal. From our review, only a handful of research reports (fewer than forty) are identifiable, using descriptors related to incarcerated fathers and incarcerated parents; a small percentage are empirical studies of basic, applied, or policy research. However, several highly informative conceptual analyses and critical commentaries on issues in the field do exist. A small number refer to findings from selected efforts throughout the country and summarize program or state activities. A slightly more significant number of published reports address parenting and incarceration or examine the nature or effects of parent incarceration on children. None is sufficient to provide the field with a model of the effect of incarceration on fathers, fathering, children, child outcomes, or family processes.

What We Know about Incarcerated Parents and Their Children: A Brief Review

As a society, we have often stated our commitment to children and families. However, it is not clear—either in public discussions or in scholarly and policy debates—that anything more than ambivalence exists toward attending to the needs of children and families of incarcerated parents. The best case in point is the absence of a systematic approach for determining the number of parents who are incarcerated. In many countries (Canada, for example) such data are routinely collected at intake and monitored over time to chart the number of men who learn of their paternity while incarcerated and the number of mothers who give birth during incarceration (Stewart and Gabora-Roth, this volume; Motiuk, 2001). Although recent studies by the U.S. Department of Justice (Mumola, 2000) offer some of the most reliable statistics, we can only estimate, at best, the number of children of incarcerated parents in the United States. The lack of both statistics and literature makes it difficult to draw any conclusions about either the size of this population or the course of research efforts.

Many controversies have surrounded the interpretation of incarceration rates over time. These patterns indicate peaks in the number of those imprisoned for drug offenses and longer sentences for repeat offenders. Beck (2000) suggests that just 10 percent of the rise in state imprisonment between 1980 and 1996 can be attributed to violent offenses and that more than 50 percent of the rise in imprisonment can be traced to the use of custodial sentences, particularly for drug offenders. This and other factors have led observers to note that the criminal justice system is a sorting ground that identifies those with the fewest economic, educational, social, and legal resources.

Converting this number into an estimate of affected children is difficult. Recent data from the Bureau of Justice Statistics (*see* Mumola, 2000) provide the most comprehensive and compelling numerical portrait of the numbers of fathers in prison and the nature of incarcerated fathers' involvement, both preincarceration and during incarceration. Johnston in 1995 estimated that 1.6 million children up to that year had an imprisoned father. A Bureau of Justice Statistics study places the number at about 1.374 million (U.S. Department of Justice, 2000).

The difference may well reflect the fact that law enforcement rarely gathers such information, and, until recently, most correctional institutions did not ask prisoners for specific information about the number or care of their children (Seymour, 1998). Seymour notes that "no specific agency or system is charged with collecting data about this population [making] it unclear how many children are affected, who they are, or where they live" (p. 470). These are issues likely to affect almost every child- and family-services agency and institution: the child welfare system, which supports children who need care; schools, which must not only respond to the learning needs of children but also be able to help create a sense of stability; and the workplace, when the parent or another family member left to care for the child must simultaneously manage employment, child care, and other forms of support.

The lack of knowledge about the number and identity of children with incarcerated parents has many ramifications. Seymour (1998) states that the child welfare community is currently unable to analyze the needs of children with incarcerated parents, to determine the services they require, or to assess the effects of incarceration upon them. Children who enter the social services or child welfare systems due to parental incarceration usually bring few records that might help the child welfare worker determine "when and why [the children] came into care and whether their entry into the system was a result of abuse or neglect prior to the parent's incarceration, as a direct result of the [primary caregiver's] arrest, or as a result of inadequate care during the primary caregiver's incarceration" (p. 475).

As Seymour suggests, the temptation to characterize a child of an incarcerated parent as "just like any other kid" misrepresents and minimizes a range of difficult and complex situations that arise around care, schooling, contact with primary caregiver, and separation trauma when a parent is incarcerated. Yet, our lack of data often denies us the opportunity to identify and understand the unique needs of these children.

When conceptualizing fatherhood during incarceration, the inclination in policy, practice, and even some research is to extrapolate our thin knowledge of incarcerated mothers and apply it to incarcerated fathers. However, the issues surrounding and facing incarcerated fathers are both convergent with and distinct from those of incarcerated mothers. Mothers and fathers are both parents. Both have been removed from their children, families, and communities. Both will live in isolated settings for a specified period of time. In some cases, both have experienced the hardships brought about by poverty, crime, lack of resources, poor schooling, and limited knowledge of and access to positive life options. Here may be where the external similarities end.

Incarcerated fathers and mothers differ, or are distinctive, in the kinds of crimes they commit (Morash, Bynum, and Koons, 1998); the societal expectations placed upon them in their roles as parents (Jeffries, Menhraj, and Hairston, 2001); the ability of communities to reabsorb them; and the expectations of their children. Morash, Bynum, and Koons (1998) suggest that women offenders have needs different from those of men, stemming in part from their disproportionate victimization from sexual or physical abuse and their responsibility for children. In addition, they are more likely than men to be addicted to drugs and to have mental illnesses. They also tend to commit a violent offense against someone close to them. Where programs for incarcerated mothers exist, they focus, as Conty (1999) suggests, on substance abuse, child visitation, parenting education, transition, aftercare, education, and health. Such programs seem to be conducive to success because of several gender-specific factors: for example, staff members who act as positive role models, opportunities to form supportive peer networks, and attention to particular needs, such as support for victimized women.

Until the recent emergence of fathers programs—either in prisons or in communities that can offer postincarceration support—incarcerated men had few of these supports. Much of this is accounted for by the societal expectation that mothers will be children's primary caregivers. In sheer numbers, support programs for mothers are greater than for fathers. However, in general, the number of support programs even for mothers is inadequate. That is, the parenting and other support programs are not proportional to the number of incarcerated women who are primary caregivers, and neither fathers nor mothers have support programs proportional to the severity of their need during or after incarceration.

Fathers also differ from mothers in a range of ways that concern more than gender differences—that is, ways that are often associated with the processes by which family life and family practices come to be shaped. For example, the bond between mother and child created by childbirth does not exist for men, although men report high levels of engagement and anticipation around childbirth and the subsequent role of attaching to newborns (Parke and Coltrane, 2001). Unlike the place of mothers, the role of fathers has not traditionally received much attention. This is not simply because the fathers in question are incarcerated or may be deemed unfit but primarily due to the public's and policymakers' ambivalence about whether fathers are essential to children's well-being and family development. This ambivalence is exacerbated by the fact that some fathers have had tempestuous and even violent relationships with the mothers of their children, or have been separated from their children and families—resulting in both punishment and safety for mothers and children.

Mumola (2001) presents these and other findings and elucidates a range of specific issues around caregiving. They include who provides care prior to and during a parent's incarceration; what the living arrangement is prior to the incarceration of a parent; the number of children; types and nature of contact; type of offense; and whether there was a previous incarceration and/or conviction. More recent discussions have focused on the reentry of offenders into families and communities (Travis, Solomon, and Waul, 2001). Inherent complexities exist, not unlike the issues raised when assessing an individual for parole and in other efforts to reintegrate ex-offenders. Aside from the problem of recidivism, we face the more fundamental issue of the ability, capacity, and willingness of families and communities to receive former inmates.

Issues in Responsible Fatherhood

Societal changes within the past twenty-five years have slowly but persistently helped to redefine traditional understanding of concepts such as "father" and "fathering," as well as fathers' roles (Parke, 1996). Most social scientists recognize the need to move beyond crude distinctions between father presence versus absence as gauges of father involvement. In general, researchers agree that what fathers do with and for their children is much more important than whether fathers simply co-reside with them or have frequent contact with them (Coltrane, 1996; Parke, 1996).

Although using marital status or living arrangements as a measure can be useful in the initial assessment of potential for father-child contact, such structural approaches leave unaddressed variations in actual father involvement in both "father-present" and "father-absent" homes (McLanahan and Sandefur, 1994). Consequently, the most important recommendation to emerge from the fatherhood literature may be that measurement strategies should move past the presence/absence dichotomy to distinguish among different forms of father-child involvement across household type and marital or legal status.

While everyone seems to agree that fathers are good for children and families, the evidence in the academic literature that fathers matter or how they matter is scant, compared to the literature on mothers or in family studies. Thus, it is safe to say that father-focused policies have not been implemented fully or long enough to determine what the returns will be.

Anecdotal evidence and some evaluation reports from fathering programs support the notion that fathers, particularly fathers of young children, are reengaging in their children's lives or, beginning at birth, are becoming more actively aware of parenting and childcare. Our inability to speak with greater confidence about the real and potential effects of these fatherhood initiatives on children and families is linked to several factors. First, despite investments in efforts such as the Fragile Families and early Head Start studies, there has been relatively little federal investment in other research efforts on fathering. Attempts to include father variables in national datasets such as the Family Household Survey and the National Longitudinal Study of Youth, as well as in other datasets, have not yet yielded significant patterns and trends. Second, insufficient time has elapsed since the implementation of many programs for them to have had an impact, on the one hand, and for researchers to garner meaningful data that would show effects over time, on the other.

Unlike other areas of human development and family support, however, the issues of father involvement are especially complex. Many public discussions focus on the concept of "responsible fathering," but research studies are still unclear about what the characteristics of a responsible or competent father actually are (Dollahite, Hawkins, and Brotherson, 1997; Gadsden, Fagan, Ray, and Davis, 2001; Levine and Pitt,1995; Pollack, 1995). In particular, Levine and Pitt suggest that a man who behaves responsibly towards his child and family:

- Waits to make a baby until he is prepared emotionally and financially to support his child

- Establishes his legal paternity if and when he does make a baby

- Actively shares with the child's mother in the continuing emotional and physical care of their child, from pregnancy onwards

- Shares with the child's mother in the continuing financial support of their child, from pregnancy onwards (Levine and Pitt, 1995, p. 5).

The field of father and family studies is growing, and such growth must include a focus on diverse cultural, class, and ethnic groups of fathers and families. A number of research studies are underway that will expand the limited literature on fathers from ethnic minority groups; low-income fathers; noncustodial, nonresidential fathers; never-married fathers; adolescent fathers; and working poor fathers. At the same time, the field continues to examine issues faced by both absent fathers and fathers present in the home, whose interactions with their children may vary by income, history, race, class, and culture and vary in ways that we have yet to understand fully.

One area of contention is the suggestion that fathering issues have been positioned only in relationship to the poor, with laws not intended to help families negotiate systems effectively but designed to legislate morals. The focus on fathers that is attached to proposed legislation on marriage promotion for low-income families thrusts the issue of who represents fathers in father-focused policy into the center of the debate.

As Duncan and Chase-Lansdale (2000) note, for example, a different, family-structure-based view of how welfare reform might promote children's well-being is featured in the preamble to welfare reform legislation, PRWORA. It identified marriage as "an essential institution of a successful society which promotes the interests of children" and "responsible fatherhood and motherhood [as] integral to successful child rearing and the well-being of children." In addition, most policies to date have focused disproportionately on the poor and have been concerned mostly with establishing paternity. Although issues such as visitation and child support collections affect children in all families, attention has been focused primarily on the performance of poor, minority fathers.

One of the strengths of the fathers and families field has been its efforts to increase attention paid to diverse populations, and its ability to find common ground among populations that may not share many other experiences or concerns. The field has stressed that it is equally important to target never-married fathers as well as divorced fathers; urban and suburban fathers; low-income and middle-class fathers; minority and white fathers; and fathers who cut across all of these descriptions. Much of the work is still in its formative stages, and not unlike other research areas, cultural and ethnic diversity, issues related to race, and the effects of institutional forms of racism are rarely the primary focus of efforts. However, for the field to address the complexity of issues, this emphasis should be continued.

Conceptualizing Father Incarceration as an Issue of Responsible Fathering: Linking Parallel Currents of Research and Practice

Throughout this chapter, we have aimed to draw links between disparate areas of research on fatherhood and parenting, in general with research on the nature and consequences of incarceration. This multidisciplinary approach, we believe, is important for developing the field of fathers and families. It highlights potentially integrative and complementary issues that, until now, have not been transformed into rigorous conceptual frameworks, empirical studies, or field-based efforts that cut across diverse domains such as social services and criminal justice. The need for this cross-fertilization of ideas is obvious in any observation of the field of family studies or the more specific area of father involvement, mothering, and parenting.

As we stated early in the chapter, it is difficult, if not impossible, to locate more than a few studies in the social sciences research base that focus on incarcerated fathers or parents and the effects on children or families. Despite the paucity of publications, the effects of and precursors to incarceration are addressed by this literature. As child and family researchers attempt to identify risk factors to the healthy development of children, they tend to include and report data about children who are put at risk by parent incarceration. However, they rarely isolate these children for a more selected analysis of the additional risk created by incarceration. Thus, it appears incarceration and its effects do not constitute a primary or easily identifiable area of inquiry within current social science research outside of social services or criminology.

We can only speculate about why this may be the case. One explanation may be that to address these issues directly, child and family researchers would need to ask study participants to self-identify either as an incarcerated parent or as the child of an incarcerated parent. The social stereotypes are significant, so that most children—and perhaps adults—may be unlikely to engage in such self-identification. Children and adult family members may perceive public or private disclosures to researchers or practitioners outside of correctional or incarcerated parent programs as exposing them to greater risk. Large samples are necessary, as well as smaller-scale studies within programs that serve families with an incarcerated parent or within other institutional settings with participants who represent a range of backgrounds.

Within the social services sector, another barrier to examining these issues is the ambivalent attitude of some practitioners toward noncustodial fathers—much less incarcerated noncustodial fathers. As previous research has demonstrated (Gadsden, Rethemeyer, and Iannozzi, 2001), social service providers in traditionally "mother-focused" areas of practice—day care, pre-schools, and elementary schools, to name a few—often have negative attitudes toward noncustodial fathers, regardless of their incarceration status.

Bias against noncustodial fathers increases the barriers to father involvement in programs and activities for their children in the best of circumstances. It also reduces the motivation for practitioners to incorporate father-oriented activities into their programs and practices. In situations where the father is incarcerated, practitioners may view these fathers as a liability rather than an asset—believing it is better to separate the child from the source of "contagion" than to encourage involvement. From the data and analysis perspective, this bias may reduce the incentives practitioners have to undertake fathering support efforts with incarcerated fathers, and even further reduce the likelihood that such efforts will be reported or analyzed.

On the other hand, it is equally uncommon for the criminology literature to investigate the impact of incarceration on anyone other than the offender and/or to assess the implications of system practices on the effectiveness of "the system" itself. Prisoners are typically described outside of their social roles and familial expectations and responsibilities. Thus, while the process of collecting data on the number of inmates in prisons and jails is relatively straightforward, collecting comparable data on the impact of incarceration on fathers and families has posed a greater challenge, not only in conceptualizing the purpose and significance of such data but also the best uses for them.

The ways in which children, families, and communities are affected or the developmental consequences of imprisonment for the offender and others left behind are rarely examined. Clear and Rose (1999) suggest that criminologists typically study the impact of incarceration by focusing on offenders' criminal behavior in an attempt to discern the rehabilitative, deterrent, and "capacitative" effects of prison sentences. As they note, this approach assumes a fundamental and straightforward relationship:

Remove the criminal, remove the problem, and in so doing create safer, healthier communities. We agree with their suggestion that the relationship is more circuitous and complex, requiring an examination of context, history, demographics, and access to social structures and opportunity for the offender and his family.

A slightly different case exists for practice, particularly social services for children, families, and, more recently, fathers. There is a slowly emerging body of work that examines this area. However, although fatherhood and parenting programs within corrections are increasing within states (*see* Jeffries, Menghraj, and Hairston, 2001), their numbers are still relatively few. Jeffries and his colleagues were able to identify 356 programs across the fifty U.S. states. As we noted earlier, much of the impetus for addressing fatherhood practice has been brought to the forefront by fatherhood practitioners themselves who, in the regular course of their work, encountered disproportionate numbers of fathers who had been in jail or who were or had been engaged in criminal activities leading to imprisonment (Kane, Gadsden, and Armorer, 1996).

Practice issues regarding incarcerated fathers are innately multilayered, with at least two embedded features. One concerns the provision of services to fathers within correctional institutions: whether programs focus on parenting, fathering, or related issues that assist men in learning how to become good parents; become engaged with their children; or make the transition back into the lives of their children, families, and communities (*see* Palm, 1998). This problem is exacerbated when men during their imprisonment learn that they have children; when relationships between the men and the mothers of their children are strained or dissolve during the incarceration; and when the children have little to no knowledge of or previous interactions with their fathers. The situation is made even more difficult when the relationships between the men and the mothers of their children have been violent, or when the relationships between the men and the children themselves have been abusive, inappropriate, or life-threatening.

In this section, we consider all of these issues within the context of two questions: (1) What are the nature and complexities of fathering/parenting from prison and the consequences of father incarceration for families and children? (2) What are the critical features of family and community reentry? Similar to Palm (this volume), we use the *Fathers and Families Core Learnings* as an organizing framework because of its utility to cover the breadth of issues in fathers and families research and its capacity to analyze the consequences of father incarceration and the potential for family and community reentry. The *Fathers and Families Core Learnings* are not a document but seven findings from the work of the National Center on Fathers and Families with fathering practitioners. They serve as a focal point of the investigation, discussion, and analysis of research, practice, and policy in the National Center on Fathers and Families (NCOFF) at the University of Pennsylvania.

The *Core Learnings* were formulated first as seven hypotheses drawn from information supplied through surveys of and interviews with practitioners throughout the country. Each hypothesis was then tested against existing research and published reports. As each hypothesis was borne out in the literature, it became a *Core Learning*. The *Core Learnings* represent primary areas of research, practice, and policy and are used to group or thread together studies that share themes on the role of fathers in family development and efficacy and their relationship to children's well-being. They also constitute the seven categories of National Center on Fathers and Families' *FatherLit Research Database* (www.ncoff.gse.upenn.edu), which houses abstracts of major studies from a wide range of disciplines on issues related to fathers and families. Thus, the *Core Learnings* also serve as both a context to reframe inquiry, practice, and policy and as a way to highlight the need for and pertinence of rigorous conceptual, theoretical, empirical, applied, and policy work in this area.

As described in Table 1, the *Core Learnings* address issues and pose questions around fathers' care, father presence, unemployment and employability, systems barriers, coparenting, role transitions, and intergenerational learning.

In 1996 seven additional *Learnings*, identified through focus groups with almost 100 practitioners throughout the country, were integrated into National Center on Fathers and Families' research effort. Listed in Table 2, they include barriers, such as poor schooling and lack of access to educational opportunities, which limit fathers' employment options; vulnerability, including conditions associated with poverty, drug use, incarceration, and family violence; intergenerational isolation and increasing sense of hopelessness; specific needs and expectations associated with the transition to parenthood and the search for meaning; lack of early preparation for the responsibilities of parenthood and family life.

Father Presence

In research and practice on fathering, the old dichotomy of father presence-father absence has been replaced with a more continuous timeframe in which father presence is thought to extend beyond physical and

Table 1. The National Center on Fathers and Families Original Seven Core Learnings

1.	Fathers' care—even if that caring is not shown in conventional ways.
2.	Fathers' presence matters—in terms of economic well-being, social support, and child development.
3.	Joblessness is a major impediment to family formation and father involvement.
4.	Existing approaches to public benefits, child support enforcement, and paternity establishment operate to create obstacles and disincentives to father involvement. The disincentives are sufficiently compelling as to have prompted the emergence of a phenomenon dubbed "underground fathers"—men who acknowledge paternity and are involved in the lives of their children but who refuse to participate as fathers in the formal systems.
5.	A growing number of young fathers and mothers need additional support to develop the vital skills to share the responsibility for parenting.
6.	The transition from biological father to committed parent has significant developmental implications for young fathers.
7.	The behaviors of young parents, both fathers and mothers, are influenced significantly by intergenerational beliefs and practices within their families of origin.

Source: National Center on Fathers and Families. 1995. *Shared Commitment: Issues from the Inaugural Meeting of the National Practitioners Network*. Philadelphia, Pennsylvania: National Center on Fathers and Families, University of Pennsylvania.

Table 2. Additional Core Learnings (Updated in 1996)

1.	Poor schooling and lack of access to educational opportunities limit the employment options of many fathers and contributes to family instability, which threatens children's well-being and school achievement.
2.	Current discussions about father involvement often minimize the significance of the vulnerable situations of many fathers and families, including conditions associated with poverty, drug use, incarceration, and family violence.
3.	Many young fathers and families experience isolation and a sense of hopelessness, but the transition to parenthood may provoke a new search for meaning in life.
4.	Preparation for the future responsibilities of parenthood and family life should begin early in a child's life.
5.	Encouraging involved fatherhood means moving away from traditional ideals that define manhood in opposition to women and developing models of good fathering.
6.	A systematic analysis of programs for fathers will help identify what elements are essential for reconnecting fathers to families.
7.	Communities' cohesiveness and power to set standards is eroding.

Source: *See* Kane, Gadsden, and Armorer. 1996. *The Fathers and Families Core Learnings: Update from the Field*. Philadelphia, Pennsylvania: National Center on Fathers and Families, University of Pennsylvania.

fiscal boundaries to functional and emotional relations with children (Marino and McCowan, 1976). As a *Core Learning*, father presence addresses two major questions: (1) What difference does a father in the home make to a child's emotional, social, and cognitive development? (From the child's point of view, what difference does it make to live with or have access to only one parent?) and (2) How does father absence affect family well-being? For example, how does father absence contribute to poverty in families?

"Father presence" is more than the mere antithesis of father absence. It encompasses a range of issues that combine the nurturing, educational, and financial roles that fathers play in children's cognitive development, physical health, and social well-being. Father presence is a rich and complex construction of fathers' roles and relationships to their children. Attached to the concept of father presence is a presumption of responsible fathering. That is, "responsible fathering" is the ideal that researchers, practitioners, and policymakers alike hold up in determining support for children, families, and fathers themselves.

The term "responsible fathering" is a not an entirely neutral concept, however. It reflects a recent shift among academics and professionals away from value-free language toward a more explicit value advocacy approach (Doherty, Kouneski, and Erickson, 1998). The term conveys a moral meaning (right and wrong), since it suggests that some fathering could be judged "irresponsible" or "nonresponsible."

Lamb and his colleagues (Lamb, 1987; Lamb, Pleck, Charnov, and Levine, 1985) offered the most influential schemata for considering fathering involvement, which has three components: (1) responsibility, (2) availability, and (3) engagement. Responsibility refers to the role that a father takes in ascertaining that the child is cared for and arranging for the availability of financial and care-giving resources (Lamb, Pleck, Charnov, and Levine, 1987, p. 125). Availability is a related concept concerning the father's potential for interaction, by virtue of being present or accessible to the child (irrespective of whether direct interaction is occurring). Engagement refers to the father's direct interaction or contact with his child through care giving and shared activities.

Numerous studies link father absence to child and adolescent problems and, similarly, literature on incarcerated parents and child welfare demonstrates a connection between child and youth problems and parent absence (though such work is usually mother-focused). The literature suggests that children whose parents are incarcerated experience a variety of negative consequences, particularly in emotional health and well-being, contact with their parents, and physical care and custody (Johnston, 1995; Hagan and Dinovitzer, 1999). The specific effects on children are dictated by a range of variables, such as the age of the child at the time of the parent's incarceration; the child's relationship with the parent prior to the parent's incarceration; the parent's familiarity with the placement or new caregiver; the nature of the parents' crime; the length of the parent's sentence; the availability of kin and other familial and community support; and the nature and degree of stigma associated with the incarceration (Gaudin and Sutphen, 1993; The Osborne Association, 1993).

Although the differential effects of father absence due to incarceration have not been examined as a separate area of study, moving away from the father presence-father absence dichotomy and focusing on the continuum of father presence behaviors may be a particularly useful and relevant approach for examining father incarceration—a situation for which we can assume some form of absence but not necessarily total unavailability. Thus, the points along the continuum—for example, father availability at one end and father unavailability at the other—are likely to inform us about the evolution of engagement and the nature of contact between incarcerated fathers and their children and families more than any attempt to divide contact into either absence or presence.

For example, an area of considerable concern for corrections and child welfare specialists is parent-child contact: parents' access to children and children's visitation. A little over 50 percent of incarcerated parents receive regular visits from their children, while others receive infrequent visits (Mumola, 2000). Efforts are typically made to ensure that parents maintain contact with their children, in the form of telephone calls; letters, in cases where the literacy level of both parent and child allows such correspondence; and electronic mail, which has some of the same limitations as letter writing. In cases where physical visits are possible, the costs of transportation and the length of the trip may prohibit any real contact. As Bloom (1995) suggests, the inhospitable nature of visiting rooms, the disruption visits cause the custodial caregiver, and the discomfort of the incarcerated parent may make such contact difficult, at best. In fact, such visits may worsen the trauma of parental absence for the child. This, of course, assumes that bringing the child and parent together is "the right thing to do" for the child, and that such interaction will enhance children's sense of knowing and belonging, as well as their psychoemotional development.

Interspersed throughout any discussion of father presence in the context of incarceration are questions about the particular ways that this type of father absence differs from other forms of absence. How does a father's absence contribute to reconfigurations in family life and in children's care giving? What does it mean for a child—in terms of emotional and other forms of well-being—when a father reenters the family and the child's life? What is the nature of the father's presence prior to incarceration, during incarceration, and postrelease, and what are the implications of the father's presence at each of these points for children's well-being and family functioning?

Fathers' Care

The concept of *fathers' care* is distinguished from that of father presence, although it may be considered a subset of father presence. Fathers' care giving focuses on whether and how a father demonstrates concern through different behaviors and practices. Research on fathers' care investigates questions related to attachment and support and to the personal, familial, and structural barriers to fathers' care giving. It asks questions about the social and developmental needs of young fathers and questions of particular interest to practitioners, such as how to define a "good" father and what kind of involvement makes a difference (Kane, Gadsden, and Armorer, 1996). Research on fathers' care giving also examines the role of fathers in the physical and psychological maintenance of children and the relationships that develop between fathers and their children throughout the life course.

When fathers give care to their children, they provide for children's basic needs, including feeding them, ensuring they get sufficient rest, and protecting them from danger. They also provide a range of other nurturing expressions and behaviors that convey to children a sense of emotional engagement, love, attachment, and security. These behaviors involve culturally appropriate physical acts of affection and comfort (such as touching, hugging, kissing, and cuddling), verbal expressions (such as comforting with reassuring words and sounds), and behaviors that help to maintain communication between children and caregivers (including listening and giving timely responses to children's concerns).

In addition, care giving involves generativity—that is, psychological and emotional investment in the care-giving role and in the children for whom one provides such care (Erikson, 1969; Erikson and Erikson, 1981). Finally, paternal care giving includes the managerial tasks that permit those nurturing and life-sustaining acts that help to ensure optimal child outcomes, especially physical, emotional, and psychological development.

The intimate nature of care giving provides a context for emotional engagement between father and child. Over the past decade, studies of father involvement have highlighted the importance of fathers' emotional connection with their children (Coltrane and Parke, 1998), suggesting that positive father involvement is an important factor in children's socioemotional development. For example, during infancy, secure attachment to the father has been associated with positive emotional development and the capacity for empathy in school-age children (Biller and Trotter, 1994).

Much of the literature on fathers' caring has been shaped by developmental psychology, sociology, and family and gender studies and has explored father participation without much attention to the processes through which men come to participate in their children's lives, and the nature of this participation (Barnett and Baruch 1987; Palkovitz, 1984). What we do know is that, within the general population, mothers still provide more childcare than fathers, suggesting that when women and their children are separated because of their mother's imprisonment, the children are likely to suffer loss of maternal support.

More than two-thirds of all women in prison had children under the age of eighteen, and 64 percent of these mothers (compared with 44 percent of incarcerated fathers) had co-resided with their children prior to their incarceration (Mumola, 2000). Of these mothers, only 25 percent said the children were living with the other parent, namely the father.

Data on fathers' care among men in prison is even less clear cut than that on mothers, although the data are far less compelling than that of the imprisoned mothers who were caring for their children prior to their incarceration. Unlike the work focused on fathers outside of corrections, however, there is a disconnect between the number of children who have a father in prison and the number of men in prison who report having children. Many men who are fathers cannot or do not always self-identify as fathers. That is, they may not know they have fathered a child or exactly how many children they have fathered, typically because the mother or the mother's family has chosen to sever ties with the incarcerated father for a variety of reasons.

Western and McLanahan (2000) note that mothers' reports are particularly informative about fathers who are hard to locate and whose incarceration risk is likely to be high. In describing the data for the Fragile Families survey, they note that because the fathers studied were disproportionately young, with little education, it seems likely that their reports understate their true incidence of incarceration. In this reference, the role of practice is particularly noteworthy, since practitioners in fathers and family programs typically collect information on whether a father has been incarcerated; in the course of their participation in programs, the fathers tend to form relationships with practitioners that reduce the perceived threat of revealing their criminal histories. In our own work with poor fathers in an urban, Midwestern city, fathers were more willing to reveal their pasts in one-on-one interviews than in responses to surveys or in focus groups, unless focus group participants were their program cohorts.

It is not uncommon for incarcerated fathers who do not have positive, noncombative relationships with their spouses or the mothers of their children to express the same kind of caring, hope, and expectation as other fathers. In many ways, their care may be enhanced by the fact that their contact with their children is irregular—if it exists at all—and their dreams of their children are created around an ideal of the child. However, if one does not know he has fathered a child, it is unlikely that he will demonstrate positive caring behaviors.

Imprisonment of a parent often disrupts intact families in which the parent and child know and are strongly attached to each other (Genty, 1998). The issues of father care reach into a range of child welfare areas, for example, permanency planning for children. Only 25 percent of incarcerated women with children left their children in the care of their children's fathers. However, 90 percent of fathers in state prison reported that at least one of their children lived with the child's mother.

Several factors make the issue of incarcerated fathers' care murky. First, if fathers are not engaged in children's lives, what is the role of the correctional system in helping them become engaged? How is such engagement complicated when a) mothers want to sever relationships with the father, b) fathers have histories of violence toward mothers, or c) fathers are known physical or sexual abusers? Second, in cases where mothers and incarcerated fathers agree that the fathers can and should demonstrate caring, how can fathers be positively engaged? Are parenting classes enough to help fathers understand children's development and fathers' responsibility to ensure children's health development? Are more focused fathering and male involvement programs necessary to help men become good fathers, develop positive parenting behaviors during and after incarceration, and identify resources that make them better fathers and family members?

In particular, researchers will need to work with practitioners to determine the dimensions of fathers' care and how these dimensions may be implemented in incarcerated father programs, translated for fathers postrelease, and measured in both settings and over time (*see The Fathering Indicators Framework*, Gadsden, Fagan, Ray, and Davis, 2001). Among the indictors that we typically associate with fathers' care are the following: being aware of children's social-emotional development; being responsive to children's emotional reactions; making efforts to make children feel safe in their presence; providing physical care to children (for example, changing diapers, grooming); and consistently arranging a safe environment and monitoring children's safety. To what degree can programs assist incarcerated fathers in exhibiting these behaviors? In what ways can research monitor, study, and inform the field on how these are accomplished within the context of correctional settings and upon family reentry?

Employment, Joblessness, and Father Reentry

Employment and joblessness are problems that affect a disproportionate number of incarcerated fathers—particularly poor, minority fathers—both before and after incarceration. Problems around employment and the intractability of joblessness often have causal links to incarceration, poor reintegration, and recidivism (Beck, 2000; Travis, Solomon, and Waul, 2001). The impact of incarceration may be most obvious for ex-offenders. Kling (1999), drawing from administrative data and unemployment insurance records, found large, temporary effects of incarceration on employment and earnings. Western and Beckett (1999) report that employment among respondents to the National Longitudinal Survey of Youth (NLSY) is close to 10 percent lower among those who have been in juvenile detention, ten years after the original incarceration and even when accumulated work experience and adult incarceration are taken into account.

Joblessness and problems of employment and employability serve as impediments to family formation and family involvement. This *Core Learning* centers on two questions: (1) What is the relationship between father involvement and joblessness, particularly among African-American fathers and other fathers of color? That is, how does joblessness and limited access to well-paying employment affect family formation choices and patterns, parenting activities, and decisions to marry?; and (2) What types of policies are necessary to respond to unemployment among young fathers, particularly African-American fathers and other fathers of color?

FATHER INVOLVEMENT AND PARENTAL INCARCERATION: CONCEPTUAL ISSUES

Research on father involvement, employment, and joblessness addresses a father's ability to obtain and sustain employment and the ways in which a history of joblessness influences a father's engagement with his children, particularly within African-American and Latino communities. More than two decades ago, Goodwin (1972) found that, across social classes, people in all ethnic groups in American society value work for similar reasons, including feelings of self-worth, survival needs, and support of children and families.

When the normal venues to obtain work are unavailable or inaccessible, many fathers—particularly young fathers with few skills, few years of schooling, and a record of incarceration—either avoid the responsibility for supporting their children or turn to informal economies (for example, unrecorded and untaxed work such as car washing, home-based instrument repair, and the drug trade) to provide the necessary income. Practitioners identified lack of education as a major contributor to young fathers' joblessness along with the young fathers' attitude toward, experience with, and exposure to work and work settings (Kane, Gadsden, and Armorer, 1996). They raised questions about how having or not having a job interfered with fathering, and how education and schooling contribute to increased employment options and to sustained father involvement.

Although all ex-offenders face these problems to some degree, minority and currently or formerly imprisoned poor men are often seen as unavailable or unsuitable as mates. Edin (2000) found from interviews with single mothers that they were reluctant to marry or live with the father of their children if he had a history of incarceration. Even outside of incarceration, involuntarily institutionalized, marginalized males may be economically unsuitable as mates due to insufficient or unstable earnings or socially unsuitable because of current participation in illegal activities or underground economies, which hold the possible result of incarceration.

Marginalization, Mason (1995) argues, also may result from insufficient access to health care and health information, as well as overrepresentation in hazardous work, for example, combat assignments in the military or hazardous industrial employment. By reducing the supply of marriageable males, he suggests, marginalization is a contributory factor to the rise of female-headed households in the United States.

Darity and Myers (1995) outline a two-stage dynamic model of African-American male marginalization. In this model, an increase in the probability of marginalization in one year lowers the ratio of men in the marriage market, which, in turn, tends to raise the probability of marginalization in the subsequent year. The embarrassment of incarceration is severe enough to serve as a disincentive to get married and increases the likelihood that women will "settle" for a former inmate. Sabol and Lynch (1997) found, for example, that the number of female-headed households was large compared to other counties when there was a large number of ex-offenders reentering communities.

Solid empirical evidence shows that, for many poor minority men, limited earnings opportunities in the mainstream economy are the primary determinant of drug dealing (Myers, 1992). Increases in joblessness tend to be associated with increases in the incarceration rate of African-American men (Myers and Sabol, 1987). In the Darity-Myers model of transitions in the African-American family structure, secular trends and cyclical shifts in the macroeconomic structure strongly influence microeconomic decision making in the marriage market through endogenous changes in the ratio of marriage-eligible males to females (*see also* Mason, 1995).

Several studies report that employed fathers, who are better able to provide for their children, are also better able to cope with parental strain than unemployed fathers. Employed fathers of all ethnic backgrounds appear to be less irritable and more actively involved than unemployed fathers. Danziger and Radin (1990) obtained data from 289 interviews with teenage mothers who were receiving public assistance on the father's willingness to assume paternal responsibilities. The most important predictor of an absent father's involvement with his children was his employment status over the last year. Grossman, Pollack, and Golding (1988) using a small sample of white intact families found that, among employed fathers, greater job satisfaction tended to improve slightly the quality of father-child relationships. However, the social impact of incarceration for fathers cannot be minimized. Unemployed young adults appear to be hardest hit psychologically by joblessness, and father incarceration decreases the real contributions of fathers, and depletes the financial and human resources available to children.

The preceding discussion highlights a number of questions that deserve greater attention from researchers and practitioners. How do issues of physical and mental health contribute to joblessness and criminal activities among incarcerated fathers? How do problems of poor health, literacy, schooling, and educational achievement generally interfere with fathers' ability to engage positively with their children? How does joblessness and access to well-paying employment affect family formation choices and patterns, parenting activities, and decisions to marry, among incarcerated fathers? What are the basic workforce investment issues that need to be addressed by current policies in relationship to incarcerated fathers?

Systemic Barriers

For nonincarcerated fathers, systemic barriers refer to features of public benefits, child support enforcement, and paternity establishment that have been perceived traditionally as barriers to fathers' positive engagement with children in families. In the context of incarcerated fathers, the primary barrier to father involvement is the father's incarceration. However, there are useful insights that may be applied from the systemic barriers literature to incarcerated fathers.

In this literature, the central assumption is that father involvement is "good" and that policy barriers to father involvement result when the policy is irrational, has impacts that are poorly understood, or is created without grappling with and reconciling competing policy objectives. The goal of publications in this literature is to find ways to reconcile the needs of policy and the needs of fathers. In the context of incarceration, the key systemic barrier may not be incarceration itself, but the complex interplay of criminal justice and related child support and welfare policies that are poorly reconciled to the central facts of incarceration and its impact on families.

In the "traditional" systemic barriers literature, both divorced and never-married fathers reportedly refer to the "system" as being counterproductive in their efforts to be "good" fathers. One might imagine that the bureaucratic nature of government systems might create obstacles. Among many young fathers and the mothers of their children, systemic approaches to paternity establishment and child support enforcement activities are met with distrust and associated with punitive, rather than supportive, effects.

This distrust is supported by the experiences of many young parents, particularly those in low-income homes and in families of color. In the past, the first contact between the institution and absent parent was often through a phone message or letter and, if that was ignored, a visit from the sheriff's office (Wattenberg, 1993; Sullivan, 1993). The requirement that the absent father appear in court was likely to deter many young men whose primary association with such courts is arrest, conviction, or imprisonment (Danziger, Kastner, and Nickel, 1993).

Noncustodial fathers often associate "the system" with efforts to create new financial obligations for them (via paternity establishment and child support orders)—efforts which rarely take into account their desire to have nonfinancial relationships with their children and which create large "overhead" expenses (like court costs) that provide no benefit to their children. These punitive associations and bureaucratic fragmentation can reinforce preexisting client attitudes regarding paternity establishment.

Incarcerated fathers face many of the same systemic barriers, but also face additional structural impediments linked to their criminal justice status. Analytically, one might divide these barriers by the cycle of incarceration itself: detention and judgment, penal incarceration, and family and community reintegration.

Detention and judgment. Men who begin their journey through the criminal justice system often do so in an abrupt manner that provides their children and family with little or no time to prepare for the impact of incarceration. In many cases—where the threat of ongoing violence or flight is high—there is good reason for this hasty removal from society. However, the trend toward detention without bail has expanded the number of children who lose their parents in an abrupt manner.

Moreover, the systems for providing care to a child who has lost his or her caregiver are skewed toward foster care. Under the Personal Responsibility and Work Opportunity Reconciliation Act (PRWORA), many state systems provide higher support payments to foster parents who take responsibility for children of incarcerated single parents than to relatives who take responsibility. Moreover, PRWORA penalizes the child for the parent's behavior by discontinuing food stamps and other forms of social welfare support after the parent has committed certain types of offenses, including those related to possession and use of relatively small amounts of illegal drugs.

In essence, the system promotes placement of children with adoptive and foster families once a parent becomes incarcerated, in contravention of practices handed down over hundreds of years (Phillips and Bloom, 1998). Lifetime bans on social support services and preference for nonkinship placement severely interrupt the ability of incarcerated men to maintain their connection to and relationship with their children.

Incarceration. During detentions and incarceration, a number of barriers exist to establishing and maintaining fathers' involvement that are not inherent to incarceration itself but are a product of policies that interact with incarceration in ways not fully appreciated. For men without known children, problems begin with establishing paternity and inhibiting the creation of initial child-parent relationships. Incarcerated men are unable to seek paternity establishment proactively.

For mothers who wish to avoid interaction with the father, birth during incarceration may increase the chances that paternity is not established. Thoennes and Pearson (1995) found in their in-hospital paternity establishment study that the chief reasons mothers were unwilling to sign a voluntary paternity acknowledgement form at the time of their child's birth was a bad relationship with the baby's father followed by concern about the father gaining custody or visitation rights. They also found that voluntary paternity acknowledgment was much more likely among parents who were financially independent at the time of the child's birth and had never been involved with Aid to Families with Dependent Children (AFDC). Finally, they found that mothers were more likely to sign voluntary paternity acknowledgment forms if the fathers were employed full-time (*see also* Sorenson, 1995).

Thus, incarceration complicates an already murky paternity establishment picture. When the father is unable to provide informal support—via in-kind services or informal cash payments—mothers may have little choice but to enter the incarcerated father into the child support system in order to receive payment at some future date.

For those fathers who already have child support obligations, incarceration can create life-long financial problems. Many men perceive their child support as unfair, punitive, and counterproductive, irrespective of their criminal justice status. Men who have children receiving welfare support are particularly likely to find the system punitive, because their payment often results in no more than $50 of benefits for their children in most states.

However, incarcerated men face particularly difficult situations. Because the Personal Responsibility and Work Opportunity Reconciliation Act emphasized collection and enforcement of child support obligations, most states continue incarcerated fathers' support obligations. Courts can modify awards for incarcerated fathers, but most inmates are unaware that modification is possible. Even then, modification is usually an expensive process—one that most inmates cannot afford. A recent National Conference of State Legislatures report (Davis, 2000) suggests that because few seek modification, most fathers leave prison with arrearages that they can never meet. The inability to meet current and past child support obligations is a known barrier to father involvement in nonincarcerated situations; there is no reason to think it is not so for those who are incarcerated.

The prison system and the prison setting itself often creates barriers to fathers' involvement. Most prisons are located far from the urban areas where their family is located. While the location of prisons cannot be changed, it is possible for the system to be more sensitive to placement when multiple prisons with the same level of security exist within a state. However, the trend toward privatized prisons located at an extreme distance from the family's home enlarges this barrier enormously, making any during-incarceration contact virtually impossible.

Release and Family Reentry. Successful release and reentry is best predicted by religion and family connections (Brenner, 1998). In this context, child support arrearages and obligations have their greatest impact. Men with arrearages are less likely to participate in family life and are likely to discount the benefits of employment, because they know a significant percentage of their earnings will go to child support. In fact, arrearages may encourage men to join the informal economy, threatening to undermine their compliance with parole-based work requirements and deepening the cycle of unemployment and child support arrearages that undermine father involvement. Finally, some men actually may be forced to return to prison if they are unable to meet child support obligations (Sachs, 2000).

Release rules are another potential barrier to postincarceration father involvement. Men on parole are often restricted by their need to meet with parole officers and/or requirements that they reside in a given location. Whether the release and parole location is coterminous with the children's location is an open question.

This summary only highlights the most salient of systemic barriers that face incarcerated men. A fuller analysis is urgently needed, with particular attention to the relationship between release requirements and economic opportunities postincarceration. Analyzing these variables would help child support agencies develop a more realistic (and hopefully dynamic) set of expectations for fathers who leave prison. The existing systemic barriers literature provides many important insights and analytic tools to assist in this inquiry.

We believe three questions need further investigation as policy and institutional research on fathering and incarceration proceeds. First, what connections can be made between and across agencies to help reconcile competing mandates that have an impact on incarcerated men? Second, how can correctional programs help men more effectively navigate the paternity and child support enforcement systems? Finally, can prison programs tap the expertise of community programs with respect to system navigation? Can prison and community programs be linked to create seamless support?

Cooperative/Collaborative Parenting (Coparenting)

Coparenting refers to the range of cooperative relationships that exist between cohabiting parents, parents separated by divorce, and never-married nonresidential parents. Practitioners highlight the significance of cooperative parenting for parents of all ages, not simply for young parents, noting that it is also relevant to families regardless of the marital status of the parents, the father's residential status, or the circumstances of a child's birth.

Clearly, however, the specific nature of a cooperative parenting arrangement depends on family type. For example, cooperative parenting among divorced parents involves renegotiating shared parental roles. Cooperative parenting also is used to describe a range of other parenting relationships, including same-sex parenting and childcare shared by a parent and a grandparent or a parent and other caregivers (Arendell, 1995).

In addition, since the mid-1990s, attention to cooperative parenting has captured the attention of researchers and practitioners working with unmarried fathers and mothers (Philadelphia Children's Network, 1996) and those participating in fathers' programs. Such attention has spurred new terms, such as "team parenting," intended to highlight the complexities that some young, low-income, never-married fathers and mothers face in sharing decision making and supporting their children.

Coparenting is a particularly complex undertaking when parents have been separated by incarceration. Relationship status prior to incarceration, length of the sentence, and changes in the lives of the nonincarcerated parent may all contribute to whether and how coparenting can and does occur. The ability of parents to construct both a plan for cooperative parenting activities and mutually respectful relationships does serve as a critical mediating factor for child well-being.

If parents are not able to coplan and coparent, fundamental parent-child activities may be compromised. For example, frequent visitation becomes problematic if the parental relationship is conflict-ridden, and fathers may reduce the frequency of visitation and the amount of child support to reduce the opportunity for conflict with the former spouse (Arendell, 1995). In fact, the character of a father's relationship with his former partner is the most salient factor in determining the frequency of visitation.

Researchers have used different approaches to define cooperative parenting. Several focus on the support that one parent gives to the other when she or he is advancing a parenting goal (Gable, Belsky, and Crnic, 1995). Others concentrate on interparental agreement (Vaughn, Block, and Block, 1988) or child-related disputes between parents (Jouriles et al., 1991). Still others refer to parenting alliances, defined as the ability of a parent to acknowledge, respect, and value the parenting roles and tasks of the partner (Cohen and Weissman, 1984).

Using the Cohen and Weissman definition, McBride and Ranes (1998) cite four features of a parenting alliance: (1) each parent has an investment in the child; (2) each parent values the importance of the other parent in fostering the child's growth and development; (3) each parent respects and values the judgments of the other parent; and (4) parents maintain an ongoing communication with one another around the needs of the child.

Among married and two-parent cohabiting couples, the term cooperative parenting, or shared parenting, typically refers to relationships in which fathers' participation in childrearing is more or less equal to that of the mother. Such involvement still appears to be rare, despite attention given to the "new father" in recent years. Divorced parents offer a different context than either married or never-married parents. After a divorce, the establishment of a cooperative parenting relationship between parents may be influenced by the nonresidence of the noncustodial parent, the personal willingness and ability of parents to establish a cooperative parenting relationship, and feelings and emotions engendered during marital dissolution.

Unlike married or divorced fathers, young unwed fathers' participation in parenting or cooperative parenting may depend on the fathers' presence at birth and paternity declaration; frequency of access and contact; cohabitation with the mother and the status of his relationship with her; the ability of the young father to provide financial support; and social and cultural expectations around fathers' parental rights. Many unmarried parents may need support in negotiating the processes by which they learn to work together for the benefit of their children.

One variant of coparenting, cited consistently in discussions about low-income, never-married fathers or in work on what Ron Mincy in the mid-1990s termed "fragile families," is the concept of "team parenting," which is intended to denote the special circumstances faced by this population of fathers and families. For these and other unmarried couples, the task of cooperative parenting or team parenting involves defining parental roles, obligations, and responsibilities outside the legal protection and culturally defined role expectations that marriage provides.

An often-noted barrier to cooperative parenting among never-married, noncustodial fathers is maternal (or maternal grandparent) gatekeeping, which occurs if maternal custodians limit father involvement and contact with the child. Gatekeeping involves determining the circumstances for the noncustodial parent's involvement (in other words, where the visits may take place and what may happen on those visits). Anger or conflict may cause a mother to restrict the amount and type of father involvement.

Although the amount and effects of the custodial guardian's gatekeeping have not been well-documented in two-parent families, anecdotal evidence of gatekeeping in divorced families has been consistently reported. What is not known is the frequency with which such gatekeeping occurs, its nature, or the extent to which gatekeeping affects children's development either positively or negatively. Obvious issues that merit examination are those surrounding self-esteem, children's perceptions of the gatekeeping (which may be construed as a type of parental conflict), and other psychological factors for the child such as depression.

In much the same way that a father's behavior toward the mother of his children may have an impact on the access that the mother or her family gives the father to his children, a father's incarceration may dictate the degree to which a coparenting plan can be created and negotiated, whether it can be implemented, and what resources are available to monitor and support implementation and follow-through. In addition, the ability to establish a plan presupposes a reasonably respectful and perhaps cordial relationship between the father and mother. In cases in which the extended family is especially combative toward the father, resources external to the family are necessary, if not essential.

The incarceration itself may be enough for families to sever the child's relationship with the father, as they attempt to limit the child's knowledge of negative pathways. Coparenting is difficult even for parents in committed relationships with few worries about resources. The problems and resulting tensions are only heightened for poor parents, adolescent and young adult parents, unmarried parents, parents whose children have special needs, minority parents, and parents with little knowledge of the structure and working of social structures and institutions. They are similarly unsettling for those with few familial, educational, or institutional resources.

Thus, a number of potential areas of study have arisen that, if pursued, will help to initiate a discourse on coparenting "through the bars" and identify practices that promote coparenting in families with an incarcerated parent. These include the ways in which programs and social services of all types could assist parents with coparenting preparation; an increased understanding of the relationships between helping parents to become "good parents" and helping them to coparent; the roles extended families and kin play in coparenting; and the roles social and correctional systems can play in promoting coparenting.

Role Transitions

The literature on role transitions focuses on how the transition to parenthood affects the life course of fathers and mothers and how life transitions affect parenting choices, behaviors, and practices. Adult and adolescent males undergo this transition within the context of dyadic relationships (either married or unmarried couples—with resident or nonresident fathers).

Throughout the developmental stages of life, males and females experience critical changes in their perspectives and social roles as they progress from birth to old age. These attitudinal and behavioral changes generally involve growth and maturation into a new set of circumstances and adaptation into different social roles. In adapting to changing social roles, we learn new norms and modify our value system. The roles we play are adjusted over time or replaced as we transition from one stage to the next. The key stages of life involving significant transformation include going to school for the first time, leaving home, getting married, and having children (Barnhill et al., 1979).

The transition to fatherhood has been studied through various theoretical lenses and can be best understood within the context of broader perspectives on parenthood as applied to fatherhood. Several decades ago, the early sociological literature described the transition to parenthood, in general, as a "crisis" (Dyer, 1963; LeMasters, 1957) characterized by anxiety, depression, and uncertainty about the future. Other work suggests that fathers experience conflicting feelings about themselves, their wives or partners, and their children during the pregnancy and after childbirth (Osofsky and Culp, 1989). While pregnancy and childbirth are unquestionably stressful events for females, they have also been described as overwhelming events for males (Cowan et al., 1985; Klein, 1985; Wente and Crockenberg, 1976).

Father Involvement and Parental Incarceration: Conceptual Issues

In his "process model of parenthood," (Belsky 1984) suggests that parental functioning is determined by multiple factors. According to this thinking, there is a reciprocal relationship between contextual stressors and support and the individual parent's personality. The sources of contextual stress and support affect parenting either directly or indirectly. They do this by first influencing the psychological well-being of the individual parent. In turn, the parent's own personality influences the contextual stress or support he or she experiences, creating a feedback loop which again affects parenting. Further, he writes, "in order of importance, personal psychological resources of the parent are more effective in buffering the parent-child relation from stress than are contextual sources of support, which are themselves more effective than characteristics of the child" (p. 83).

In the process model of parenthood, an incarcerated father would be exposed to a range of contextual factors that neither acknowledge nor support his role as father. The required structures associated with incarceration are in themselves not inviting settings for fathers to connect with their families (Phillips and Bloom, 1998) and are not designed to encourage meaningful interaction that fathers making the transition to fatherhood outside of corrections would otherwise experience. The experience of prison is a transition that is transformative to adult male development. For some men, the additional role of father may strain the transition to the role as prisoner.

For other men, the role of father may serve as a source of solace which allows them to create and play out "an imagined self" in which they construct possible relationships with their children and families in the hope that these relationships can be realized once they are released or are given a second chance. For still other men, the role of father is as likely to serve as an excuse for their incarceration or as a stimulus to seek support in making the transition.

The full range of feelings and experiences associated with role transitions when a father is incarcerated is not known. The timing of new fatherhood and of incarceration undoubtedly plays a critical role in whether and how well a father adapts to his roles as father, incarcerated man, and absent father. A father's transition is potentially made more difficult if he does not welcome his role as a new father. However, for some young men, the new role as father becomes a deciding factor in behavior change—both the desire not to engage in criminal activities and the desire to make meaningful change.

Young fathers who participate in fathers' programs often report that their incarceration was the event that transformed their behavior as fathers. After this transformative event, they established some sort of domestic relation with their children, mostly with visitation rights and weekend overnights, together with financial support (Gadsden, Wortham, Wojcik, Ray, and Pinderhughes, 2001). If we accept the premise that the role transition to fatherhood as a part of a normative developmental sequence is fraught with inner conflicts and uncertainties for any father, we might expect that these feelings of uncertainty are heightened for fathers who have the weight of poverty, youth, and limited employment skills and educational preparation to sustain employment. This may be true even when they reportedly welcome the birth of a child.

In work on role transitions for nonincarcerated fathers, researchers note that while some upheaval and emotional distress is likely to occur, particularly among first-time fathers (Klein, 1985), these reactions are common to most significant role transitions. For example, young adults often experience anxiety, uncertainty, and fear on moving out of their parent's home, or leaving for college. Both of these are seen as socially accepted, expected, and sanctioned transitions.

The transition to prison disrupts these expectations and is not sanctioned. Progressing through a normative life events sequence often involves learning new skills, norms, and modes of adaptation, and a readjustment of priorities. Add to that transition the transition to parenthood, another critical life event, and there is exacerbated disruption of customary behavior (McHale and Huston, 1985). Such life events typically involve fundamental changes in interpersonal relationships and affect how people view themselves, their future, and their significant others.

Practitioners in fathers' programs—particularly those in programs serving low-income, young fathers—note that role transitions require changes in attitudes and that maturity and age play a role in how successfully the young father will make the transition to parenthood (Kane, Gadsden, and Armorer, 1996). This, they suggest, raises questions about what role age and maturity play in the transition to committed fatherhood, motherhood, and parenthood, and whether and how these transitions can be built on as points of entry for teaching and learning.

The practitioners' questions are particularly relevant for conceptualizing the impact of role transitions to incarceration and to incarcerated fathers, especially adolescent and young adult fathers for whom fatherhood has become the proxy or substitute for normal progression into adulthood. Young fatherhood both opens up the possibility for maturing and creates barriers that result in poor schooling, limited educational attainment, and poor job skills. Although there are cultural, gender, and individual variations in the transition through the life cycles, we invariably proceed through a relatively orderly and predictable set of developmental stages.

However, the orderliness of life transitions is broken down by early parenthood, especially when it occurs before completing secondary school and acquiring marketable job skills. Researchers such as Rapoport asserted as early as 1963 that referring to parenthood as a "crisis" exaggerates reality because becoming a parent, however stressful it may be, is a normal aspect of adult life. Rapoport suggests adding the descriptor "normal" to the term crisis and using "normal crisis" as a more accurate depiction of parenthood.

Incarceration over the short or long term interrupts this "normal crisis," and complicates the transition to fatherhood in ways that we do not yet understand fully. Whether and how the transition differs from that of nonincarcerated men and whether and how social class and race are translated within the transition are also areas of study still to be examined.

The role transitions literature offers many insights into the social and psychological changes that occur with incarceration, regardless of parental status. We believe both the fathering and the criminal justice literatures could be enriched by examining five questions that "mine" this intersection. What are the nature and range of feelings men experience at role transitions? What can we learn from general experience to help men going to prison? How do the timing of fatherhood and incarceration intersect? How do fathers adapt to being a father, an absent father, and an inmate concurrently? How can programs use the period of "state change" which comes with new fatherhood to influence both parenting and nonparenting behaviors?

Intergenerational Learning

Intergenerational learning assumes that families of origin play a critical role in defining and shaping the practices, choices, and behaviors of parents—in other words, that the behaviors of parents are influenced significantly by the beliefs and practices of earlier generations or behaviors within family cultures—and that the behaviors and attitudes of parents in the current generation will affect subsequent generations. Practitioners in father- and family-focused programs have indicated that this learning is the foundation for all others (Kane, Gadsden, and Armorer, 1996).

Intergenerational patterns of criminal behaviors in families (statistics show large numbers of second and third-generation inmates) are a part of the public image of families with an incarcerated parent, and perhaps of society's expectations of the child of an incarcerated parent. However, when considering patterns of intergenerational learning, researchers, policymakers, and practitioners should avoid any tendency to suggest that children are biologically predisposed to criminal behavior.

When researchers use the term intergenerational learning, they apply it typically as an all-encompassing concept for several kinds of human relationships across different generations. In educational research, the study of intergenerational learning focuses on the ways in which parents and other family members contribute to or affect children's academic performance, school attendance, discipline, and valuing of schooling and education (*see* Gadsden, 1995). Developmental psychologists focus on cognitive transfer that influences children's linguistic patterns or psychosocio-emotional well-being—from the inheritability of intelligence to parenting and environmental factors (Coles and Coles, 1988).

References to intergenerationality among families with an incarcerated father or mother tend to focus almost entirely on the frequency with which children of incarcerated parents "follow in their parents' footsteps," that is, enter the criminal justice system as juveniles or adults. It is difficult and misleading, however, to isolate the presence of an incarcerated parent alone as the sole causal factor in the criminal behavior of a child.

The confluence of a number of factors contributes to the behavior of a second-generation inmate, ranging from poverty and poor schooling to erratic placements due to parents' incarceration. The more basic and fundamental question is, What are the myriad influences on the learning of a child? The question posed by Fishel (1991), "What do children's lives reveal about their parents?" is not sufficient to examine the complex set of relationships that exist between incarcerated father and child or across different generations.

Whole generations and subsequent ones may be affected by different and difficult life circumstances. Difficult life circumstances result in families sometimes changing their perspectives and self-perceptions; that is, in their constructing a collection of behaviors and practices that are associated internally and externally with the family or with hardships in the family. Reiss' (1981) family paradigms, for example, are defined by family members and include the shared, implicit beliefs that families have about themselves, their social worlds, and their relationship to social structures. Paradigms, he argues, are affected by the life views of family members; that is, views of the world as ordered or disorganized, predictable or unpredictable, and fair or inequitable.

Stack and Burton (1993) expand on their multigenerational research to focus on "kinscripts." Kinscripts are developed on the premise that families have their own agenda, their own interpretation of cultural norms, and their own histories. The framework is developed around three critical issues: (1) temporal and interdependent factors in family role transitions, (2) creation and intergenerational transmission of family norms, and (3) negotiation, exchange, and conflict within families over the life course.

Gadsden's (1998) work with multiple generations of African-American and Puerto Rican families highlights the concept of family cultures, cumulative life texts, and artifacts of individual family members that contribute to life-course perspectives, decisions, and behaviors of the family unit. Intergenerational practices and learning within families are formed around an interplay of accepted ethnic traditions, cultural rituals, sociopolitical histories, religious practices and beliefs, and negotiated roles within families over time. Issues of race and culture are deeply embedded in family cultures, which in turn are manipulated by societal events and affected by shifts in family mobility. When families face stresses, they may move from implicit assumptions about their family processes, to stated alternatives to those processes, and then to individual and family techniques for survival (Germain, 1994).

Individually or collectively, these frameworks have the potential to shed light on intergenerational learning among families with an incarcerated father or mother, mostly because they attend to issues such as family members' perception of the world; shared experiences over multiple generations; accepted culture; family belief and practices; intersections between family values, community expectations, and societal practices, particularly around race and discrimination; and the approaches that are used to respond to stressors and crisis. In this way, the frameworks open the door for a more expansive discussion of intergenerationality among incarcerated fathers. Thus, we conduct intensive investigations of the kinds of conditions and experiences that cut across different generations and the ways in which verbal and physical messages mediate the power and lure of social environments other than the family to which children and other family members are exposed.

A discussion of intergenerational learning for incarcerated fathers inserts incarceration into any paradigm or examination of the issues as a singularly important dimension—depending on the experiences of the family and community, as a crisis moment or a natural event—that may be used alone to explain the choices and behaviors of children and family members or that combine with other high-risk variables within the family, community, and society to create a negative intergenerational effect that results in incarceration for second and third generations.

The more nuanced and complex questions surround a series of interrelated issues that must be studied both individually and as a system:

- the similarities between and among different generations
- the circumstances and contexts that provide presenting and welcoming conditions for the development of antisocial or criminal behaviors
- the nature of the relationship that existed between the inmate father or mother and the child
- the types of kin resources
- the child's access to good schools and community support
- the social class of the subsequent generations of offenders

The configuration of these factors creates knowledge of both the risk of intergenerational transmission of antisocial behavior and opportunities to discourage behaviors and practices that may lead to criminal behavior.

In posing these issues, we urge researchers, practitioners, and policymakers alike to refrain from seeking a set of immutable and defining characteristics that result in the labeling of children rather than promoting change in the conditions that place them at risk. Rather, we suggest that greater emphasis be placed on systematic study of families—those where there is an incarcerated parent and those where the parent is not incarcerated—to study the types of circumstances, cultural beliefs, social practices, and familial experiences to which children are exposed; the specific circumstances that lead to some children becoming incarcerated and others not; and the role of parents, kin, and communities in mitigating potentially harmful exposure.

In addition, we suggest that the focus on intergenerationality among incarcerated fathers be attached to the still-emerging body of work on intergenerationality among fathers in general. What fathers convey to their children, what children hear, and how they translate what they hear within their own lives are all fundamental to understanding when and how change occurs, and to situating change over the life course of the family (Gadsden, forthcoming). In such cases, practice-derived research is critical, as is better experimental work. However, the topic also lends itself to intensive reviews of practice, longitudinal data collection, and ethnographic/qualitative as well as quantitative analysis.

Scholars in the criminal justice tradition have long been concerned about multigenerational patterns of incarceration; the intergenerational learning literature offers one set of theories to address the process by which patterns of incarceration are transmitted from one generation to another. We believe both areas of study could be enhanced by addressing four questions. First, is the process of intergenerational learning different in families that have a parent who is/has been incarcerated? Second, do prisoners come from families with cultures that are systematically different from the general population? Third, how do institutional practices contribute to or reduce the intergenerational effects of incarceration? Finally, what facets of family culture tend to facilitate child identity formation that is open to antisocial behaviors?

Closing Considerations

What are the nature and complexities of fathering/parenting and the consequences of father incarceration for children and families? How does the process of reentry affect the real and perceived chances that an ex-inmate will be able to reunify and reintegrate himself into a family—a family to which he may have had limited exposure prior to incarceration and which may have changed significantly over time? How do children fare during father incarceration and father reentry? How are the cultures of families and communities shaped and reshaped by the changes resulting from the process of reentry?[1]

The answers to these questions are complex to determine, and, most importantly, do not lie in any single discipline or domain. That is, they are not the preserve of criminal justice or child welfare, of psychologists or policy analysts, of educators or sociologists, of practitioners or researchers. Within practice, they are not the sole purview of social services or family support programs, of child-serving agencies or fathering programs. Because the issues of incarceration and reentry encompass developmental, interactional, and systemic/structural issues, they have the potential to help us locate the ways in which child and family risk are affected and how that ultimately affects the likelihood and the realities of incarceration.

Parenting programs are a common feature of women's correctional settings, and, in a very few cases, of men's facilities. The presence of these programs represents a response to a perception that criminal behavior equals bad parenting and an attempt to provide men with some type of support that helps them to access and use the family as a unit that provides grounding. There is no evidence that these programs do harm, and modest evidence that they do good. However, in the absence of positive familial and community supports—whether these supports lie in the families or communities of origin or in what anthropologists such as Carol Stack (1974) and John Ogbu (1993) refer to as "fictive kin"—the effect of such programs will be limited and, ultimately, marginalized. As Hairston and Lockett (1987) note, for the prisoner, such family ties serve three important functions: the maintenance of the family unit, the enhancement of individual family members' well-being, and the facilitation of the prisoner's postrelease success. Both family structure and family relationships are affected negatively by incarceration (Adalist-Estrin, 1994; Hairston, 1998). Marital disruption and father absence are created by incarceration for fathers who live with their families.

The assumption that all absence is bad for children and families has been hotly contested by researchers, practitioners, policymakers, and advocates for children, women, and families. There is ample literature suggesting that father or parent absence may protect children from a range of environmental and social toxins that would be introduced if one or both parents were involved (Gadsden, Fagan, Ray, and Davis, 2001). As Hagan (1996) notes, the most obvious cases are those involving the incarceration of negligent, violent, and abusive parents for which the imprisonment of the parents benefits children by removing serious risks of current and future harm.

We do not know how many children for whom this is the case. In particular, we do not know how many of these children were in contact with their fathers and whether and how the absence of an already estranged father is exacerbated when he is imprisoned. Nor is it clear whether and how such engagement in the absence of a preexisting relationship should and can take place, or what the nature of the engagement might be on the father's reentry into the family or community. Hence, the apparently difficult questions surrounding the effects of penal sanctioning on children and families and the accompanying effects of ensuing father absence become more complicated when multiple family forms are examined. This is also true when examining the multiple types of father absence and different relationships and interactions that are created by and within families to accommodate the absence of a father, or to explain to a child that an absent father is incarcerated.

The imprisonment of a working-class father who lives with his children and family presents a set of images and issues that are different from those of an upper-middle-income father who lives with his children and family. The situation is considerably different for these two types of fathers and for those of a never-married father who has had irregular visits with his children, or another who interacts daily with his children. In all cases, family ties are important; in each they may differ. Although there is some work which suggests that, despite cultural differences, there are shared experiences across different groups of fathers, the imprisonment of a low-income African-American father results in a different set of experiences and effects for the father and his children and family than the imprisonment of a middle-income African-American father. Neither may share anything more than fatherhood.

There are no simple questions or simple answers. For fathers who are uninvolved with their children preincarceration, imprisonment may weaken the hopes of children and families, who, in addition to coping with erratic involvement, also wrestle with social labeling and possibly shame. Determining how these issues interact or differentially affect the well-being of children requires the collective, collaborative, interdisciplinary, and cross-domain efforts of researchers, practitioners, and policymakers.

Endnote

[1] Based on the work presented in this paper, it is possible to develop a preliminary set of recommendations for research on incarcerated fathers in the field of fathers and families. These research threads were fully developed following the discussion that occurred at the National Center on Fathers and Families Roundtable, *Constructing and Coping with Incarceration: Perspectives from the Field*, held on November 15 and 16, 2001.

References

Adalist-Estrin, A. 1994. Family Support and Criminal Justice. In Sharon L. Kagan and Bernice Weissbourd, eds. *Putting Families First: America's Family Support Movement and the Challenge of Change*. San Francisco: Jossey-Bass.

Arendell, T. 1995. *Co-parenting: A Literature Review*. Philadelphia, Pennsylvania: Research Report Series, National Center on Fathers and Families, University of Pennsylvania.

Barnhill, L., G. Rubenstein, G. and N. Racklin. 1979. From Generation to Generation: Fathers to Be in Transition. *The Family Coordinator.* 28: 229-235.

Barnett, R. C. and G. K. Baruch. 1987. Determinants of Fathers' Participation in Family Work. *Journal of Marriage and the Family.* 49: 29-40.

Beck, A. J. 2000. Prisoners in 1999. *Bureau of Justice Statistics Bulletin.* Washington, D.C.: U.S. Department of Justice, Bureau of Justice Statistics, NCJ 183476.

Belsky, J. 1984. The Determinants of Parenting: A Process Model. *Child Development.* 55: 83-96.

Biller, H. B. and R. J. Trotter. 1994. *The Father Factor.* New York: Simon and Schuster.

Bloom, B. 1995. Public Policy and Children of Incarcerated Parents. In K. Gabel and D. Johnston, eds. *Children of Incarcerated Parents.* New York: Lexington Books.

Brenner, E. 1998. *Fathers in Prison: A Review of the Data.* NCOFF Brief. Philadelphia, Pennsylvania: National Center on Fathers and Families, University of Pennsylvania.

Cavanaugh, K. R. and D. Pollack. 1998. Child Support Obligations of Incarcerated Parents. *Cornell Journal of Law and Public Policy.* 7(2): 531-553.

Child Welfare League of America. 1999. *Children with Incarcerated Parents: A Fact Sheet.* Washington, D.C.: Child Welfare League of America.

Clear, T. R. and D. R. Rose. 1999, July. *When Neighbors Go to Jail: Impact on Attitudes about Formal and Informal Control.* Washington, D.C.: National Institute of Justice., U. S. Department of Justice.

Cohen, R. S. and S. H. Weissman. 1984. *Parenthood: A Psychodynamic Perspective.* New York: Guilford.

Coles, M. and R. Coles. 1988. *The Development of Children.* New York: Freeman.

Coltrane, S. 1996. *Family Man: Fatherhood, Housework, and Gender Equity.* New York: Oxford University Press.

Coltrane, S. and R. Parke. 1998. *Reinventing Fatherhood: Toward Historical Understanding of Continuity and Change in Men's Family Lives.* Philadelphia, Pennsylvania: National Center on Fathers and Families, University of Pennsylvania.

Conty, C. 1999. *The Women's Prison Association: Supporting Women Offenders and their Families.* Washington, D.C.: National Institute of Justice, U.S. Department of Justice.

Cowan, C. P., P. A. Cowan, G. Heming, E. Garrett, W. S. Coyish, H. Curtis-Boles, and A. J. Boles. 1985. Transitions to Parenthood: His, Hers, and Theirs. *Journal of Family Issues.* 6: 451-481.

Danziger, S. K., C. K. Kastner, and T. J. Nickel. 1993. The Problems and Promise of Child Support Policies. In R. I. Lerman and T. J. Ooms, eds. *Young Unwed Fathers: Changing Roles and Emerging Policies.* Philadelphia, Pennsylvania: Temple University Press.

Danziger, S. K. and N. Radin. 1990. Absent Does Not Equal Uninvolved: Predictors of Fathering in Teen Mother Families. *Journal of Marriage and the Family.* 52: 636-642.

Darity, W. A., Jr. and S. L. Myers, Jr. 1995. Family Structure and the Marginalization of Black Men: Policy Implications. In M. B. Tucker and C. Mitchell-Kernan, eds. *The Decline in Marriage among African Americans: Causes, Consequences, and Policy Implications.* New York: Russell Sage Foundation.

Davis, Jenna. 2000. Barring Fatherhood: Incarcerated Fathers and Their Children. In D. Reichert, ed. *Connecting Low-Income Fathers and Families: A Guide to Practical Policies.* Denver, Colorado: National Conference of State Legislatures.

Doherty, W. J., E. F. Kouneski and M. F. Erickson. 1998. Responsible Fatherhood: A Review and Conceptual Framework. *Journal of Marriage and the Family.* 60: 277-292.

Dollahite, D. C., A. J. Hawkins and S. E. Brotherson. 1997. Fatherwork: A Conceptual Ethic of Fathering as Generative Work. In A. J. Hawkins and D. C. Dollahite, eds. *Generative Fathering: Beyond Deficit Perspectives.* Thousand Oaks, California: Sage Publications.

Duncan, G. and L. Chase-Lansdale. 2000. Welfare Reform and Child Well-being. In R. Blank and R. T. Haskins, eds. *The New World of Welfare.* Washington, D.C.: Brookings Institution Press.

Dyer, E. D. 1963. Parenthood as Crisis: A Re-study. *Marriage and Family Living.* 25: 196-201.

Edin, K. 2000. Few Good Men. *American Prospect.* 11: 26-31.

Erikson, E. H. 1969. Adult Stage: Generativity Versus Stagnation. In R. Evans, ed. *Dialogue with Erik Erikson.* New York: Dutton.

Erikson, E. H. and J. M. Erikson. 1981. On Generativity and Identity. *Harvard Educational Review.* 51(2): 249-269.

Fishel, E. 1991. *Family Mirrors: What Our Children's Lives Reveal about Ourselves.* Boston, Massachusetts: Houghton Mifflin.

Gable, S., J. Belsky, and K. Crnic. 1995. The Determinants of Co-Parenting in Families with Toddler Boys: Spousal Differences and Daily Hassles. *Child Development.* 66: 629-642.

Gadsden, V. L. 1995. Literacy and Poverty: Intergenerational Issues within African American families. In H. E. Fitzgerald, B. M. Lester, and B. Zuckerman, eds. *Children of Poverty: Research, Health and Policy Issues.* New York: Garland Press.

Gadsden, V. L. 1995. Introduction: Literacy and African American Youth: Legacy and Struggle. In V. L. Gadsden and D. A. Wagner, eds. *Literacy among African American Youth.* Cresskill, New Jersey: Hampton Press.

Gadsden, V. L. 1998. Black Families within Intergenerational and Cultural Perspective. In M. L. Lamb, ed. *Nontraditional and Traditionally Understudied Families: Parenting and Child Development.* New York: Lawrence Erlbaum.

Gadsden, V. L. Forthcoming. *Fathers within a Life Course Perspective.* Philadelphia, Pennsylvania: Research Report Series, National Center on Fathers and Families, University of Pennsylvania.

Gadsden, V. L., K. R. Rethemeyer, and M. Iannozzi. 2001. *Bay Area Fathering Initiatives: Portraits and Possibilities.* Philadelphia, Pennsylvania: National Center on Fathers and Families, University of Pennsylvania.

Gadsden, V., S. Wortham, T. Wojcik, A. Ray, and H. Pinderhughes. 2001, April. How Urban Fathers Represent the Transition to Fathering: A Discourse Analysis of Fathering Narratives. Paper presented at the biennial meeting of the Society for Research in Child Development. Minneapolis, Minnesota.

Gadsden, V. L., J. Fagan, A. Ray, and J. E. Davis, eds. 2001. *The Fathering Indicators Framework: A Tool for Quantitative and Qualitative Analysis.* Philadelphia, Pennsylvania: Research Report Series, National Center on Fathers and Families, University of Pennsylvania.

Gaudin, J. M. and R. Sutphen. 1993. Foster Care vs. Extended Family Care for Children of Incarcerated Mothers. *Journal of Offender Rehabilitation.* 19: 129-147.

Genty, P. M. 1998. Permanency Planning the Context of Parental Incarceration: Legal Issues and Recommendations. *Child Welfare League of America.* 77: 543-559.

Germain, C. B. 1994. Emerging Conceptions of Family Development over the Life Course. *Families in Society.* 74: 259-267.

Goodwin, L. 1972. *Do the Poor Want to Work? A Social Psychological Study of Work Orientations.* Washington, D.C.: Brookings Institution.

Grossman, F. K., W. S. Pollack, and E. Golding. 1988. Fathers and Children: Predicting the Quality and Quantity of Fathering. *Developmental Psychology.* 24: 82-91.

Hagan, J., and R. Dinovitzer. 1999. Collateral Consequences of Imprisonment for Children, Communities, and Prisoners. In Tonry, M. and J. Petersillia, eds. *Crime and Justice: A Review of Research, Volume 26.* Chicago, Illinois: University of Chicago Press.

———. 1999a. Unintended Consequences of Sentencing: Children. Paper presented at the Research Workshop of The Israel Science Foundation on Empirical Research and Legal Realism—Setting the Agenda. Haifa, Israel. June, 1999.

Hagan, J., A. R. Gillis, and D. Brownfield. 1996. *Criminological Controversies.* Boulder, Colorado: Westview Press.

Hairston, C. F. 1998. The Forgotten Parent: Understanding the Forces that Influence Incarcerated Fathers' Relationships with Their Children. *Child Welfare.* 77: 617-639.

Hairston, C. F. and P. W. Lockett. 1987. Parents in Prison: New Directions for Social Services. *Social Work.* 32: 162-163.

Jeffries, J., S. Menghraj, and C. F. Hairston. 2001. *Serving Incarcerated and Ex-offender Fathers and Their Families.* New York: Vera Institute of Justice.

Johnston, D. 1995. Effects of Parental Incarceration. In K. Gabel and D. Johnston, eds. *Children of Incarcerated Parents.* New York: Lexington Books.

Johnson, D. J. 1995. *Father Presence: A Literature Review.* Philadelphia, Pennsylvania: National Center on Fathers and Families, University of Pennsylvania.

Jouriles, E. N., C. M. Murphy, A. M. Farris, D. A Smith, J. E. Richters, and E. Waters. 1991. Marital Adjustment, Parental Disagreements about Child Rearing, and Behavior Problems in Boys: Increasing the Specificity of the Marital Assessment. *Child Development.* 62: 1424-1433.

Kane, D., V. Gadsden, and K. Armorer. 1996. *Fathers and Families Core Learnings: An Update from the Field.* Philadelphia, Pennsylvania: National Center on Fathers and Families, University of Pennsylvania.

Klein, B. 1985. Fathering: The First Time. *Social Work.* 30: 264-267.

Kling, J. 1999. The Effect of Prison Sentence Length on the Subsequent Employment and Earning of Criminal Defendants. Discussion Paper No. 208. Princeton, New Jersey: Woodrow Wilson School, Princeton University.

Lamb, M. E. 1987. Introduction: The Emergent American Father. *In The Father's Role: Cross-cultural Perspective.* Hillsdale, New Jersey: Lawrence Erlbaum.

Lamb, M. E., J. H, Pleck, E. Charnov, and J. A. Levine. 1985. Paternal Behavior in Humans. *American Zoologist.* 25: 883-894.

LeMasters, E. E. 1957. Parenthood as Crisis. *Marriage and Family Living.* 19(4): 352-355

Levine, J. A. and E. Pitt. 1995. *New Expectations: Community Strategies for Responsible Fatherhood.* New York: Families and Work Institute.

Lynch, J. P. and W. J. Sabol. 1998. Assessing the Longer-run Consequences of Incarceration. Paper presented at the Twentieth Annual Research Conference of Public Policy Analysis and Management, New York. (September, 1998).

———. 2001. *Prisoner Reentry in Perspective: Crime Policy Report.* Washington, D.C.: The Urban Institute.

Marino, C. D. and R. McCowan. 1976. The Effects of Parent Absence on Children. *Child Study Journal.* 6(3): 165-181.

Mason, P. L. (1996). *Joblessness and Unemployment: A Review of the Literature.* Philadelphia, PA: National Center on Fathers and Families, University of Pennsylvania.

McBride, B. A. and T. R. Ranes. 1998. Parenting Alliance as a Predictor of Father Involvement: An Exploratory Study. *Family Relations.* 47: 229-236.

McHale, S. M. and T. L. Huston. 1985. The Effect of the Transition to Parenthood on the Marriage Relationship: A Longitudinal Study. *Journal of Family Issues.* 6: 409-433.

McLanahan, S. and G. Sandefur. 1994. *Growing Up With A Single Parent: What Hurts, What Helps.* Cambridge, Massachusetts: Harvard University Press.

Morash,, M., T. S Bynum, and B. Koons. 1998. Women Offenders: Programming Needs and Promising Approaches. *National Institute of Justice Research in Brief.* Washington, D.C.: National Institute of Justice.

Motiuk, L. 2001. Commentary and Response to Lynn Stewart's Paper: What Works in the Treatment of Family Violence in Correctional Populations: Issues and Directions. September. Meeting of the International Community Corrections Association. Philadelphia, Pennsylvania

Mumola, C. 2000. *Incarcerated Parents and Their Children.* Bureau of Justice Statistics, Special Report. Washington, D.C.: U. S. Department of Justice, NCJ 182335.

Myers, S. 1992. Crime, Entrepreneurship, and Labor Force Withdrawal. *Contemporary Policy Issues.* 10: 84-97.

Myers, S. and W. J. Sabol. 1987. Unemployment and Racial Differences in Imprisonment. *Review of Black Political Economy*. Summer-Fall, 16: 1-2.

National Center on Fathers and Families. 1994. The Fathers and Families Core Learnings. *Shared Commitment: Issues from the Inaugural Meeting of the National Practitioners Network on Fathers and Families*. Philadelphia, Pennsylvania: National Center on Fathers and Families, University of Pennsylvania.

National Center on Fathers and Families, University of Pennsylvania. 1997-2002. FatherLit Research Database (www.ncoff.gse.upenn.edu).

Ogbu, J. 1993. Differences in Cultural Frame of Reference. *International Journal of Behavioral Development*. 16(3): 483-506.

Osofsky, H. J. and R. E Culp. 1989. Risk Factors in the Transition to Fatherhood. In S. H. Cath, A. Gurwitt, and L. Gunsberg, eds. *Fathers and Their Families*. Hillsdale, New Jersey: The Analytic Press.

Palkovitz, R. 1984. Parental Attitudes and Fathers' Interactions with Their 5-Month-Old Infants. *Developmental Psychology*. 20: 1054-1060.

Palm, G. 1998. *Developing a Model of Reflective Practice for Improving Fathering Programs*. Philadelphia, Pennsylvania: National Center on Fathers and Families, University of Pennsylvania.

Parke, R. and S. Coltrane. 2001. Father Presence Category. In V. L. Gadsden, J. Fagan, A. Ray, and J. E. Davis, eds. *The Fathering Indicators Framework: A Tool for Quantitative and Qualitative Analysis*. Philadelphia, Pennsylvania: Research Report Series, National Center on Fathers and Families, University of Pennsylvania.

Philadelphia Children's Network. 1996. *End-of-Project Report, Co-Parenting Program*. Philadelphia, Pennsylvania: Philadelphia Children's Network.

Phillips., S. and B. Bloom. 1998. In Whose Best Interest: The Impact of Changing Public Policy on Relatives Caring for Children with Incarcerated Parents. *Child Welfare: Journal of Policy, Practice, and Programs*. 77(5): 531-541.

Pollack, W. S. 1995. A Delicate Balance: Fatherhood and Psychological Transformation. In J. L. Shapiro, M. J. Diamond, and M. Greenberg, eds. *Becoming a Father: Contemporary, Social, Developmental, and Clinical Perspectives*, 1st ed. New York: Springer Publishing Company.

Rapoport, R. 1963. Normal Crises, Family Structure, and Mental Health. *Family Process*. 2: 68-80.

Reiss, D. 1981. *The Family's Construction of Reality*. Cambridge, Massachusetts: Harvard University Press.

Sabol, W. J. and J. P. Lynch. 1997. *Crime Policy Report: Did Getting Tough on Crime Pay?* Washington, D.C.: The Urban Institute.

Sachs, N. P. 2000. Is There a Tilt Toward Abusers in Child Custody Decisions? *Journal of Psychohistory.* 28(2): 203-227.

Seymour, C. 1998. Children with Parents in Prison: Child Welfare Policy, Program, and Practice Issues. *Child Welfare.* 75: 469-493.

Sorensen, E. 1995. *Noncustodial Fathers: Can They Afford to Pay More Child Support?* Washington, D.C.: Urban Institute.

Stack, C. 1974. *All Our Kin.* New York: Harper and Row.

Stack, C. B. and L. M. Burton. 1993. Kinscripts. *Journal of Comparative Family Studies.* 24: 157-170.

Sullivan, M. 1993. Young Fathers and Parenting in Two Inner-city Neighborhoods. In R. I. Lerman and T. J. Ooms, eds. *Young Unwed Fathers: Changing Roles and Emerging Policies.* Philadelphia, Pennsylvania: Temple University Press.

Thoennes, N. and J. Pearson. 1995. Mediation and Domestic Violence: Current Policies and Practices. *Family and Conciliation Courts Review.* 33: 6-29.

Travis, J., M. A. L. Solomon, and M. Waul. 2001. *From Prison to Home: The Dimensions and Consequences of Prisoner Reentry.* Washington, D.C.: The Urban Institute.

U.S. Department of Justice, Bureau of Justice Statistics. 2000. *Incarcerated Parents and Their Children.* Special Report NCJ 182335. Washington, D.C.: Department of Justice, August 2000, p. 2, Table 2. Table adapted by SOURCEBOOK staff.

Vaughn, B. E., J. H. Block, and J. Block. 1988. Parental Agreement on Child Rearing during Early Childhood and the Psychological Characteristics of Adolescents. *Child Development.* 88: 1020-1033.

Wattenberg, E. 1993. Paternity Actions and Young Fathers. In R. Lerman and T. Ooms, eds. *Young Unwed Fathers: Changing Roles and Emerging Policies.* Philadelphia, Pennsylvania: Temple University Press.

Wente, A. S. and S. B. Crockenberg. 1976. Transition to Fatherhood: Lamaze Preparation, Adjustment Difficulty and the Husband-Wife Relationship. *Family Coordinator.* October, 351-357.

Western, B. and K. Beckett. 1999. How Unregulated is the U.S. Labor Market? The Penal System as a Labor Market Institution. *American Journal of Sociology.* 104: 1030-1060.

Western, B. and S. McClanahan. 2000, June. Fathers Behind Bars: The Impact of Incarceration on Family Formation. Working Paper 00-08-FF. Princeton, New Jersey: Bendheim-Thoman Center for Research on Child Wellbeing, Princeton University.

Parent Education for Incarcerated Parents: Understanding What Works

4

Glen F. Palm
Professor, Child and Family Studies
St. Cloud State University
St. Cloud, Minnesota

The increasing population of incarcerated parents in federal and state prisons and local jails has a profound impact on the lives of about 2 million children under age eighteen (Johnston, 2000; Mumola, 2000). Children of incarcerated parents are six times more likely than their peers to end up in prison (Jacobs, 1995). Parent education as an intervention to this growing population can be described best as a two-generation program with important long-term goals for both incarcerated parents and their children (Layzer and St. Pierre, 1998). For incarcerated parents, the long-term goals are rehabilitation and reintegration into society as productive citizens and responsible parents. For children, the goals are prevention of poor developmental outcomes and prevention of criminal behavior (Lange, 1997). Parent education programs provide a number of potential pathways towards these long-term goals. Current programs and practices in parent education for incarcerated parents reflect different theories and assumptions about the most direct and effective pathways towards achieving these long-term goals.

This review of literature will examine program philosophy, program practices, and empirical research from parent education to understand the utility and possibilities of this work for supporting incarcerated parents and their children. The review begins with a description of the background and context, including definitions of parent education, gender-related concerns, and demographic issues. It then focuses primarily on information from three important perspectives: (1) theories and conceptual frameworks that explain how parent education works, (2) research on the outcomes/effectiveness of different parent education programs, and (3) effective program practices and critical learnings from practitioners. The review concludes with a discussion of critical practice issues and the need for reflective practice in addressing these issues.

Background and Context
Defining Parent Education

Parent education has many different meanings (Carter, 1996) and is embedded in a number of different institutions—from education, to health care, to social service, to correctional facilities (Cooke and Thomas, 1986). Definitions of parent education may be narrow in their frame of reference, focusing mostly on the delivery of parenting "knowledge" to passive learners (Johnston, 1995; Canning and Fantuzzo, 2000). Such definitions make a clear distinction between parent support and education, often creating a false dichotomy.

The diversity and wide range of goals of parent education reflect both the complexity of the parenting role in contemporary society and different ideas and values related to parent-child relationships (Smith, Cudaback, Goddard, and Myers-Walls, 1994). Parent education practice has incorporated ideas from different disciplines including early education, developmental psychology, family studies, adult education, health care, and criminal justice (Carter, 1996). Parent education is most often conducted within the context of small groups where support and education work together in a complementary manner (Boudouris, 1996; Browne, 1989; Campbell and Palm, 2001; Doherty, 1995; Harris, 1996).

Parent education is, by necessity, distinguished from other forms of parent and family involvement. One distinction is between parent education and family life education, particularly in relationship to incarcerated parents. Klein, Bartholomew, and Bahr (1999) make a case for family life education as a more comprehensive approach than parent education for incarcerated parents since family education addresses economic and social support issues beyond the parent-child relationship and parenting skills focus. However, although family life education is a broader concept than parent education. Many programs (for example, Early Childhood Family Education in Minnesota) combine many aspects of family life education under parent education (Powell and Cassidy, 2000). This more encompassing perspective on parent education reflects the trend towards a more ecological and contextual view of child development and parenting.

This review will focus on literature about incarcerated parents and related parent education efforts in juvenile/criminal justice and early education. The operational definition of parent education created by the author for this review is "any educational program that focuses directly on strengthening parent-child and family relationships through parents learning new ideas, skills, and attitudes." This operational definition is purposefully broad and inclusive to cover the various efforts that are described in the literature. A broad view of parent education reflects the trend towards a more ecological and contextual view referred to in the previous paragraph and advanced as early as the 1970s by Bronfenbrenner (1979). The ecological perspective includes the multiple social systems that interface both directly and indirectly with children and families. The systems that may directly impact incarcerated parents include early childhood programs, the school system, social service programs, faith-based programs, the court system, and correctional systems. The systems that may indirectly impact families with incarcerated parents are public policy and public opinion on crime, violence, and incarceration. Program descriptions for incarcerated parents also reflect this more comprehensive approach to combining parent education with other family support efforts (for example, Genisio, 1996; Martin and Cotten, 1995; Boudouris, 1996; Johnston, 1997), noting that parent education must consider family, cultural, and social contexts.

Discussions about parenting and education have evolved beyond the narrow stereotype of parent education as a fixed knowledge base of child development and generic parenting skills that professionals "teach" to parents. Although a broad and inclusive definition of parent education has been adopted for this review, it is important to remember that parent education does have important boundaries and limits to what it can or should be expected to accomplish for incarcerated parents and their families. The parenting role itself encompasses many different family tasks and intersects with various aspects of adult identity (Palkovitz and Palm, 1998).

Gender Issues: Parent Education for Mothers and Fathers

Parent education has been offered as both intervention and prevention programs for mothers and fathers alike. However, when offered as a service for both parents, the emphasis is generally on mothers as participants (Johnson and Palm, 1992). Over the past ten years, considerable attention has been given to creating parenting programs specifically designed for fathers that address both generic parenting concerns as well as issues that are more specific to fathers' development and roles (*see* Johnson and Palm, 1992; Kliman and Kohl, 1984; Levine and Pitt, 1995; Fagan and Hawkins, 2001). Since correctional facilities are gender-segregated, parenting programs typically have been implemented for either mothers or fathers.

The literature describes several important differences between incarcerated mothers and fathers (*see* Koban, 1983, Johnston, 1995). Some of the literature advocates for parity in services to mothers while at the same time making a case for the unique needs of mothers based upon assumptions about gender differences found in the practice literature (Koban, 1983, Johnston, 1997, Boudouris, 1996). These assumptions are as follows:

1. Mothers are already connected to their children and living with them prior to incarceration, making the incarceration of mothers more traumatic for children.

2. Mothers are more invested in parenting as part of their identity and face a more traumatic adjustment when they are deprived of their maternal role through incarceration.

3. Mothers have custody of children and are likely to return as their primary caregivers after incarceration.

4. Mothers do not enjoy the same level of support from male partners/marriage that men do. (Koban, 1983; Boudouris, 1996; Johnston, 1997)

These assumptions can be supported with data on mother and father differences reported by Koban (1983) and cited by Johnston (1997). Koban (1983) reports two major conclusions from the comparison of mothers and fathers in Kentucky prisons. First, mothers had a closer relationship to children prior to incarceration. More children lived with mothers prior to incarceration, 74.3 percent for mothers compared to 24.5 percent for fathers. More mothers than fathers also reported plans to reunite with their children after incarceration (83.3 percent for mothers and 68.4 percent for fathers). Second, mothers' relationships with their children are more stressful when fathers are incarcerated. Mothers are left with the sole responsibility of taking care of the children, ensuring that the children visit the father, and maintaining the household.

Differences in and beliefs about traditional sex roles and families have been used to support increases in parenting programs for incarcerated mothers (Blinn, 1997; Boudouris, 1996). In contrast, programs for fathers have been limited primarily because fathers have been seen as less central to the lives of their children and thus less deserving or in need of parent education classes (Hairston, 1998).

Johnston (1997) notes that some of these differences between incarcerated mothers and fathers are beginning to fade, at least as indicated in shifts in demographic data on mothers and fathers. She attributes this change not to women becoming more like men in their parenting patterns but to the dissolution of family based on repeated parental incarcerations. However, the blurring of distinct mother and father differences in the population of incarcerated parents can be attributed to a number of factors besides incarceration itself, including changes in family formation, increase in the number of working mothers, and increased expectations for fathers to be involved in their children's lives.

Over the last twenty-five years, changes in family structure and gender roles around parenting have permeated U.S. society and families at all socioeconomic levels. Some of these changes are reflected in the recent national study of incarcerated parents (Mumola, 2000). Koban (1983) reported that 75.4 percent of mothers and 25 percent of fathers lived with their children prior to incarceration. Mumola (2000) reported that 64 percent of mothers and 44 percent of fathers lived with their children prior to incarceration. The difference between mothers and fathers living with their children prior to incarceration was 50 percent in Koban's research from 1983 and dramatically decreased to 20 percent in Mumola's study in 2000. Most mothers (64 percent) still live with their children prior to incarceration and an increasing number of fathers (44 percent) also live with their children prior to incarceration.

There appears to be increased social pressure for greater father involvement in children's lives (Blankenhorn, 1995; Dollahite and

Hawkins, 1997) accompanied by policy changes to hold unmarried and divorced fathers responsible for child support payments. In addition, the traditional roles of both mothers and fathers are in flux (Palm and Palkovitz, 1988), and these changes may have important implications for parenting programs in correctional facilities.

Hairston (1998) presents a strong case for more services including parent education for incarcerated fathers. As the fatherhood role becomes more valued and central to male identity and social institutions demonstrate their valuing of fathers' contributions, incarcerated fathers will benefit more from parent education classes. However, it appears that focusing on differences between mothers and fathers as a basis for advocating for more services for one group versus the other is counterproductive at this point. Both mothers and fathers are important to children and families, and both have critical needs for parent education. Yet, there are still some unique issues for each group that should be addressed with different program content and methods (see Turner and Eichenlaub, 1998).

Demographic Background Features of Incarcerated Parents

Not unlike other parents, incarcerated parents face a myriad of issues in fulfilling their parental responsibilities. The severity of these issues points to the need for other services and programs that support individual development: for example, educational/vocational programs, substance abuse treatment, and mental illness treatment. Parent education practitioners understand this need for collaboration with other service providers and see how services such as adult basic education can open up new job opportunities that help parents to fulfill their provider role (Palm, 2001). Any review of the demographic backgrounds of incarcerated mothers and fathers demonstrates the need for services beyond the boundaries of parent and family education that are necessary to carry out the functions of responsible parenthood.

For example, incarcerated parents may struggle with substance abuse problems. In a study conducted by the Bureau of Justice Statistics, Mumola (2000) notes that 85 percent of parent inmates reported some type of drug use and 25 percent were alcohol-dependent. Similarly, other studies suggest that drug and alcohol abuse are implicated in both crime and family violence (Gilgun, 1994). Often, substance abuse treatment may be a prerequisite to an incarcerated parent receiving parent education or a service that is coordinated with a parenting program (*also see* the chapter by Stewart and Gabora-Roth in this volume).

Limited educational attainment and preparation also constitutes a serious problem. The majority of inmates—66 percent of men and 62 percent of women—have completed fewer than twelve years of schooling (Owen and Bloom, 1995). This low level of educational attainment limits job opportunities as well as the ability of parents to support educational achievement in children. Thus, adult basic education should be a critical component of rehabilitation for many incarcerated parents. Family literacy programs are a particularly good resource. Family literacy programs for incarcerated parents link adult literacy and parent education with developing literacy skills in young children (Genisio, 1996; Gonzalez, 1995; Martin and Cotten, 1995). The advantages are clear: Increased educational attainment can lead to better jobs and an increased ability to support children financially. Family literacy programs also help parents to value education and provide skills to guide and support their child's educational development.

Family violence has been the norm for many incarcerated parents who grew up in physically, sexually, or emotionally abusive family situations. Harlow (1999) reported that 57 percent of female inmates experienced physical or sexual abuse before their incarceration. This compares to about 16 percent of male inmates. In a different study of male inmates, Gilgun (1994) reports a much higher rate of physical abuse (37 percent) and sexual abuse (26 percent), suggesting that a significant number of both male and female inmates may be dealing with histories of family violence. Male inmates appear to discount family violence patterns in which they are abused, which may explain the differences in the two reports (Palm, 2001). Abusive parenting behaviors are risk factors that can be directly addressed through parent education (Showers, 1993) and through appropriate therapeutic interventions for parents and children.

A final challenge or risk factor that most incarcerated parents face is the lack of family stability accompanied by strained family communication. Only one in four incarcerated parents is married, and these marital relationships are fragile from long periods of incarceration of one spouse. Co-parenting skills as well as legal information on custody, visitation, and child support may be incorporated into parent education programs to help address the needs of these parents. Incarcerated parents often need additional legal assistance, marriage, and co-parenting support services to manage relationships in a fragile family system.

These risk factors combine to limit the influence of parent education as the sole or primary generator of long-term change for parents and children. Most inmates will require additional intervention services.

Individual needs should be carefully assessed to determine if an incarcerated parent will benefit from parent education classes. Moreover, parent education specialists should remind themselves that parenthood can be a powerful motivation for change in individual behavior (Palm and Palkovitz, 1998), and programs should build upon parenthood as a strong motivator. This generative force (Snarey, 1993) can be activated through parent education classes for some incarcerated parents (Enos, 2000). However, parent education alone cannot address all of the issues that incarcerated parents bring with them as they attempt to establish and maintain positive relationships with their children, but it can be an essential component of an intervention plan for many incarcerated parents.

Parent education for incarcerated parents appears to be available in a number of correctional facilities for women in the United States. Boudouris (1985) reported that 93 percent of institutions that responded to a survey in the 1980s indicated that they had or were planning parenting programs. This increased to 97 percent of 86 institutions surveyed in the mid-1990s (Boudouris, 1996). Although the majority of institutions for women reported offering parenting programs, it is not clear how accessible these programs are or what percentage of incarcerated parents actually attends parent education classes. Johnston (1995) reports that only 14 percent of women prisoners were enrolled in a parenting program in 1991. Less is known about the availability of parenting programs for fathers, but the number of programs appears to be increasing (Brenner, 1999; Hairston, 1998; Knitzer and Bernard, 1997).

The literature from the mid-1980s to the present describes a variety of parenting programs for both mothers and fathers that use different theories, strategies, and program formats (*see* Boudouris, 1985, 1996; Blinn, 1997; Giveans, 1988; Lange, 1997; Palm, 2001). In the next section, the conceptual domains that inform theories, frameworks, and models in the field and that form the philosophical foundation for parenting programs for incarcerated parents are examined.

Conceptual Domains in Parent Education

Parent education specialists have not systematically developed theories of change in parents, children, and families based on educational interventions. As a field, parent education tends to borrow and integrate a variety of theories, conceptual frameworks, and models from different disciplines. In this review, we will refer to these theories, frameworks, and models as conceptual domains. These conceptual domains represent basic assumptions about parent-child relationships and parent education for incarcerated parents. Medway (1989) and Todres and Bunston (1993) identified three major parent education programs/curricula that present different theoretical approaches to helping parents change negative behaviors. These include the following: (1) Behavioral Skills Training, (2) Parent Effectiveness Training (PET), and (3) Systematic Training for Effective Parenting (STEP). The literature on parent education for incarcerated parents uses specific features of these approaches and the conceptual domains listed below as the foundation for current practices. Most contemporary parent education programs have developed a more eclectic approach, combining a range of ideas about effective parenting.

The conceptual domains that are used by parent education specialists focus on key concepts and causal connections that provide explanations for changes in parenting behavior that are intended to lead to long-term positive outcomes for incarcerated parents and their children. Five important conceptual domains that emerge from the literature are discussed below. Most programs combine two or more frameworks into a blend of assumptions, content, and strategies.

1. Attachment theory. The early process of attachment between parent and child and the maintenance of this relationship is seen as a critical link to healthy child development. The assumption is that incarcerated mothers need to have regular contact with their children to maintain this bond and the security that it provides to a child in order to ensure healthy growth and development (Bowlby, 1969; Boudouris, 1996). This is especially important during the earliest years of a child's development. Programs that are based on this theory generally advocate for frequent parent-child visitation and include shared activities for parents and children (Clement, 1993; Blinn, 1997). Parent education programs also may focus on communication skills that will assist parents in maintaining a supportive and loving relationship with their child. The mother-child bond is sacred in this framework; incarceration is seen as an intrusion into this sacred territory. Proponents of this theory often propose a range of alternatives to mother-child separation—from infants residing in prisons with mothers to mothers serving sentences in settings for incarcerated adults other than prisons (Boudouris, 1996).

2. Parenting Skills Training. Parenting Skills Training programs are based on behavioral skills training and assume that effective parenting strategies can be taught directly to parents. Both the STEP and PET programs focus on developing specific communication techniques to help parents maintain close relationships with their children (Showers, 1993;

Harrison, 1997). Several approaches may be used. For example, some programs address active listening as a critical communicative skill that helps parents to express their understanding and acceptance of their child's feelings. Behavioral strategies such as parents' reinforcing their child's behaviors and ignoring misbehavior are skills that are taught to parents to learn alternative ways to manage a child's behaviors. Filial therapy is another example of a program that teaches specific parenting skills derived from play therapy techniques (Harris and Landreth, 1997; Landreth and Lobaugh, 1998). These skills focus on helping parents develop empathy, understanding, and acceptance of a child's behavior. They also appear to be a good match for incarcerated parents who may find it difficult to understand the trauma that their child experiences due to separation resulting from parent incarceration.

The focus in parenting skills training is generally on communication and behavior management skills which may be adapted for incarcerated parents to address the limited types of contact they have with their children. Parenting skills training is seen as a direct way to change parenting behavior and gives parents concrete techniques for guiding and improving a child's behavior.

3. Self-Esteem and Self-Development. The focus on parents as individuals is another important conceptual domain for parent education for incarcerated parents. The basic assumption here is that parents must develop a healthy adult identity and self-esteem before they can be effective and loving parents. For some parents, this may include other educational and therapeutic interventions to address mental illness, a history of abusive parenting, substance abuse, and lack of vocational or job skills (*see* Blinn, 1997). The development of self-esteem is seen as a prerequisite for becoming a responsible and caring parent. However, the focus on self-esteem, adult identity, and personal development is not always accepted as legitimate when incarceration is seen primarily as punishment instead of rehabilitation. Parenting programs may find it more effective to emphasize benefits to children that result from an increase in parent self-esteem. The larger issue of helping parents to construct a positive adult identity that includes vocational goals, moral values, and generative caring for children also addresses the needs of incarcerated parents (Erikson, 1968; Snarey, 1993).

4. Social Support and Empowerment. This conceptual domain acknowledges the importance of social support systems for incarcerated parents (*see* Dunst, 1985; Johnston, 1995). Programs that draw upon this conceptual area often use peers as group facilitators because they have a direct understanding through personal experience of the problems and issues of parenting while incarcerated (Turner and Eichenlaub, 1998). Peer understanding and support can assist parents in identifying relevant resources and strategies that foster effective parenting. Peer support from other parents is also a powerful force in helping parents to understand difficult parenting issues. Parents frequently report that knowing that other parents are facing similar issues reduces parenting stress (Campbell and Palm, 2001). Programs may include a specific peer support group component to encourage direct parent-to-parent support. This approach empowers parents to set their own goals and agenda and can be a direct path to parents changing attitudes and behavior.

5. Parenting Beliefs and Attitudes. This conceptual domain focuses on the beliefs and attitudes that parents have developed from their experiences as a child and from their interactions with peers in their current social and cultural context. Work in this area assumes that parents must first examine their beliefs about children and child-rearing before they are motivated to learn and adopt new skills (Powell, 1986). Some of the beliefs are related to knowledge about child development while others may be connected to family and cultural values. Changing parental attitudes that have been connected to abusive behavior—physical, sexual, and emotional—continues to be an important goal in a number of programs (*see* Browne, 1989; Harrison, 1997; Harm and Thompson, 1997; Martin et al., 1993; Moore and Clement, 1998). For example, parents may come to a parent education program with very strong beliefs about the importance and effectiveness of physical punishment. However, parents will not adopt alternative strategies to physical punishment if they do not first change their belief or attitude about the necessity for physical punishment. Exploring and changing beliefs about child-rearing is most likely to occur when parents have developed trust and believe that parent educators will understand and respect their decisions related to parenting beliefs and behaviors.

Synthesizing the Five Conceptual Domains. These five different conceptual domains and the assumptions that undergird them provide potential pathways to the long-term goals of maintaining parent-child relationships, increasing positive child outcomes, and preventing future criminal behavior. Each domain provides a way of thinking about pathways that can lead towards long-term program goals. However, there are many barriers and challenges that divert incarcerated parents and their children from achieving these long-term goals. No one pathway or starting place can ensure long-term success for all incarcerated parents and their children. Thus, many programs use more than one of the frameworks outlined in an eclectic manner to provide multiple pathways and to achieve long-term goals for programs and participants.

One way to think about the multiple conceptual domains is to consider an ecological model as a meta-framework to integrate all of the areas (*see* Garbarino, 1995). The ecological model brings a more sophisticated, systemic understanding of parent-child relationships that can be translated to help us understand the specific risks and protective factors that influence long-term parent and child outcomes. This model emphasizes the complexity of parent-child relationships and points to the problem with frameworks which suggest that changing parenting attitudes or behavior will lead directly to changes in a child's behavior. First, children are active partners in parent-child relationships and changes in parenting skills will impact individual children differently (Shonkoff and Phillips, 2000). Second, the social and family context significantly affects the behaviors of parents and children. The ecological model is useful in framing approaches to increase protective factors for children and parents and as a strategy for reaching long-term outcomes; it encompasses and integrates concepts from the other frameworks by describing short-term outcomes such as changes in parenting attitudes as potential protective factors that can reduce child abuse.

Issues from Research

Although the body of empirical research that focuses on parent education for incarcerated parents has steadily grown during the 1990s, the research base is still limited and is primarily focused on short-term program outcomes for parents. These begin to test some of the conceptual models that guide practice. Eleven studies were reviewed that were published between 1989 and 1999 and that used at least a pretest and posttest design. The majority of these studies (nine out of eleven) had experimental and control groups. The sample size in the experimental groups was between fifteen and forty-four in ten of the eleven studies. Most experimental groups represented one or two-parent education classes. Seven of the eleven studies focused on incarcerated mothers and the remaining four studies examined incarcerated fathers. Showers (1993) was the only large-scale study and included close to 500, 203 of whom formed the experimental group and a comparable number in the control group. All of the studies that are reviewed focused on short-term outcomes in parents.

The designs and results of the eleven studies are summarized in Table 1 (Incarcerated Mothers) and Table 2 (Incarcerated Fathers).

All of the studies addressed parent attitudes and beliefs (for example, developmental expectations, empathetic awareness, belief in corporal punishment, respect of child's feelings, parent attachment, and parental sense of competence). The attitudes that were studied are related to risk of family violence and abusive behavior towards children (Showers, 1993). In these studies, changes in parenting attitudes indicate that parents are adopting beliefs that have been linked to positive parenting practices. The Adult and Adolescent Parenting Index (Bavelok, 1984) was used in six of the eleven studies for this purpose. The Parenting Stress Index (PSI) and the Porter Parental Acceptance Scale were both used in two of the studies. At least some parenting attitudes changed in a statistically significant manner in nine of the eleven studies that were reviewed. Some studies (for example, Browne, 1989; Moore and Clement, 1998) reported the results of parenting attitudes by breaking down differences into specific subscales while other studies (Harrison, 1997; Spring, 1999) only provided a total score report for a parent-attitude measure. It appears that incarcerated fathers were more likely to exhibit positive changes in attitudes than mothers. Both father and mother changes were mixed, with some studies (for example, Landreth and Lobaugh, 1998) reporting a number of positive changes and others (for example, Spring, 1999) reporting no differences after parents attended a parent education program. (*See* Tables 1 and 2 for a complete summary of study designs, curricula used, and results for mothers and fathers).

The research on parent education programs also examined changes in self using measures of self-esteem (for example, Index of Self Esteem) in seven of the reviewed studies. Of these seven studies, five reported significant changes in at least one subscale that reflected self-esteem or attitudes about self. Two of the studies (Harrison, 1997; Moore and Clement, 1998) reported no significant changes in relationship to parent self-esteem and parent self-development. The conceptual domain of parent self-esteem is an important area in parent education as discussed in the previous section of this chapter. Parent self-esteem has been related to positive adult identity and generative caring for children.

Another area that was examined in the studies was parent knowledge of child development, which is important to effective parenting. Parent education programs have focused on increasing parent knowledge of child development as a way to influence parent understanding of children and reasonable expectations for children (Smith et al., 1994). Parent knowledge of child development was assessed in four of eleven studies. Positive changes were reported in three of the four studies. Only Spring (1999) failed to show a significant growth in knowledge of child development.

A final area that was measured in two of the reviewed studies was parenting skills. This is a more difficult area to assess and document change, especially with the limited contact between incarcerated parents and their children. Harris and Landreth (1997) reported positive changes in videotaped observations of parental acceptance and empathy. Showers (1993) reported changes in parent responses to situations that indicated that new problem-solving skills had been developed. These are important indicators of parents' ability to change their behavioral interactions with their children and adopt more positive parenting practices.

These reported changes in parenting attitudes, knowledge, and skills indicate that parenting programs had a positive impact on incarcerated parents. The changes reported are short-term indicators that parents can learn new ideas, attitudes, and skills related to effective parenting. Two of the studies also examined child outcomes (self-esteem), and one demonstrated positive changes in children. This is a promising area for future research although changes in child behavior may not be easy to influence or detect since incarcerated parents may have limited or no contact with their children.

There are still many more questions than answers about program efficacy. Some of the next generation of research questions should include larger samples where individual and group characteristics such as parent age, culture/ethnicity, mental health status, parents who have histories of being abused, and education levels can be controlled and more carefully examined. Only Showers (1993) had a large enough sample to look at race/ethnicity as a variable. Backgrounds and preparation of parent group leaders, different levels of program intensity, and program content and format should also be explored in a more systematic manner. The evidence that parenting programs can be effective in creating short-term changes has begun to accumulate. The uneven quality of the results suggests that more information on program participant characteristics, group leaders, and long-term impacts should be studied to have a better understanding of program efficacy with different groups of parents.

In addition to more carefully controlled quantitative studies, qualitative studies should be undertaken to improve our understanding of the actual dynamics of parent and family changes (for example, First and Way, 1995; Glasser, 1993). Enos (2000) provides an excellent example of the type of qualitative study that adds some depth of understanding to the different ways that incarcerated mothers approached the parenting role and processed their parent education experience. She describes four different trajectories of mother careers that show how mothers have managed their parenting roles before and after incarceration. These include: (1) Motherhood Accepted, (2) Motherhood Terminated, (3) Mother on Leave, and (4) Sporadic and Shared Motherhood. These descriptions emphasize some of the family and cultural context differences that may influence parent involvement in programs and the efficacy of parent education programs. The results also demonstrate the interaction of social context with potential parenting education impacts. Incarcerated parents have diverse backgrounds and life experiences that have an impact on their current commitment to parenthood.

Different levels of role commitment and attitudes about the importance and centrality of parenthood are important factors in the potential impact of any parent education program. Parents in groups that this author teaches often comment at the end of a class on the lack of commitment they see in another class member as a real distraction for the class.

The research agenda for parent education including both quantitative and qualitative studies is full with many important questions. In addition, long-term outcomes will need more attention to understand better some of the hypothesized causal chains of program impacts such as the nature and rates of recidivism. There are also clear limits to what empirical research of parenting programs for incarcerated parents can explain about practice. Assessment of program outcomes is a complex task that includes understanding diverse populations, varying lengths of incarceration, and different program models delivered by parent educators with different levels of understanding and preparation. In this context, it becomes difficult to control important program factors and make valid generalizations that can guide practice. The research agenda should begin to address more defined practice issues that can help to improve practice. For example, how does the program intensity in terms of number of hours influence specific program outcomes such as changes in parenting attitudes? How does experience and training of a parent educator influence program outcomes?

Practice and the Learnings from Practitioners

The final perspective that informs what works comes from practitioners who gain knowledge and insight through direct experience. They refine and test their ideas as they work directly with parents. The literature on practice is primarily descriptive with some recommendations for practice and anecdotal accounts of program successes. The literature has been analyzed to identify some important core learnings (National Center on Fathers and Families, 1995; Kane, Gadsden, and Armorer, 1997) that emerge from the published literature. The discussion of core learnings for parent education in this section draws on the philosophy and content of the Fathers and Families Core Learnings (National Center on Fathers and Families, 1995) (*see* the chapter by Gadsden and Rethemeyer in this volume). The core learnings described below offer specific implications for practice. This section concludes with a brief discussion of some critical practice questions that need to be more carefully studied and discussed by practitioners, researchers, and policymakers.

1. Incarcerated parents care deeply about their children.

Concern about their children can be a primary motivator for incarcerated parents to improve their own lives to care for their children (Clement, 1993; Garcia Coll, Surrey, Buccio-Notaro and Molla, 1998; Newby, 1997; Palm, 2001). Parent education can be a critical link to acknowledging this care and to reinforcing the importance of good parenting for children as a way to demonstrate this care. Since incarcerated parents are often stripped of the social role and identity of parenthood through incarceration, it is important to recognize and acknowledge this caring as a strength and protective factor. Parents can be given opportunities and support to express this caring through parent education. Palm (2001) describes an exercise where a group of incarcerated fathers create a list of activities they can do while incarcerated to demonstrate their care for their children.

2. The needs of and services for incarcerated mothers and fathers are different.

The emphasis on parenting services for mothers is based on the importance of the mother-child bond, the significance of motherhood to female identity (Boudouris, 1996; Blinn, 1997; Garcia Coll, Surrey, Buccio-Notaro and Molla, 1998), and the close relationship that most mothers and children shared prior to incarceration (Gabel and Johnston, 1995). Gender roles continue to evolve and gender differences continue to be important to consider when designing parent education programs (Palm, 1997). Mothers and fathers will articulate different needs based on social beliefs about parent roles, parent relationships prior to incarceration, and gender socialization about parenting (Palm, 1996).

3. Sensitivity to cultural values and beliefs should be integrated into parent education programs for incarcerated parents.

The demographic realities of state and federal prisons (Mumola, 2000) dictate that racial/ethnic diversity be directly addressed in the design of parent education programs. Cheng Gorman, and Balter (1997) reviewed some of the parent education curricula that have been developed for different cultural groups in the United States. The initial review of research studies shows limited support for the efficacy of culturally specific curriculum materials. The sample of studies was small, and there were many methodological issues that make it difficult to draw conclusions from this meta-analysis of studies. There is a clear understanding that parent education content must be relevant and acceptable to all populations and should reflect sensitivity to cultural history and immediate social context. A few culture-specific curricula exist that have been designed for African-American and Hispanic parents (Cheng Gorman, and Balter, 1997). These curricula need further evaluation and refinement. Similarly, studies on Native American and Asian-American populations are needed to guide our understanding and development of parent education materials.

4. The parent educator is a critical component of effective parent education programs.

Kumpfer and Alvarado (1998) estimate that the quality of the trainer accounts for 50 to 80 percent of the quality of the program. Yet, both the research studies and the practice literature are often unclear about the importance of the role of the trainer or parent educator in program efficacy. Most of the research on parent education programs continues to focus on the curriculum or curriculum model as the critical or defining aspect of a program. The background of the parent educator including educational preparation, characteristics, and experience have not been studied in any systematic manner. The practice literature in parent education (for example, Braun, Coplon, Sonnenschein, 1984; Clarke, 1984) addresses some of the desired characteristics of parent educators such as being caring, a good listener, and nonjudgmental.

Efforts to develop specific preparation programs for parent educators have described in detail the knowledge, skills, and dispositions needed as competencies for parent education (*see* Powell and Cassidy, 2000). Although there is no agreement about the importance or necessity of a professional parent educator, parent education specialists typically share the belief that the character, skills, and knowledge of the trainer are an essential but understudied component of parent education programs.

5. Parent education must be integrated into more comprehensive family interventions that include children.

Parent education services as currently designed may be able to attain some of the short-term outcomes for parents but will fail to help parents and children meet the long-term outcomes. The literature (for example, Kumpfer and Alvarado, 1998; Layzer and St. Pierre, 1998) identifies additional child and family services that complement and reinforce parent education efforts. The program descriptions clearly indicate that current practices include a variety of efforts to include family members (see Boudouris, 1996; Perez, 1996; Blinn, 1997; Sheridan, 1996). Mustin (1988) describes the importance of family members as a rich resource for reaching the long-term goals of rehabilitation and reintegration of incarcerated parents into the community. Parent education programs that include a filial therapy approach (for example, Harris and Landreth, 1997) have clearly demonstrated the effectiveness of including children. There appear to be many creative efforts to work with the family system. Moreover, parent education with the focus on parent-child relationships should continue as an essential component of these efforts.

6. Parent education services must incorporate developmental sensitivity to both adults and children.

The trend in parent education towards more diverse program offerings based on child and parent developmental stages (for example, Carter, 1996; Long, 1997) has started to appear in programs for incarcerated parents (Bowling, 1999). Parent educators will encounter young parents who have different developmental needs than older parents and parents of infants and toddlers who have different needs and interests than parents of adolescents. Limited resources in most correctional settings have led to a "one size fits all" parenting program where the skilled practitioner must work to adapt a curriculum to meet the individual needs and interests of all parents.

Expanding the Role of Parent Education: Critical Practice Issues

There are a number of important issues that need further clarification and discussion to move parent education practice with incarcerated parents forward. These issues will be presented as practice-focused questions that have generated different responses and resulted in different program practices. The questions tap into some of the more complex and controversial issues in parent education practice with incarcerated parents. These are issues that come from practice and should be addressed through reflective practice strategies that bring together parent educators, researchers, and policymakers (Palm, 1998).

1. What are the similarities and differences in the needs of incarcerated mothers and fathers?

There appears to be a common core of generic parenting needs for both mothers and fathers around maintaining communication with children, understanding child development, and recognizing the emotional responses of children to parental incarceration. Both mothers and fathers also have a need to develop vocational skills to be able to serve as a provider for their children, and both have needs for additional services related to substance abuse, mental illness, limited educational attainment, and family violence.

Although there are many common issues that are important for both genders, there are also some important differences that should be addressed in parenting programs (Everhard, 1995). For example, fathers may be at a different starting place in maintaining a close relationship with their children. They typically have not spent as much time with their children prior to incarceration and may have to work harder at establishing a relationship through all the barriers that incarceration brings. Fathers also frequently are not connected to their children in a legal manner through marriage or the establishment of legal paternity. They need legal advice about establishing paternity, custody, visitation, and child support payments. Many fathers worry about another man taking over their identity as the child's father (Palm, 1996).

Mothers also face some unique issues concerning custody and termination of parental rights. Mothers are concerned about who is taking care of their children and how to keep their children out of the foster care system. Mothers who have established a close emotional bond with their children may be depressed about the loss of both the contact with their child and the loss of the role that they played (Enos, 2000).

Practitioners must work with parents to identify the specific issues that are most important and immediate before addressing some of the more common parenting issues such as behavior management. Gender differences will be an important factor to consider in defining needs, determining appropriate content, and adapting curriculum materials. Changes in gender roles will continue in many ways to influence mothers' and fathers' need for parent education. Gender differences do not have to become gender stereotypes, but they continue to exist and have a significant impact on parent education needs (Palm, 1997).

2. Who should deliver parent education services?

The parent educator is a critical component for determining program effectiveness. The field of parent education has struggled with the necessity of a professional parent educator *versus* a peer leader. Recent research on home visitation programs favor a professional as a more effective deliverer of services (*see* Shonkoff and Phillips, 2000). It would be easy to make a logical case for a professional parent educator to work with incarcerated parents because incarcerated parents are a "high need" group; someone with appropriate training and preparation would be better prepared to handle the complexity and demands of working with a population with multiple needs. The limitation associated with professional parent educators is the extended time it may take for an incarcerated parent to build a trusting relationship with a professional who seems so different from themselves.

The case for a peer parent educator is made on the basis of their ability to be understanding and empathic while more quickly being able to build a relationship with inmate parents based on some common bonds. Peers may also serve as a more salient role model. The limitations associated with the peer model focus on peer models' lack of a deeper understanding of content and minimal preparation in facilitating and teaching. Peer models may base their advice primarily on their own narrow experiences, not from a broader understanding of children and families. In addition, they may not always be a good match as a role model. Peer leaders take more time to train and supervise and require carefully developed curriculum materials (Lange, 1997). The question of who should deliver services requires careful attention and considerable discussion to determine how to staff parent education programs. It may be that both types of "leaders" have important and perhaps complementary roles to play in providing effective parent education services.

3. Which incarcerated parents will benefit most from parent education?

Practitioners often note that it is not clear whether all incarcerated parents are equally good candidates to benefit from parent education classes. Enos's (2000) study of incarcerated mothers clearly describes some of the important differences that incarcerated parents may bring to parent education. Screening and assessing parents prior to participating in a program may be one practical approach to consider (Palm, 2001). However, which characteristics should we look for when we screen parents? Should all parents be given a chance to participate in parent education if they feel it would be beneficial (Ayre, 1996)? There are also ethical questions about parent-child relationships, parent rights, and the best interests of the child. How do we assess parents and the potential harm they may cause to children if the parents become reconnected to a family?

Family systems are very complex and fragile, and it is feasible that parent education of incarcerated parents may create positive changes in a parent that have negative impacts on family life. For example, a father who has not been involved in his young child's life may attend a parent education class and decide that he now wants to play an active role in supporting his child. The child's mother may have moved on to a different relationship and may have developed a stable family situation. The father's possible reconnection with the child is seen as undesirable to the mother and her new partner. Whose rights and needs are most important in this situation? More thinking about screening and assessment of inmate parents and family systems may help not only to improve chances of program success but also to avoid some of the potential negative results of parent education.

4. What are the potential cost benefits of parent education programs for incarcerated parents?

The field has not addressed the question of the cost-benefits of parent education programs. The potential high costs of maintaining incarcerated parents and the long-term costs to children of incarcerated parents who may follow in their parents footsteps and require expensive services along the way make the potential benefits of parent education programs a critical factor to consider. Short-term and relatively low-cost investments in parent education programs may make this service a very good long-term investment even if it is not effective for most incarcerated parents (*see* Reynolds, Temple, Robertson, and Mann, 2001). The potential long-term cost of the incarceration of two generations is very high. However, an important question is what level of program efficacy is reasonable or necessary to make the investment in parent education a wise choice? If we are able to target the parents and families who are most likely to benefit from parent education, it would increase program effectiveness and improve the cost-benefit ratio.

5. How does program intensity impact program outcomes in parent education programs for incarcerated parents?

The issue of program intensity has not been addressed in the research literature on incarcerated parents, which reflects a wide range of program intensity from 10 to 15 hours (Showers, 1993) to almost 100 hours (Browne, 1989). The practice literature suggests that at least 32 hours (16 hours of parent education and 16 hours of parent support discussion) are needed for programs to be effective (Johnston, 1995). Related parent-education practice literature suggests a minimum of 45 hours of parent education for high-risk parents (Kumpfer and Alvarado, 1998). This is an important research and practice question that should be studied in a more systematic manner to determine how the level of services affects both short and long-term outcomes. It may be that initial parent education programs can be of moderate length and that parent support services are needed to support continued progress and help parents face new developmental and transitional issues.

6. How can cultural differences be addressed most effectively in parenting classes with incarcerated parents?

The demographics of the current prison population clearly point to the need to address the parenting issues and beliefs of ethnic minority populations. In some communities, the strategy has been to create parent education groups for specific minority populations. This is reflected in the Cheng Gorman, and Balter (1997) review of culturally sensitive programs. The critique of traditional parent education programs as being designed for white and middle class parents (Alvy, 1994) has relevance to the programs used for incarcerated parents. This review of research on parent education programs reveals that some of the curricula, such as STEP, that were used may not be "culturally sensitive." The demographics of each sample of parents included some identification of minority parents, but only one study was able to examine race/ethnicity as a factor (Showers, 1993). The conclusions in this study were that parent education was effective for both "black and white parents."

The problem does appear broad, however. As a researcher-practitioner, this author has worked with mixed cultural groups in which the majority of parents were identifiable as African-American, white, Latino (primarily Mexican-American), and Native American. Some inmates also identify themselves as biracial, and many have children who are biracial. This mixture of different cultural/ethnic backgrounds provides both an opportunity and challenge for parent educators. It also raises questions for practice. How should we approach a group that consists of parents from different cultural backgrounds? What kinds of adaptations do we make to parent education curriculum materials? Do we choose a curriculum for African-American parents? Do we create a curriculum specifically designed for incarcerated parents without any specific focus on race/ethnicity? Should we be creating parenting curriculum materials that are both multicultural and address the specific issues of incarcerated mothers and fathers? The simplistic practice guideline to be culturally sensitive (Family Resource Coalition of America, 1996) does not provide any real guidance to these practical questions. Practitioners and researchers must begin to address the pragmatic issues behind culturally sensitive practice to understand which approaches are effective. This is an area where it is easy to criticize both practice and research for their lack of cultural awareness and sensitivity. The field needs to move beyond these simplistic critiques and identify strategies that work for all of the different ethnic groups of incarcerated parents.

Conclusion

This chapter began with the basic question about what works in parent education programs for incarcerated parents. The review touched on three different perspectives: (1) conceptual domains, (2) research, and (3) practice. Each provides some insight into thinking about and understanding what works in parent education programs. Parent education employs a number of conceptual frameworks and theories that guide current practice. The existing conceptual domains provide some guidance to practice, but many of the basic assumptions have mixed support. The ecological model was introduced as a way to integrate and provide a context for understanding different frameworks. This model identifies risk and protective factors for both incarcerated parents and their children and helps to clarify the contributions of the current eclectic blend of frameworks that are represented by current practice.

The research base is small but provides some evidence of positive short-term outcomes. Research suggests that programs have had some moderate success with the primary short-term goals of changing parenting attitudes and increasing parent self-esteem. There are many new research questions that need to be addressed to understand which specific factors influence program efficacy. There is also a need for more qualitative research to provide new insights into the dynamics of parent education and how it actually promotes changes in parents, children, and families.

The practice literature at this point is also limited. It is clear that practitioners in the field are dedicated and caring, and they strongly advocate for both incarcerated parents and their children. The practice literature and the author's experience as a researcher-practitioner suggest that practitioners need more opportunities for communication and support around practice. The core learnings that were identified are intended to be a starting point for establishing principles to guide practice.

The chapter concludes with a discussion of critical practice questions. These are presented to stimulate dialog and promote reflective practice. Kirby and Paradise (1992) describe reflective practice as the "integration of research, theory and experience in the formulation of solutions to problems of practice that are complex and unique." This concept invites practitioners, researchers, and policymakers to join together to examine the different perspectives on parent education that have been presented in the chapter and find ways to address the issues that come from practice to improve practice and program effectiveness.

In conclusion, parent education is one important strategy for addressing the needs of incarcerated parents—both mothers and fathers. It can directly affect parent attitudes, knowledge, and skills to improve parent-child and family relationships. This can be a pathway to the long-term goals for both parents and children that were defined at the beginning of the chapter. The real power of parent education programs as an intervention strategy for incarcerated parents comes from the potential deep caring and goodness that exists in the parent-child relationship. As one incarcerated father stated: "Fatherhood has brought maturity, more value to life. Kids come before you. It has brought me away from things, friends, drugs . . . my number one priority (now) is my family." It is this transformative potential of parenthood combined with a growing research base that continues to support parent education services as an important pathway to change for incarcerated parents and their families.

Table 1A. Summary of Parent Education Studies on Mothers

Study	Participants	Design	Time	Curriculum
Browne (1989)	20/29 completed	E: OXO	2 X 2 hr. for 24 weeks	Education for parenthood
Showers (1993)	203- E 275- C	E: OXO C: O O	1.5 hrs. for 10 weeks	Systematic Training for Effective Parenting (STEP)
Martin, Cotton, Browne, Kupper, Kurz, and Robertson (1993)	36-E t1-t2	E: OXOXO	2 X 1.5 hr. for 8 weeks	Motheread
Harris and Landreth (1997)	12- E 10- C	E: OXO C: O O	2 X 2 hr. for 5 weeks	Filial Therapy
Harm and Thompson (1997)	44/80 completed	E: OXO	15 weeks	Nurturing Program
Moore and Clement (1998)	20- E 20- C	E: OXO C: O O	2 hr. for 9 weeks	Mothers Inside Loving Kids (MILK)
Spring (1999)	30- E 30- C	E: OXO C: O O	2 hr. for 12 weeks	Project Reach

E = Experimental
C = Control
R = Random Assignment
O = Observation
X = Treatment

Table 2A. Summary of Parent Education Studies on Fathers

Study	Participants	Design	Time	Curriculum
Bayse, Allgood, and Van Wyck (1991)	27- E 27- C	E: ROXO C: RO OXO	2.5 hrs. for 4 weeks	Eclectic - How to Keep the Family Alive
Harrison (1997)	15- E 15- C	E: ROXO C: RO O	2.5 hrs. X 2 for 6 weeks	Nurturing Program/STEP
Landreth and Lobaugh (1998)	16- E 16- C	E: ROXO C: RO O	1.5 hrs. for 10 weeks	Filial Therapy
Wilczak and Markstrom (1999)	21- E 21- C	E: OXO C: O O	1.5 hrs. for 8 weeks	Systematic Training for Effective Parenting (STEP)

E = Experimental
C = Control
R = Random Assignment
O = Observation
X = Treatment

Table 1B. Summary of Parent Education Studies on Mothers—Continued

Study	Instruments	Results
Browne (1989)	Self-Evaluation Inventory (SEI)	+
	—Self-esteem	0
	—Self-criticism	0
	—Self-control	0
	—Locus of Control	0
	—Efficacy scale	
	Adult Adolescent Parenting Inventory (AAPI)	+
	—Developmental Expectations	0
	—Empathetic Awareness	+
	—Belief in Corporal Punishment	0
	—Role Reversal 20/29 completed	
Showers (1993)	Child Behavior Management Scale	+
	Recidivism (E=1.5%, C=19%)	+
Harris and Landreth (1997)	Measurement of Empathy in Adult-Child Interaction (MEACI)	+
	Porter Parental Acceptance Scale (PPAS)	+
	Parenting Stress Index (PSI)	0
	Filial Problem Checklist	+
Harms and Thompson (1997)	Index of Self-Esteem	+
	Adult Adolescent Parenting Inventory (AAPI)	
	—Developmental Expectations	+
	—Empathetic Awareness	+
	—Belief in Corporal Punishment	+
	—Role Reversal	+
Moore and Clement (1998)	Index of Self-Esteem	0
	Adult Adolescent Parenting Inventory (AAPI)	
	—Developmental Expectations	0
	—Empathetic Awareness	0
	—Belief in Corporal Punishment	0
	—Role Reversal	0
	Nurturing Quiz	+
Spring (1999)	Project REACH Parent Education Instrument	0
	Index of Parental Attitudes	0
Martin and Cotton (1993)	T1-T2	
	CES-Depression Scale	0
	Self Evaluation	
	—External Locus of Control	+
	—Negative Self-Evaluation	+
	—Positive Self-Evaluation	0
	Adult Adolescent Parenting Inventory (AAPI)	
	—Developmental Expectations	+
	—Empathetic Awareness	+
	—Belief in Corporal Punishment	0
	—Role Reversal	0
	Reading Behavior (interview)	0

+ = Significant positive difference
0 = No change/difference

Table 2B. Summary of Parent Education Studies on Fathers—Continued

Study	Instruments	Results
Bayse, Allgood and Van Wyck (1991)	Selfism Scale	+
	Family Adaptability & Cohesion Evaluation Scale (FACES)	
	—Cohesion	+
	—Adaptability	0
	—Distance from Center	+
Harrison (1997)	Adult Adolescent Parenting Index	+
	Index of Self Esteem	0
	Harter's Self Perception Profile (child)	0
	Harter's Self Perception Profile (adolescent)	0
Landreth and Lobaugh (1998)	Porter Parental Accceptance Scale	
	—Respect for Child's Feelings	+
	—Appreciation of Child Uniqueness	+
	—Child's Need for Autonomy & Independence	+
	—Unconditional Love	+
	Parenting Stress Index (PSI)	
	—Parent Domain	+
	—Child Domain	0
	Joseph Preschool & Primary Child's Self Concept	+
	Filial Problem Checklist	+
	Parental Locus of Control	
	—Parental Efficacy	+
	—Parental Responsibility	0
	—Child Control	0
	—Believe in Fate	+
	—Parent Control of Child Behavior	0
Wilczak and Markstrom (1999)	Content Test	+
	Cleminshaw-Guidubaldi Parent Satisfaction Scale	
	—Spouse Support	0
	—Child Parent Relationship	0
	—Parent Performance	+
	—Discipline/Control	0
	—General Satisfaction	0

+ = Significant positive difference
0 = No change/difference

References

Alvy, K. 1994. *Parent Training Today: A Social Necessity.* Studio City, California: Center for Improvement of Child Caring.

Ayre, E. 1996. They Won't Take No for an Answer: The Relais Enfants-Parents. ERIC Document. ED 399 038.

Bavelok, S. 1984. *Adult-Adolescent Parenting Inventory*. Eau Claire, Wisconsin: Family Development Resources, Inc.

Blankenhorn, D. 1995. *Fatherless America*. New York: Basic Books.

Blinn, C. 1997. *Maternal Ties: A Selection of Programs for Female Offenders*. Lanham, Maryland: American Correctional Association.

Boudouris, J. 1985. Prisons and Kids: Programs for Inmate Parents. ERIC Document. ED 269 123.

———. 1996. *Parents in Prisons: Addressing the Needs of Families*. Lanham, Maryland: American Correctional Association.

Bowlby, J. 1969. *Attachment and Loss: Vol. 1 Attachment*. New York: Basic Books.

Bowling, G. 1999. The MELD for Young Dads Program. *Family and Corrections Network Report Issue*. 20: 10-11. Palmyra, Virginia.

Braun, L., J. Coplon, and P. Sonnenschein. 1984. *Helping Parents in Groups: A Leader's Handbook*. Boston: Resource Communications, Inc.

Brenner, E. 1999. Fathers in Prison: A Review of the Data. *Family and Corrections Network Report*. 20: 4-7. Palmyra, Virginia.

Bronfenbrenner, U. 1979. *The Ecology of Human Development*. Cambridge, Massachusetts: Harvard University Press.

Browne, D. C. H. 1989. Incarcerated Mothers and Parenting. *Journal of Family Violence*. 4: 211-221.

Campbell, D. and G. Palm. 2001. Group Parent Education: Facilitating Parent Learning and Support. Unpublished manuscript. St. Cloud, Minnesota: St. Cloud State University.

Canning, S. and J. Fantuzzo. 2000. Competent Families, Collaborative Professionals: Empowered Parent Education for Low Income, African-American Families. In J. Gillespie and J. Primavera, eds. *Diverse Families, Competent Families*. Binghamton, New York: The Haworth Press.

Carter, N. 1996. *See How We Grow: A Report on the Status of Parenting Education in the U.S.* Philadelphia, Pennsylvania: The Pew Charitable Trusts.

Cheng Gorman, J. and L. Balter. 1997. Culturally Sensitive Parent Education: A Critical Review of Quantitative Research. *Review of Educational Research*. 67(3): 339-369.

Clarke, J. I. 1984. *Who Me Lead A Group?* San Francisco: Harper and Row.

Clement, M. J. 1993. Parenting in Prison: A National Survey of Programs for Incarcerated Women. *Journal of Offender Rehabilitation.* 19(1-2): 89-100.

Cooke, B. and R. Thomas. 1986. Summary of Profile of Parent Education Study. In J. Parsons, T. Bowman, J. Comeau, R. Pitzer, and G. Schmitt, eds. *Parent Education State of the Art Monograph.* White Bear Lake, Minnesota: Minnesota Curriculum Services Center.

Doherty, W. J. 1995. Boundaries between Parents and Family Education and Family Therapy: The Levels of Family Involvement Model. *Family Relations.* 44(4): 353-358.

Dollahite, D. and A. Hawkins. 1997. Generative Fathering: Beyond Deficit Perspectives. Thousand Oaks, California: Sage Publications.

Dunst, C. 1985. Rethinking Early Intervention. *Analysis and Intervention in Developmental Disabilities.* 5(1-2): 165-201.

Enos, S. 2000. Mothering from the Inside: Parenting in a Women's Prison. Albany, New York: State University of New York Press.

Erikson, E. 1968. *Identity, Youth and Crisis.* New York: Norton.

Everhard, L. 1995. Notes on Parenting Programs for Incarcerated Fathers. *Family and Corrections Network Report.* Nos. 8, 7 and 10. Palmyra, Virginia.

Fagan, J. and A. Hawkins. 2001. *Clinical and Educational Interventions with Fathers.* New York: The Haworth Press.

Family Resource Coalition of America. 1996. *Guidelines for Family Support Practice.* Chicago, Illinois: Family Resource Coalition of America.

First, J. and W. Way. 1995. Parent Education Outcomes: Insights into Transformative Learning. *Family Relations.* 44: 104-109.

Gabel, K. and D. Johnston. 1995. Incarcerated Parents. In K. Gabel and D. Johnston, eds. *Children of Incarcerated Parents.* New York: Lexington Books.

Garbarino, J. 1995. *Raising Children in a Socially Toxic Environment.* San Francisco: Jossey-Bass.

Garcia Coll, C., J. Surrey, P. Buccio-Notaro, and B. Molla. 1998. Incarcerated Mothers: Crimes and Punishments. In J. Garcia Coll, J. Surrey, and K. Weingarten, eds. *Mothering Against the Odds: Diverse Voices of Contemporary Mothers.* New York: Guilford.

Genisio, M. 1996. Breaking Barriers with Books: A Father's Book-Sharing Program from Prison. *Journal of Adolescent and Adult Literacy.* 40(2): 92-100.

Gilgun, J. 1994. *A Survey of Minnesota Prison Inmates: Risk and Protective Factors in Adolescence.* Minneapolis, Minnesota: Minnesota Citizens' Council on Crime and Justice.

Giveans, D. 1988. The Positive Effects of Child Development Classes on Incarcerated Fathers. *Nurturing Today.* 10(1): 16-17.

Glasser, I. 1992. Parenting Programs for Imprisoned Mothers. *Practicing Anthropology.* 14(3): 17-21.

Gonzalez, M. 1995. When Bonds Are Broken: Family Literacy for Incarcerated Fathers and Their Children. ERIC Document. ED 395 123.

Hairston, C. F. 1998. The Forgotten Parent: Understanding the Forces that Influence Incarcerated Fathers' Relationships with Their Children. *Child Welfare.* 77(5): 617-639.

Harlow, C. W. 1999. *Prior Abuse Reported by Inmates and Probationers.* Washington, D.C.: U.S. Department of Justice.

Harm, J. and P. J. Thompson. 1997. Evaluating the Effectiveness of Parent Education for Incarcerated Mothers. *Journal of Offender Rehabilitation.* 24(3/4): 135-152.

Harris, Z. 1996. How to Help the Children when Mothers Go To Jail: Parenting Classes with Incarcerated Mothers and Mother-Child Play Sessions in a Country Jail Setting. *American Jails.* 9(6): 31-34, 36.

Harris, Z. and G. Landreth. 1997. Filial Therapy with Incarcerated Mothers: A Five Week Model. *International Journal of Play Therapy.* 6(2): 53-73.

Harrison, K. 1997. Parental Training for Incarcerated Fathers: Effects on Attitudes, Self-esteem, and Children's Self-perceptions. *The Journal of Social Psychology.* 137: 588-593.

Jacobs, A. 1995. *Protecting Children and Preserving Families: A Cooperative Strategy for Nurturing Children of Incarcerated Parents.* New York: New York Women's Prison Association.

Johnson, L. and G. Palm. 1992. *Working with Fathers: Methods and Perspectives.* Stillwater, Minnesota: Nu Ink.

Johnston, D. 1995. Intervention. In K. Gabel and D. Johnston, eds. *Children of Incarcerated Parents.* New York: Lexington Books.

———. 1997. Developing Services for Incarcerated Mothers. In C. Blinn ed. *Maternal Ties: A Selection of Programs for Female Offenders*. Lanham, Maryland: American Correctional Association.

———. 2000. Incarcerated Fathers and Their Children. Paper presented at the North American Conference on Fathers Behind Bars and on the Street, Durham, North Carolina.

Kane, D., V. Gadsden, and K. Armorer. 1997. *The Fathers and Families Core Learnings: An Update from the Field*. Philadelphia, Pennsylvania: University of Pennsylvania, National Center on Fathers and Families.

Kirby, P. and L. Paradise. 1992. Reflective Practice and Effectiveness of Teachers. *Psychological Reports*. 70: 057-58.

Klein, S., G. Bartholomew, and S. Bahr. 1999. Family Education for Adults in Correctional Settings: A Conceptual Framework. *International Journal of Offender Therapy and Comparative Criminology*. 43(3): 291-307.

Kliman, D. and R. Kohl. 1984. *Fatherhood, U.S.A*. New York: Garland.

Knitzer, J. and S. Bernard. 1997. *Map and Track: State Initiatives to Encourage Responsible Fatherhood*. New York: National Center on Children in Poverty.

Koban, L. A. 1983. Parents in Prison: A Comparative Analysis of the Effects of Incarceration on the Families of Men and Women. *Research in Law, Deviance and Social Control*. 5: 171-183.

Kumpfer, K. and R. Alvarado. 1998. Effective Family Strengthening Interventions. *Juvenile Justice Bulletin*. November. 1-15.

Landreth, G. L. and A. F. Lobaugh. 1998. Filial Therapy with Incarcerated Fathers: Effects on Parental Acceptance of Child, Parental Stress, and Child Adjustment. *Journal of Counseling and Development*. 76: 157-165.

Lange, S. M. 1997. Parenting Training in Corrections: Mission, Methods, Materials and Best Practices. ERIC Document. ED 418 264.

Layzer, J. and R. St. Pierre. 1998. Improving the Life Chances of Children in Poverty: Assumptions and What We Have Learned. *Social Policy Report*. Society for Research in Child Development, 12(4): 1-25.

Levine, J. and E. Pitt. 1995. *New Expectations: Community Strategies for Responsible Fatherhood*. New York: Families and Work Institute.

Long, N. 1997. Parent Education/Training in the USA: Current Status and Future Trends. *Clinical Child Psychology and Psychiatry*. 2-4: 501-515.

Martin, S., N. Cotten, D. Browne, L. Kupper, B. Kurz, and E. Robertson. 1993. Evaluation of the Motheread Program. Unpublished report. University of North Carolina at Chapel Hill.

Martin, S. and U. Cotton. 1995. Literacy Intervention for Incarcerated Women: The Motheread Program. *Corrections Today.* 57(7): 120, 122, 123.

Medway, F. 1989. Measuring the Effectiveness of Parent Education. In M. Fine, ed. *The Second Handbook on Parent Education.* San Diego: Academic Press.

Moore, A. R. and M. J. Clement. 1998. Effects of Parenting Training for Incarcerated Mothers. *Journal of Offender Rehabilitation.* 27(1/2): 57-72.

Mumola, C. 2000. *Incarcerated Parents and Their Children.* Bureau of Justice Statistics Special Report, NCJ 182335. Washington, D.C.: Bureau of Justice Statistics.

Mustin, J. 1988. The Family: A Critical Factor for Corrections. *Nurturing Today.* 10(1): 6-7.

National Center on Fathers and Families. 1995. *Core Learnings.* Philadelphia, Pennsylvania: National Center on Fathers and Families, University of Pennsylvania.

Newby, G. 1997. Las Comadres: A Parenting Education/Foster Parenting Program. In C. Blinn, ed. *Maternal Ties: A Selection of Programs for Female Offenders.* Lanham, Maryland: American Correctional Association.

Owen, B. and B. Bloom. 1995. Profiling Women Prisoners. *The Prison Journal.* 75: 65-85.

Palkovitz, R. and G. Palm. 1998. Fatherhood and Faith in Formation: The Developmental Effects of Fathering on Religiosity, Morals and Values. *The Journal of Men's Studies.* 7(1): 33-52.

Palm, G. 1996. Understanding the Parent Education Needs of Incarcerated Fathers. Paper presented at the National Council on Family Relations Conference. Kansas City, Missouri.

———. 1997. Promoting Generative Parenting through Parent and Family Education. In A. J. Hawkins and D. C. Dollahite, eds. *Generative Fathering: Beyond Deficit Perspectives.* Thousand Oaks, California: Sage Publications.

———. 1998. Developing a Model of Reflective Practice for Improving Fathering Programs. Philadelphia, Pennsylvania: National Center on Fathers and Families, University of Pennsylvania.

———. 2001. Parent Education for Incarcerated Fathers. In J. Fagan and A. Hawkins eds. *Clinical and Educational Interventions with Fathers.* New York: The Haworth Press.

Palm, G. and R. Palkovitz. 1988. The Challenge of Working with New Fathers: Implications for Support Providers. In R. Palkovitz and M. Sussman, eds. *Transitions to Parenthood.* New York: The Haworth Press.

Perez, J. A. 1996. Inmate Parenting Contact Visitation Programs: Why Implement Them? *American Jails.* 10(5): 31-33, 35-36.

Powell, D. 1986. The Assumptions of Parent Education. In J. Parsons, T. Bowman, J. Comeau, R. Pitzer, and G. Schmitt, eds. *Parent Education State of the Art Monograph.* White Bear Lake, Minnesota: Minnesota Curriculum Services Center. pp. 12-18.

Powell, L. and D. Cassidy. 2000. *Family Life Education.* Mountain View, California: Mayfield Publishing Company.

Reynolds, A., J. Temple, D. Robertson, and E. Mann. 2001. Age 21 Cost-benefit Analysis of the Title-I Chicago Child-Parent Center Program: Executive Summary. http://www.waisman.wisc.edu/cls/clsexecsumr.html.

Sheridan, J. 1996. Inmates May Be Parents, Too. *Corrections Today.* 58(5): 100, 102-103.

Shonkoff, J. and D. Phillips. 2000. *From Neurons to Neighborhoods: The Science of Early Childhood Development.* Washington, D.C.: National Academy Press.

Showers, J. 1993. Assessing and Remedying Parenting Knowledge among Woman Inmates. *Journal of Offender Rehabilitation.* 20(1/2): 35-36.

Smith, C., D. Cudaback, W. Goddard, and J. Myers-Walls. 1994. *National Extension Parent Education Model.* Manhattan, Kansas: Kansas State University.

Snarey, J. 1993. *How Fathers Care for the Next Generation: A Four-Decade Study.* Cambridge, Massachusetts: Harvard University Press.

Spring, J. B. 1999. The Effect of Parent Education on Knowledge of Parenting Skills and Attitude Change of Incarcerated Mothers. *Dissertation Abstracts International: Section B: The Sciences and Engineering.* 60(6-B): 3022.

Todres, R. and T. Bunston. 1993. Parent Education Program Evaluation: A Review of the Literature. *Canadian Journal of Community Mental Health.* 12(1): 225-257.

Turner, R. and M. Eichenlaub. 1998. Long Distance Dads: The Fatherhood Workshop. Incarcerated Fathers Program, State Correctional Institution at Albion: Pennsylvania Department of Corrections.

Wilczak, G. and C. Markstrom. 1999. The Effects of Parent Education on Parental Locus of Control and Satisfaction of Incarcerated Fathers. *International Journal of Offender Therapy and Comparative Criminology.* 43(1): 90-102.

WHAT WORKS: CHILDREN OF INCARCERATED OFFENDERS

5

Denise Johnston, M.D.
Director, Childhood Trauma Project
The Center for Children of Incarcerated Parents
Eagle Rock, California

To determine "What Works" for children of incarcerated offenders, the outcomes that are desired for these children must be identified. This, in turn, requires an understanding of the effects of parental incarceration. A simple prerequisite for that understanding is information about parent and child issues among criminal offenders prior to their arrest and confinement. Without such information, data collected on families during and immediately after parental incarceration may have limited practical and predictive value. This chapter focuses on these child and parent issues, examining them over the course of the pre- to postincarceration of parents. It begins with a review of empirical research on incarcerated parents and their children.

Empirical Research on Incarcerated Parents and Their Children

Three Eras of Research

Only a small minority of professional publications about incarcerated parents and their children report on empirical studies. Empirical research is important because it involves actual observation, measurement, or testing of the subjects of study. There have been three overlapping eras of empirical research on the effects of parental incarceration: a criminology era; an advocacy era; and the current era, which has been focused on developmental, family, and community issues. The number of studies in each of these periods is extremely limited.

The criminology era includes work conducted from the early years of the twentieth century and suggested that children of criminal parents were likely to become criminals themselves. That observation was and remains a primary basis for much of the attention paid to children of incarcerated parents and to the parenting issues of their mothers and fathers (Adalist-Estrin, 1993; Blumstein, Cohen, Roth, and Visher, 1986; Brennan, Mednick, and Kandel, 1993; Farrington, 1989; Farrington and Hawkins, 1991; Robins, 1979; U.S. Senate, 2001). Early in the twentieth century, some investigations recorded findings (Breckenridge and Abbott, 1912) about housing and other social conditions related to juvenile delinquency or incarceration, but other subsequent studies were directed at identifying risk factors for juvenile delinquency (Glueck and Glueck, 1950; Loeber and Dishion, 1983; McCord and McCord, 1959; Otterstrom, 1946; Robins, West and Herjanic, 1975).

Most major investigations reported since the middle of the last century were conducted on the wives and families of male prisoners (Bakker, Morris and Janus, 1978; Blackwell, 1959; Schneller, 1978; Swan, 1981). The current literature cites no studies of children of criminal offenders from the criminology era that actually involved direct examination or observation of the children themselves or the content of their lives.

The advocacy era began concurrently with the women's movement in the 1970s and reflected that era's interest in the conditions of women's lives. Advocacy research was usually conducted by women on women and quickly became focused on what has always been a topic of major importance to women prisoners: their children. As a body of work, advocacy research led to the first wave of public attention to the children of incarcerated parents.

With a couple of notable exceptions (for example, Kolman, 1983; Stanton, 1980), advocacy-era research described the children, parent-child relationships, and parenting of women prisoners by talking with or surveying these mothers (Baunach, 1979; Gibbs, 1971; Johnston, 1991; LaPointe, Picker, and Harris, 1985; McGowen and Blumenthal, 1978). Some researchers also collected information from the children's caregivers or other interested adults (Bloom and Steinhart, 1993; Henriques, 1982; Hungerford, 1993; Hunter, 1984; Sack, Seidler, and Thomas, 1976). Several studies used similar methodologies to compare children of male and female offenders (Fritsch and Burkhead, 1982; Koban, 1983; Sack, Seilder, and Thomas, 1976). Although there was greater focus on children, data were typically collected on parents or other caregivers. Little of the work emanating from advocacy efforts actually collected data by observing, examining records about, or interviewing substantial numbers of the children themselves.

The third era spans the period from the early 1990s to the present. During these years, investigators have begun to study children of prisoners/criminal offenders as index subjects of research. Index subjects of research are those subjects who are identified as the focus of the research; are selected and assessed directly rather as a consequence of their relationship to other subjects; and whose qualities and/or performance are measured directly rather than reported upon by others. A number of such studies are described in later sections of this chapter; several represent significant advances in research on these children. Catan (1992) was the first to measure developmental outcomes among children of prisoners; she studied infants living in the prison nurseries of Great Britain. The Children of Offenders Study (Johnston, 1992) used interviews, observations, and standardized instruments to collect and examine data on child functioning in multiple domains. Kampfner (1995) also observed, interviewed, and tested children as part of her research.

The current era also includes a series of studies that more substantively examine incarcerated parents, using professional observations and standardized measurements in addition to information collected by parent surveys. These include investigations of incarcerated fathers (Adalist-Estrin, 1986 and 1993; Lanier, 1993) as well as mothers (LeFlore and Holston, 1990).

Clinical and Evaluation Studies

In addition to these studies, researchers in other fields have conducted a few clinical studies of children whose parents also happened to be incarcerated (Gabel and Schindledecker, 1993; Sack, 1977). However, these studies are limited in their usefulness in describing the large majority of children of prisoners, most of whom are not in treatment for mental illness. Such studies, nevertheless, have been widely cited in descriptions of this population. As a result, they have helped to shape an image of the children of incarcerated parents as a disordered population.

Also, beginning in the late 1970s, descriptions of the content and evaluation of programs for incarcerated parents and/or their children appeared in the literature (Browne, 1989; Datesman and Cales, 1983; Glasser, 1990; Hairston and Lockett, 1985); some contain information collected by direct observation, testing, and interviews of the children of prisoners (Keay, 1989; Key and Eyres, 2000; Landreth and Lobaugh, 1998). The selection of the child subjects of these studies from the small segment of the families of incarcerated parents that participate in such programs limits the usefulness of collected data in understanding the whole or even significant numbers of children of prisoners.

Empirical Research Findings on Parenting by Criminal Offenders

Although research on parenting by criminal offenders is receiving increased attention, very little solid information on how criminal offenders parent is available. The dearth of research is reflected in the kinds of conclusions that have been drawn. For example, in his careful and extensive review of empirical research that examined familial influences on criminal behavior, Raine (1993) stated: "Parents who are criminals are invariably bad parents, and this bad parenting, along with other social disadvantages of being criminal, translates itself into poor parental supervision, parental absence, poor discipline, and child abuse and neglect" (p. 245). Yet, Raine cited no research in support of this statement. In fact, with the exception of episodes of parental absence, there is no work that establishes that "bad parenting" characterizes criminal offenders.

On the contrary, there is some evidence that cases of child abuse or neglect occur at roughly the same rate among families of criminal offenders as among their neighbors (Johnston, 1992). Although the concern about the potential for child abuse among criminal offenders has driven the development of services for incarcerated parents and their children (Browne, 1989; Hairston and Lockett, 1985), there have been almost no studies on that aspect of parenting among criminal offenders.

Much of the research on parenting among criminal offenders has been conducted on imprisoned women and has consisted of the collection of demographic data and measurements of attitudes, beliefs, concerns, and "characteristics" of parenting and the maternal role, as reported by the mothers (Baunach, 1979; Bonfanti, Felder, Loesch, and Vincent, 1974; DuBose, 1977; Gibbs, 1971; Koban, 1983; Lundberg, Sheekley, and Voelker, 1975; McGowan and Blumenthal, 1978; Zalba, 1964; Zeitz, 1963). These studies found that maternal attitudes, beliefs, and concerns of incarcerated women were normative. For example, LeFlore and Holston (1990) found that the women studied did not differ from their matched, nonoffender peers in the community. None of these studies included actual observations or measurements of parenting practices.

Several researchers have attempted to produce more concrete documentation of parenting by women offenders. Zalba (1964) verified data reported by mothers about the preincarceration care they gave their children and found their reports to have flaws; for example, the mothers studied reported a lower than actual level of child involvement with juvenile probation and the Youth Authority, (p. 49). In some instances, other authors found that women prisoners idealized their previous maternal performance (Bonfanti et.al., 1974). Stanton (1980) conducted one of the few studies that have measured parent knowledge of children's lives among women offenders. She studied fifty-four mothers in jail and twenty-one mothers on probation, finding that more than one-third of the jailed women had limited knowledge of their children's school lives and friends, although all but four were serving sentences of less than one year. Significantly, the subjects of this research were selected because they had lived with their children prior to incarceration; they did not represent a cross-section of women prisoners. Hunter (1984), who studied paroled women and their children, found that more than four in five drug-abusing mothers reported that their children's closest relationships prior to maternal incarceration were with other adults; a large majority of these women also reported that their children had a significant male figure in their lives prior to maternal incarceration but that these men did not live with the children.

In perhaps the only study to conduct systematic observations of parenting behaviors among women offenders, Kolman (1983) examined mother-child interactions among a group of previously incarcerated mothers and their young children in structured settings. She found the mothers studied to be somewhat rigid and over-controlling in their parenting style; however, there was no comparable information produced about their preincarceration parenting. There have been few other studies that have focused specifically on parent-child interaction within families of criminal offenders outside of prison. Studies that have collected the most extensive data about the lives of children of criminal offenders (for example, Johnston, 1992, 1993; Johnston and Carlin, 1996; Project SEEK, 1997) generally have not examined parent-child interactions or concrete aspects of parenting.

Empirical Research Findings on the Children of Prisoners

Empirical data on children of prisoners and children of criminal offenders who are not incarcerated is extremely limited. Most publications that include information about these children have been focused on incarcerated mothers (Baunach, 1979; Henriques, 1982; Hunter, 1984; Johnston,1991; Kolman, 1983). The great majority of substantive empirical studies on the topic of "children of incarcerated parents" have not involved any type of direct observation, assessment, interview, or examination of the children themselves (Bloom and Steinhart, 1993; Fritsch and Burkhead, 1982; Hungerford, 1993; McGowan and Blumenthal, 1978; Morris, 1965; Prison Visitation Project, 1993; Sack, Seidler, and Thomas, 1976; Virginia Commission on Youth, 1992; Zalba, 1964). While there have been other studies that included information about these children, virtually all were either investigations of the predictors of delinquency (Glueck and Glueck, 1950; Loeber and Dishion, 1983; McCord and McCord, 1959; Otterstrom, 1946; Robins, West, and Herjanic, 1975) or reports on programs for children of prisoners (Harm and Thompson, 1995; Project SEEK, 1997.) None was designed to provide descriptions of the children themselves. Only five publications describing these children have reported on empirical research that involved direct examination or observation of the children.

Friedman and Esselstyn (1965) studied academic performance among 117 children of men incarcerated in Santa Clara County, California, comparing the children of incarcerated men with a control group of children of nonincarcerated men. The children were identified through their jailed fathers. Demographic descriptors of the children, other than race, and criminal justice histories of the fathers whose children were in the control group were not recorded; in addition, selection criteria were not described for either group of children. Subjective teacher evaluations of child performance were used as the outcome measures. No grades or other objective performance records were reported, and numerical data were not presented in the report. The obvious methodological limitations of this study made its findings of little use in developing an understanding of the children of prisoners.

In an elegant study, Stanton (1980) compared children of jailed mothers and children of probationer mothers to distinguish the effects of maternal incarceration from those of maternal crime and criminal justice involvement. Stanton collected comprehensive demographic and placement data on the 172 children studied: for example, school performance, child knowledge of the maternal legal situation, welfare status, and child legal socialization. Interviews were conducted with the children, the mothers, the children's caregivers, and school personnel. The children studied were accessed through their mothers. Only women offenders who had lived with their children prior to arrest, and their school-age children, were selected for study. Stanton found that the children she studied had experienced multiple disruptions in their lives, not all due to maternal incarceration. The children had extensive exposure to the criminal justice system; slightly more than one-third were present at maternal arrest, many had criminal family members other than the mother, and some had experienced their own "trouble" with law enforcement.

In spite of this exposure to the criminal justice system, the children had limited understanding of their incarcerated mothers' circumstances. In addition, although the children studied performed poorly in school, Stanton found their poor performance to be due to long-term factors such as family socio-economic status and the mothers' past criminal behavior, rather than to the current maternal incarceration. The children's economic status did not change with maternal incarceration. Although most mothers and their children were reunified, there was a high incidence of subsequent mother-child separation.

Three other studies are of particular significance in the study of children of offenders. First, in Great Britain, Catan (1992) studied seventy-four babies born to mothers in prison and raised for thirteen to nineteen weeks in prison nurseries, comparing them to thirty-three babies born to mothers in prison but placed in the community with family members or foster parents. She compared the growth and development of both cohorts with a larger group of contemporary British babies, conducting a series of developmental assessments. The study found no generalized developmental delays in either study group. Transient and reversible declines in motor and cognitive development in the nursery group were found and attributed to environmental and childcare limitations. Catan also found that infants who were placed in the community experienced multiple placements and caregivers, visited their mothers infrequently, and were about half as likely as the nursery babies to live with their mothers after the mothers were released from prison.

Second, Johnston (1992, 1993 and Johnston and Carlin, 1996) began a longitudinal study of children of criminal offenders in 1991. The first group of fifty-six middle school children studied was selected for a therapeutic services program on the basis of behavior that appeared to be leading them towards early entry into the criminal justice system; elementary school children and the siblings of selected children were also included in the study group in the second and subsequent years of the project. Almost all of the first study group were the children of previously or currently incarcerated parents: 79 percent had a previously or currently incarcerated father, and 46 percent had a previously or currently incarcerated mother. About one in five had experienced incarceration of both natural parents concurrently or sequentially. Data were collected from child, parent/caregiver and teacher interviews; child developmental assessments; reviews of school records; classroom, playground, and home behavior observations; health records; standardized measurements of child intellectual functioning, school behavior, and development; and clinical psychological assessments.

The study produced a range of findings about the children's families. Investigators found that the children had experienced extensive exposure to the criminal justice system, with almost one in three having a currently incarcerated parent and the majority reporting arrest and/or incarceration of multiple family members. Only 9 percent of the children had lived continuously with the same primary caregiver since birth. Slightly more than one-third lived with their mothers and no other adults, 18 percent lived with their mothers and their mothers' partners, 11 percent lived with both natural parents, 11 percent lived with grandparents, and 11 percent lived with a maternal aunt. Only 4 percent were in foster care with unrelated caregivers. In addition, the study revealed that the whereabouts of 4 percent of the mothers, and 25 percent of the fathers was unknown. More than 10 percent of the children had a deceased father, more than 11 percent had experienced parental or sibling bereavement, and more than 40 percent had experienced the violent death of a family member. Parental rights to the children studied had been terminated for about 25 percent of the mothers and 4 percent of the fathers.

The study was one of the first to describe the lives of children of incarcerated parents. More than one-third of the children had experienced prenatal drug exposure, and those children were more likely than the others to be living apart from a natural parent, to have a parent whose rights to the children had been terminated, to have been separated from their primary caregivers and from siblings, and to have experienced child abuse or neglect. However, there was no relationship between prenatal drug exposure and parental/family member incarceration, child clinical diagnosis, child behavioral problems, or child school problems. None of the children had previously been identified as developmentally delayed, but minimal to moderate delays were found in 14 percent of children during the study. More than 75 percent of the children experienced substance abuse or dependency in the home, and more than 40 percent experienced family member gang involvement. Only 9 percent were found to have no emotional difficulties or relationship problems. The majority, including siblings of index subjects, exhibited anxiety states, irritability, aggression, and/or withdrawal. One in three was involved in delinquent behavior and one in three was gang-affiliated.

For older children, mean grade point averages declined from 2.4 on a scale of 4 in Grade 5 to 1.7 in Grade 7. Lastly, upon psychological assessment, 75 percent of the children were found to meet the criteria for one or more clinical disorders, including adjustment, oppositional-defiant, and dysthymic disorders. Despite the breadth of the study, the findings are limited in their applicability to the general population of the children of criminal offenders, in large part because of the high annual per capita crime rate (1:12-14) for residents in the communities where the children lived and the selection criteria for the first study group.

Third, Kampfner (1995) conducted two studies of children of women prisoners, interviewing children and collecting their observations for each investigation. In the first study, a group of thirty-six children who were participating in a mother-child prison visitation program were examined and compared to a group of matched controls whose mothers were not incarcerated. This study found children of prisoners to be affected profoundly by traumatic experiences and lacking in emotional supports when compared to children in a control group. In the second study, fifty children were observed and interviewed while visiting their imprisoned mothers. These children ranged in age from five to sixteen years and lived in inner-city areas and in poverty; approximately, 10 percent had changed placements two or more times during maternal incarceration. About 75 percent of the children reported clinical symptoms suggestive of depression and/or traumatic stress reactions. The study did not present data on the living arrangements of the children prior to maternal incarceration. The lack of descriptive data on selection methods for both groups prohibits broad application of these study findings.

In general, information about the effects of parental incarceration is largely unavailable as a result of both conceptual and methodological barriers to empirical research on families involved in the criminal justice system. The lack of useful information has had a profound effect on practice with and policy related to these families. These issues are described in the next section.

Conceptual Barriers to Research

The traditional focus of the criminal justice system and several assumptions related to this focus have created conceptual barriers to the development of useful empirical research on parenting among criminal offenders. Among these areas are the tendency to focus on the isolated offender, assumptions about offenders' families, and assumptions about the effects of parental incarceration on children.

Focus on the Isolated Offender

Traditionally, the U.S. criminal justice system has focused on the isolated male offender, to the exclusion of interest in and information about the parents, spouses, partners, children, extended families, neighborhoods, and communities of offenders. Offenders have typically been defined, classified, and studied by their crimes rather than by individual and family characteristics. The importance of individual criminal behavior within this perspective logically leads to concentration of attention on the prison where recidivists and offenders who have committed many and/or major crimes are usually found. The emphasis on prison-based research, and the difficulty in identifying offenders who have not been caught, has produced a relative disregard for the study of adult offenders prior to incarceration. As a result, there have been virtually no efforts to collect information on how offenders parent in the community or the status of their children in those circumstances.

From this adult-oriented perspective, and as reflected in the great majority of publications about them, children of criminals have been assumed to be of significance primarily in relationship to the offender, and parental criminality or incarceration has been assumed to be a central influence in the children's lives. These assumptions have never been proven or examined carefully and have been recently brought into question by federal research (U.S. Department of Justice, 2000) which supports earlier studies (Hunter, 1984; Johnston, 1992; and McGowan and Blumenthal, 1978). Zalba (1964) suggested that a majority of these children do not live with their offending parents prior to parental incarceration. Similarly, although it is assumed that criminality shapes parent and family issues. Raine (1993) suggests that there is significant evidence that parental status affects patterns of offending and decreases the likelihood that a prisoner will have been convicted of a violent crime (U.S. Department of Justice, 2000).

Assumptions about Family Configurations among Criminal Offenders

From the program and advocacy literature on incarcerated parents, it is clear that "reunification"—meaning "parents and children living together again"—is seen as a major goal of services for prisoners and their families (Barry, 1985; Block and Potthast, 1998; Bertram, Lowenberg, McCall, and Rosenkrantz, 1982; Cannings, 1990; McCarthy, 1980; and Rosenkrantz and Joshua, 1982). Underlying this body of work and practice are two assumptions:

- most prisoners lived with all or most of their children prior to incarceration

- most prisoners have the option or want to return to the preincarceration family configuration following release.

Existing research data dispute these assumptions. Little discussion about the differences in preincarceration household patterns has occurred. The majority of male prisoners have children from two or more mothers (Hairston, 1989, 1995; Lanier, 1987) and, therefore, lived apart from at least one-half of their children prior to paternal incarceration (Koban, 1983; U.S. Department of Justice, 2000). Most incarcerated fathers also experience the dissolution of their marital and nonmarital partnerships during incarceration (Hairston, 1995), suggesting that even in the best of circumstances, parent-child "reunification"—in the sense of everyone living together again—is not an option for these men and all of their children. Earlier studies have similarly reported that many women prisoners did not live with their children prior to maternal incarceration (Baunach, 1979; Bloom and Steinhart, 1993; McGowan and Blumenthal, 1978; Task Force on the Female Offender, 1990; and Zalba, 1964). The most recent government data on prisoners' families (U.S. Department of

Justice, 2000) support these earlier findings. Approximately 26 percent of women and 53 percent of men currently in federal prison, and 42 percent of women and 64 percent of men in state prisons did not live with their children prior to incarceration.

The assumption that most children of prisoners, and specifically most children of women prisoners, lived with their parents prior to parental incarceration is based on an interpretation of the term "living with children" used in data collection to mean "living with all children." Each of the children in a prisoner's family may not have been living with the parent who reported that he or she was "living with children." Hunter (1984) carefully examined preincarceration placement of children of women prisoners and found that while 82 percent of the fifty-five women studied were reported to be "living with all their children," only 62 percent of the children had actually lived with their mothers and all of their siblings prior to maternal incarceration. Data on child living arrangements prior to maternal incarceration reveals that 27 to 60 percent of the children of women prisoners were not residing with their mothers (Baunach, 1979; Bloom and Steinhart, 1993; McGowan and Blumenthal, 1978; and Zalba, 1964).

Another problem concerns the application of the descriptive phrase, "living with children," to mean "providing primary care for children" (Barry, 1985; Bertram et al., 1982). This relationship has not been firmly established. Zalba (1964) found that women prisoners overstated the degree of their responsibility for the care of their children prior to incarceration. Similarly, while eight in ten of the women studied by Hunter (1984) reported living with all of their children, fewer than six in ten were actually their children's primary caregivers.

Assumptions about the Effects of Parental Incarceration on Children and Families

Another assumption is that the extensive needs and problems of the children and families of criminal offenders are primarily caused by parental incarceration (Bakker, Morris, and Janus, 1978; Fishman, 1982; Johnston, 1993; Little, 1993; Locey, 1999; Rosenkrantz and Joshua, 1982). This assumption developed in part because early studies sought information about the effects of maternal incarceration from prisoners who were often experiencing a variety of powerful emotional reactions to their status as incarcerated parents. That literature reflects these mothers' anguished concern that their children were also suffering from their confinement

(Baunach, 1979; Bertram et al., 1982; and DuBose, 1977) and has shaped public perception of the children's lives and needs.

The greatest support for this assumption, however, comes from the literature on intergenerational criminality. Strong studies, like that of Robins, West, and Herjanic (1975), found that about 50 percent of the variance in delinquency was explained by parental arrests particularly by parental *adult* arrests and that arrests of both parents produced the highest rates of child delinquency. Raine (1993), in his extensive review of the literature on familial influences on offending, agrees with the strength of this effect. But, such studies have difficulty explaining why about half of the children in families with two arrested parents do not become delinquent.

In an ongoing study of more than 600 children of criminal offenders in Los Angeles County, the Center for Children of Incarcerated Parents (Johnston, 1992, 1993; Johnston and Carlin, 1996) found that the characteristics that distinguish these children from their peers and the factors that are causally related to intergenerational crime and incarceration do not include parental incarceration. These conclusions are consistent with research that has examined the conditions of life for children and families of offenders (Johnston, 1995; Schneller, 1978; Swan, 1981; Tennessee Department of Corrections, 1995; and Prison Visitation Project, 1993) and found that these children live in environments and have experiences that produce risk, irrespective of the current location of a parent. These include: poverty, communities with high levels of crime and violence but low levels of resources, families with high levels of stress and limited access to resources, parental substance dependency and other compulsive behaviors, mental health problems among parents and caregivers, multiple family members involved in the criminal justice system, and childhood trauma—for example, bereavements, abuse, the witnessing of violence, caregiver-child separations, and multiple placements.

Clearly, parental incarceration must have effects on children, and these effects are likely to be strongest if the incarcerated parent and child had a meaningful relationship prior to the parents' incarceration (Johnston, 1993) or if both parents are criminal (Raine, 1993; Robins, West, and Herjanic, 1975). The only study to attempt to distinguish the effects of parental incarceration from parental crime and arrest (Stanton, 1980) examined only children who had lived with their mothers prior to incarceration. This study found very few significant differences between children of mothers who had gone to jail and children of mothers who had been placed on probation after arrest. However, the study also found that children of mothers who had been incarcerated shared several characteristics. For example, these children were less likely than their peers to seek police assistance when fourteen-to-eighteen years of age and to want to become police officers. The children were also less likely to be living with their mother again after she completed her sentence and to tell others about their mother's criminal status. However, they were more likely to have a low level of academic performance, to be on welfare after their mother completed her sentence, and to be separated from their mother again.

The applicability of these findings to children who have not recently or never lived with their incarcerated parent is unknown. There have been no other studies that have specifically attempted to differentiate the effects of parental incarceration from the effects of other hurtful circumstances that are common in the lives of children of criminal offenders.

Methodological Barriers in Research

Similar to the problems around conceptual frameworks in research, the selection of research methods used to study children of criminal offenders has also been influenced by unproven assumptions. These include using prisoners as index subjects for research on children, and issues of consent and reporting.

Using Prisoners as Index Subjects for Research on Children

The assumption that children and families of offenders are of significance as a result of their relationship to the offender has led to the study of prisoners' families and children by surveying or interviewing incarcerated parents (Bloom and Steinhart, 1993; Fritsch and Burkhead, 1982; Johnston, 1991; Koban, 1983). As discussed, this approach has often produced inaccurate or idealized data about children and/or parent-child relationships. The multiple separations and disruptions that characterize the lives of families of most criminal offenders do not negate the importance of the normal parental feelings of these parents (Baunach, 1979; Bonfanti, et al., 1974; Leflore and Holston, 1990), the eloquent voices of prisoners who have had close relationships with and long for their children (Bertram, Lowenberg, McCall, and Rosenkrantz, 1985; Boudin and Greco, 1993; Clark, 1995), or the right of incarcerated parents to attempt family reunification (Barry, 1985; Barry and Reid-Green, 1990). However, these characteristics do point to limitations of using incarcerated parents as the primary source of information on their children. This analysis is supported by the work of Stanton (1980) and other studies of incarcerated mothers (such as Johnston, 1991; and Zalba, 1964) that have found that many of the mothers studied did not have basic information—including developmental milestones, school grade, and the names of children's teachers and friends—about their children.

Identifying Representative Samples for Study

The traditional focus on the isolated offender has created another important barrier to studying children of criminal offenders: in other words, the inability to identify representative samples of such children for study. Virtually all published research on prisoners' children has been done on samples of opportunity and self-selected samples of prisoners. Most pillars of empirical data that support the field of "children of incarcerated parents" have been collected from nonrepresentative samples of prisoners at one or more correctional institutions (for example, Adalist-Estrin, 1986; Bloom and Steinhart, 1993; Fritsch and Burkhead, 1982; Gibbs, 1971; Koban, 1983; Sack, Seidler, and Thomas, 1976). Many other studies collected data from incarcerated mothers and fathers who were participants in special programs for parents in prison (for example, Dressel and Barnhill, 1994; Hairston, 1989; Kampfner, 1995).

Prior to 2001, there had been only a few empirical studies on incarcerated parents and their children that attempted to address the bias inherent in using self-selected or program-related samples of prisoners as the index subjects of research on their children. Each of these studies attempted to examine an entire population of prisoners. In 1964, Zalba studied all of California's women prisoners and their children, obtaining detailed information from a random sample of 26 percent of the entire group and documenting information provided by random samples of women from two California counties. In 1978, McGowan and Blumenthal attempted to survey all 9,379 women prisoners in 74 of 77 U.S. correctional facilities housing 25 or more women. The information they collected on about 3,121 women was uneven, including both aggregate data provided by institutions and responses from individual prisoners. In 1990, Hairston interviewed fifty-eight mothers among eighty jailed women in a Midwestern metropolitan jail. Thirty-eight of the fifty-eight mothers were mothers of dependent children. In 1991, the Center for Children of Incarcerated Parents (Johnston, 1991) interviewed 100 of the 114 mothers held in the Riverside, California, County Jail.

Although all of these studies contributed to our understanding of the issues, with the exception of Zalba's (1964) study, which probably no longer can be duplicated, there have been no studies of families of incarcerated parents or their children that have examined representative samples of these populations. Indeed, no mechanism for the identification of such samples has been seriously proposed.

Issues of Consent and Accurate Reporting

There are also methodological issues related to institutional and environmental constraints on research with prisoners. These issues become apparent when comparing recent federal data on the proportions of incarcerated parents among prisoners and the mean numbers of their children (U.S. Department of Justice, 2000) with data from other large but nongovernmental studies of similar populations (Baunach, 1979; Bloom and Steinhart, 1993; Hunter, 1984; McGowan and Blumenthal, 1978; Zalba, 1964) and small nongovernmental studies (Hairston, 1989; Sack, Seidler, and Thomas, 1976).

True confidentiality and anonymity can be difficult to provide for subjects of studies in correctional settings. Data collection methods that require prisoners to write responses on paper may not provide the confidentiality that prisoners need to report information about their families. On the other hand, the costs of interview methods, particularly for large-scale studies, may be prohibitive for all but government researchers with whom prisoners are least likely to share accurate information. For example, even in a study conducted by a private, nonprofit agency from the local community (Johnston, 1991), 14 of 114 mothers in a large county jail would not participate in the research because of issues of confidentiality. Those who refused to participate feared that correctional and other public authorities would have access to their responses, leading to the possibility that Child Protective Services would remove their children from current informal placements arranged by the mother (four of fourteen mothers), law enforcement could locate an adolescent child wanted by the police (one of fourteen mothers), and/or they would lose legal custody of a child due to their incarceration (twelve of fourteen mothers).

Parenting among Criminal Offenders, Children of Criminal Offenders: Research from the Center for Children of Incarcerated Parents

The Center for Children of Incarcerated Parents is conducting three projects that are directly or indirectly examining parenting among criminal offenders, a fourth focuses on children of criminal offenders and foster care, and a fifth examines the lives of children of criminal offenders in the community.

Service-related Research

The Center for Children of Incarcerated Parents regularly collects client and outcome data for all of its projects and services. They are currently conducting three projects with or related to incarcerated mothers.

- The first is the Attachments Project. Attachments provides developmental interventions for infants, children, and mother-child dyads living in correctional settings. Attachments has been offered at five residential, mother-child correctional facilities in southern California since 1997.

- The second is the MotherRight Project, which offers a comprehensive program of services including parent and family life education, psycho-educational interventions, a trauma-focused mothers' support group, and mentoring for mothers. MotherRight has been offered at four residential, mother-child correctional facilities since 1999.

- A third project is the Center's Mother-Child Correctional Programs Symposia, a series of semiannual meetings attended by all U.S. programs providing mother-child residential services to women prisoners and their infants or children.

Clients in the Center's Attachments and MotherRight projects include all southern California residents of the California Department of Corrections mother-child programs. One of the benefits of collecting service data in these settings is that client participation is predicated on formal verification of parental rights, child custody and placement status, and childcare prior to maternal arrest/incarceration by the correctional agency.

In collecting data on more than 400 mother-child dyads over five years, the Center has found that women in these programs have an average of 2.8 children each, in other words, more children per woman than the national and the national prisoner averages. More than one-half of the mothers in the programs were not living with any of their children prior to incarceration. Many of the mothers who were living with one or more of their children prior to incarceration were living with an "allo-parent" co-caregiver or were living with their own parent who cared for both the mother and her children. More than 20 percent of the mothers had never parented any of their children. Lastly, the majority of mothers and children developed strong, healthy bonds during their participation in the program. Mothers often reported that their relationships to these infants and children who participated in the program were stronger than their relationships to their other children.

The Center's Mother-Child Correctional Programs Symposia series has resulted in the development of preliminary guidelines for practice in these settings by symposia participants and the production of a national study of all such programs (Johnston and Michalak, forthcoming). Participants have learned a great deal from these symposia about mother-child programs and efforts. For example:

- Mother-Child Correctional Programs (MCCPs) have been in existence for almost 100 years, with strong evidence of their safety and stability.

- There have been no negative effects of the locked correctional environment on infants; the development of children in these programs appears to be normal, and the programs studied have had no incidents of significant harm to children by either parents or other prisoners.

- While most of the programs studied have similar admission criteria and exclude women with offense histories of violence, major felonies, arson, or sexual crimes, the programs that have individualized criteria and no automatic exclusions by offense history have had the same outcomes as other programs with more restrictive criteria. This suggests that conditions of confinement for incarcerated mothers may be significantly modified without dire results for correctional or community security, regardless of the prisoners' offense history.

The Children of Criminal Offenders and Foster Care Study

This investigation is focused on families involved in the child welfare system. It compares children of criminal offenders to children of nonoffenders. Three cohorts of families in one southern California county have been studied:

- all families with children in long-term foster care with a private foster care agency

- the first 400 children who entered the child welfare system in April 1997

- the first 400 children who entered the child welfare system in April 1998, following the passage of the federal Adoptions and Safe Families Act

A comprehensive history of each child's placements, custody status, family configurations, parent-child contact and separation, other types of childhood trauma, and family involvement in the criminal justice system is being collected.

The first phase of the study was completed in 1999. The Center is currently collecting data on the second cohort of families. It is anticipated that the study will be completed in 2002. Although still in progress, this research has yielded some new and important information. Investigators have found that:

- Approximately 80 percent of all children in long-term foster care have a parent who is a criminal offender; if offenders who have offended against their children are included, the percentage increases to 90 percent.

- If only current parental incarceration had been considered, less than 40 percent of the same group would have been identified as children of criminal offenders. This includes 33 percent with a currently incarcerated father and 10 percent with a currently incarcerated mother (a different male to female ratio than the one to ten seen in the correctional system).

- If only parental incarceration at the time of entry into the child welfare system had been considered, less than 15 percent of the same group would have been identified as children of criminal offenders.

- Approximately 85 percent of women offenders with children in long-term foster care have committed primarily or exclusively drug offenses.

- The number of terminations of parental rights per cohort has increased dramatically following the passage of the Adoptions and Safe Families Act.

Clearly, one of the most profound effects of incarceration on parenting is its increasing potential to end the parent-child relationship through legal means; yet, there is limited published research that directly examines this phenomenon to date.

The Children of Criminal Offenders Study Part II

Conducted in a racially and ethnically diverse city of 200,000 in northeast Los Angeles County, this second investigation included interviews with 190 randomly selected public school students and their parents or caregivers. The full report of this study is in preparation.

The study focused on the children's life experiences, including parent-child experiences, and compared children of criminal offenders to all other children. The children in the study group lived in one zip code area and were representative of their school populations except in the area of race/ethnicity. *See* Table 1.

Table 1. Study Participant Profile

CHARACTERISTIC	TOTAL STUDY POPULATION N=190	
	N	%
African-American	105	55.2
European American	25	13.2
Latino	30	15.8
Biracial	22	11.6
All children of criminal offenders	50	26.3
Children of male offenders	38	20.0
Children of female offenders	29	15.3
Children of both male and female offenders	17	8.9
Father ever incarcerated	23	12.1
Mother ever incarcerated	20	10.5

Table 2. Parental Offender Status* by Race/Ethnicity

Race/Ethnicity	Parent Ever Involved in Criminal Activity %	Parent Ever Incarcerated %
African-American	34.4	24.8
European American	8.0	0
Latino	16.7	16.7
Biracial	22.7	13.6
All	26.3	17.9

* During child's lifetime

At the time of the interviews, enrollment in the school district from which study participants were drawn included about 35 percent African-American children compared to 55.3 percent of the study participants who identified as African American and about 45 percent Latino children compared to 15.8 percent of study participants who identified as Latino.

A large proportion of all the children studied (26.3 percent) reported that their parents had been involved in criminal activity, but there were significant differences in this proportion by race, as shown in Table 2. Similarly, while one in six (17.9 percent) of all the children studied reported parental incarceration during their lifetimes, this proportion varied from 0-24.8 percent in different racial and ethnic groups.

The study also found that many children of criminal offenders have never lived and/or currently do not live with their parent who is an offender as shown in Table 3. Among children who had experienced parental incarceration, less than one-half were currently living with their parents who had been incarcerated.

Table 3. Living Arrangements of Children of Criminal Offenders N = 50

Race/Ethnicity	Ever Lived With Offender Parent	Currently Live With Offender Parent
Children of all male offenders	61.5%	36.8%
Children of all female offenders	81.8%	51.7%
Children of two criminal offenders		47.1% w/ either parent
Children of fathers who have been incarcerated		13.0%
Children of mothers who have been incarcerated		50%
Children of two parents who have been incarcerated		0% w/ both parents 0% w/ fathers 11.1% w/ mothers

"What Works" for Children of Prisoners

There are several efforts that need to be made before identifying the best or even promising practices for children of prisoners and other children of criminal offenders. First, research on children of criminal offenders must be brought into line with research on children conducted in other fields. Studies in other child-focused fields have their foundation in developmental theory and the understanding that child development is shaped by children's experiences. Child-focused research efforts also have children as the index subjects of study and are conducted in the communities where children live and develop. Such an approach will address many of the incorrect assumptions that have shaped prison-based research on children of prisoners and the resulting outcome data.

Second, careful consideration must be given to issues of race and ethnicity in collecting and interpreting data on parental incarceration and children of criminal offenders. The disproportionate involvement of families of color in both the criminal justice and child welfare systems makes it almost impossible to report aggregate data on family and parenting issues among criminal offenders and their children responsibly. As shown by the Center's "Children of Criminal Offenders, II" study, aggregate data obscures dramatic racial and cultural influences on criminal justice system involvement. These disparities are highly likely to be related to significant differences in the social, political, and economic contexts of child development; therefore, they cannot be ignored in reporting information about children's lives.

Third, in interpreting research data on incarcerated parents and their children, evidence that prisoners' families were in many cases neither intact nor cohesive prior to parental incarceration has often been unrecognized or has been disregarded. False assumptions about the family configurations of criminal offenders have led to the formulation of policy and the design of low-cost interventions and services for families of criminal offenders. Without a history of recent primary parenting, simple "family reunification" cannot apply to the majority of incarcerated parents and their children, and a more complex understanding of and approach to the postincarceration needs of these families is necessary.

Fourth, in the absence of data suggesting causality, and in consideration of the strong evidence that prisoners often have not regularly lived with or provided primary care for their children, the relationship between parental incarceration and child outcomes needs to be redefined. Criminality and incarceration of a parent might be best conceptualized like other conditions of children's lives—such as being the son of an unwed, teenaged, African-American mother—that confer risk but are not in themselves the actual cause of negative developmental outcomes.

Fifth, it is likely that what works to improve the well-being of other children will also work for children of prisoners. Children's outcomes are the result of the sum of developmental resources and developmental insults. Interventions that increase children's developmental resources will improve outcomes. Some of the most effective of these that also work to decrease criminal justice system involvement include: functional family therapy (Alexander, Barton, Schiavo, and Parsons, 1976; Alexander and Parsons, 1973; Klein, Alexander and Parsons, 1977); mentoring (U.S. Department of Justice, 1997); and multisystemic therapy (Hennegler, 1997). Similarly, interventions that decrease children's exposure to developmental insults will also improve outcomes. The most effective of interventions include home visiting (Larson, 1980; Olds, Henderson, Tatelbaum, and Chamberlain, 1986) and multidimensional treatment foster care (Chamberlain, 1990). Programs that both increase developmental resources and prevent or decrease the effects of developmental insults will improve the well-being of any child, including children of prisoners. Perhaps the best-documented and most effective comprehensive program of services for children of prisoners (Project SEEK, 1997) uses this approach.

Other interventions have been found to be effective in preventing juvenile offending and adult criminality (Greenwood, Model, Rydell, and Chiesa, 1996; Mihalic, Irwin, Elliott, Fagan, and Hansen, 2001; Wasserman, Miller, and Cothern, 2000). Given the high rate of intergenerational incarceration, these are all likely to be of value with some or many children of prisoners and other children of criminal offenders, even though the developmental insults and loss of developmental resources that are specifically due to parental incarceration rather than to other parental, familial, social, and economic factors among criminal offenders have not been delineated.

Finally, although the above interventions are likely to be helpful without any further research on children of prisoners, it is also important to continue to examine and define the effects of parental crime/arrest/incarceration to know when to intervene. For example, we already have some information that will allow us to predict which families are likely to be most affected by parental crime/arrest/incarceration. Although only about half of all children who have had both mothers and fathers involved in the criminal justice system will be living with any birth parent, this number declines to one in ten when both parents have been incarcerated. If people who are or become criminal offenders are experiencing obstacles to effective parenting, and if their children have high levels of unmet needs prior to or early in the parents' criminal justice system involvement, should we be waiting until the parents are incarcerated to identify and assist these families?

Conclusions and Recommendations for Research

The families of criminal offenders are clearly disadvantaged and in disarray prior to parental incarceration. Yet, society has only given attention to their needs after the parent has entered the correctional system and in response to the risk posed by their children. A more appropriate response would be to identify and attempt to meet the needs of families before or early in their involvement in the justice process. One step towards this end would be to examine the lives and needs of these children the way we do those of other children, rather than through the lens of their parents' current circumstances.

Review of the literature suggests that there have been significant conceptual and methodological barriers to empirical research on the effects of crime and incarceration on parenting and on the children of criminal offenders. To address these barriers, the Center for Children of Incarcerated Parents has developed a series of guidelines for such investigations. These guidelines are intended to lead to research that provides more generally useful information on these populations, and will support the development of realistic, useful interventions for children and families.

1. Research on parenting by, and children or families of, criminal offenders should be grounded in a developmental perspective in which children or families are index subjects.

2. Research should identify representative samples of criminal offenders and their families for study OR indicate the extent to which another type of sample represents or differs from the larger population.

3. Research design should recognize the wide variety of family configurations that occur—before, during, and after parental incarceration—among criminal offenders and their children.

4. Research protocols should consider the potential effects of the correctional environment on the accuracy of prisoner reporting about child and family issues.

5. Research design should recognize the multiple individual, familial, and community factors that influence long-term outcomes among children of criminal offenders.

6. For most children of criminal offenders, parental incarceration should be considered as a marker for highest risk but not necessarily a major influence in children's lives.

References

Adalist-Estrin, A.1986. Parenting from Behind Bars. *Family Resource Coalition Report.* 51:12-13.

———. 1993. Moral Development and Attachment: Disruptions that Create Cycles of Criminal Behavior. Paper presented at the 4th Annual North American Conference on the Family and Corrections, Quebec City, Quebec.

Alexander, J. F., C. Barton, R. S. Schiavo, and B. V. Parsons.1976. Systems-behavioral Intervention with Families of Delinquents. *Journal of Consulting and Clinical Psychology.* 44: 456-664.

Alexander, J. F. and B.V. Parsons. 1973. Short-term Behavioral Intervention with Delinquent Families. *Journal of Abnormal Psychology.* 81: 219-225.

Bakker, L. J., B. A. Morris, and L. M. Janus. 1978. Hidden Victims of Crime. *Social Work.* 23: 143-148.

Barry, E. 1985. Reunification Difficult for Incarcerated Parents and their Children. *Youth Law News.* 5: 14-16.

Barry, E. and C. Reid-Green. 1990. The Foster Care System and the Children of Incarcerated Parents: A Summary of Concerns. In E. Barry, ed. *Custody Issues for Incarcerated Parents: A Practitioner's Guide.* San Francisco: Legal Services for Prisoners with Children.

Baunach, P. J. 1979, November. Mothering from Behind Prison Walls. Paper presented at the annual meeting of the American Society of Criminology, Philadelphia.

Bertram, J., C. Lowenberg, C. McCall, and L. Rosenkrantz. 1982. *My Real Prison Is . . . Being Separated from My Child.* San Francisco: Prison MATCH.

Blackwell, J. E. 1959. The Effects of Involuntary Separation on Selected Families of Men Committed To Prison From Spokane, Washington. Unpublished doctoral dissertation. State College of Washington.

Block, K. J. and M. J. Potthast. 1998. Girl Scouts Behind Bars: Facilitating Parent-Child Contact in Correctional Settings. *Child Welfare*. 775: 561-578.

Bloom, B. and D. Steinhart. 1993. *Why Punish the Children: A Reappraisal of the Children of Incarcerated Mothers in America*. San Francisco: National Council on Crime and Delinquency.

Blumstein, A., J. Cohen, J. Roth, and C. Visher. 1986. *Criminal Careers and "Career Criminals."* Washington, D.C.: National Academy Press.

Bonfanti, M. A., S. S. Felder, M. L. Loesch, and N. J. Vincent. 1974. *Enactment and Perception of Maternal Role of Incarcerated Mothers*. Unpublished master's thesis, Louisiana State University.

Boudin, K. and R. Greco. 1993. *Parenting from Inside/Out: The Voices of Mothers in Prison*. Bedford Hills, New York: The Children's Center at Bedford Hills Correctional Facility.

Breckenridge, S. P. and E. Abbott. 1912. Chicago Housing Problems. *American Journal of Sociology*. 16: 289-308.

Brennan, P., S. A. Mednick, and E. Kandel. 1993. Congenital Determinants of Violent and Property Offending. In D. Pepler and K. H .Rubin, eds. *The Development and Treatment of Childhood Aggression*. Hillsdale, New Jersey: Erlbaum.

Browne, D. 1989. Incarcerated Mothers and Parenting. *Journal of Family Violence*. 42: 211-221.

Cannings, K. 1990. *Bridging the Gap: Programs and Services To Facilitate Contact between Inmate Parents and Their Children*. Ottawa: Ministry of the Solicitor General of Canada.

Catan, L. 1992. Infants with Mothers in Prison. In R. Shaw, ed. *Prisoners' Children*. London: Routledge.

Chamberlain, P. 1990. Comparative Evaluation of Specialized Foster Care for Seriously Delinquent Youths. *Community Alternatives: International Journal of Family Care*. 2: 21-36.

Clark, J. 1995. The Impact of the Prison Environment on Mothers. *The Prison Journal*. 753: 306-329.

Datesman, S. K. and G. L. Cales. 1983. I'm Still the Same Mommy: Maintaining the Mother-Child Relationship in Prison. *Prison Journal*. 632: 142-154.

Dressel, P. and S. Barnhill. 1994. Reframing Gerontological Thought and Practice: The Case of Grandmothers with Daughters in Prison. *The Gerontologist*. 34: 685-691.

DuBose, D. G. 1977. Incarcerated Mothers and Their Children in Texas. Unpublished manuscript.

Farrington, D. P. 1989. Early Predictors of Adolescent Aggression and Adult Violence. *Violence and Victims*. 4: 79-100.

Farrington, D. P. and J. D. Hawkins. 1991. Predicting Participation, Early Onset, and Later Persistence in Officially Recorded Offending. *Criminal Behavior and Mental Health*. 1: 1-33.

Fishman, S. 1982. The Impact of Incarceration on Children of Offenders. *Journal of Children in Contemporary Society*. 15: 89-99.

Friedman, S. and T. C. Esselstyn. 1965. The Adjustment of Children to Parental Absence Due to Imprisonment. *Federal Probation*. 29: 55-59.

Fritsch, T. A. and J. D. Burkhead. 1982. Behavioral Reactions of Children to Parental Absence Due to Imprisonment. *Family Relations*. 30: 83-88.

Gabel, S. and R. Shindledecker. 1993. Incarceration in Parents of Day Hospital Youth: Relationship to Parental Substance Abuse and Suspected Child Abuse/Maltreatment. *International Journal of Partial Hospitalization*. 81: 77-87.

Gibbs, C. 1971.The Effect of Imprisonment of Women upon Their Children. *British Journal of Criminology*. 11: 113-130.

Glasser, I. 1990. *Maintaining the Bond: The Niantic Parenting Programs*. Niantic, Connecticut: Families in Crisis.

Glick, R. and V. V. Neto. 1977. *National Study of Women's Correctional Programs*. Washington, D.C.: National Institute of Law Enforcement and Criminal Justice.

Glueck, S. and E. Glueck. 1950. *Unraveling Juvenile Delinquency*. Cambridge, Massachusetts: Harvard University Press.

Greenwood, P. W., K. E. Model, C. P. Rydell, and J. Chiesa. 1996. *Diverting Children from a Life of Crime: Measuring Costs and Benefits*. Santa Monica, California: RAND.

Hairston, C. F. 1989. Men in Prison: Family Characteristics and Family Views. *Journal of Offender Counseling, Services and Rehabilitation*.141: 23-30.

———. 1995. Fathers in Prison. In K. Gabel and D. Johnston, eds. *Children of Incarcerated Parents*. New York: Lexington Books.

Hairston, C. F. and P. Lockett. 1985. Parents in Prison: A Child Abuse and Neglect Prevention Strategy. *Child Abuse and Neglect.* 9: 471-477.

Harm, N. and P. Thompson. 1995. *Children of Incarcerated Mothers and Their Caregivers: A Needs Assessment.* Little Rock, Arkansas: Centers for Youth and Families.

Hennegler, S. W. 1997. *Treating Serious Antisocial Behavior in Youth: The MST Approach*. Bulletin. Washington, D.C.: U.S. Department of Justice, Office of Justice Programs, Office of Juvenile Justice and Delinquency Prevention.

Henriques, Z. 1982. *Imprisoned Mothers and Their Children.* Washington, D.C.: University Press of America.

Hungerford, G. 1993. *Children of Inmate Mothers in Ohio.* Columbus, Ohio: Ohio State University.

Hunter, S. M. 1984. The Relationship between Women Offenders and Their Children. *Dissertation Abstracts International.* University Microfilms No. 8424436.

Johnston, D. 1991. *Children of Jailed Mothers.* Pasadena, California: Pacific Oaks College, Center for Children of Incarcerated Parents.

———. 1992. *Children of Offenders.* Pasadena, California: Pacific Oaks College, Center for Children of Incarcerated Parents.

———. 1993. *Children of the Therapeutic Intervention Project.* Pasadena, California: Pacific Oaks College, Center for Children of Incarcerated Parents.

———. 1995. Effects of Parental Incarceration. In K. Gabel and D. Johnston, eds. *Children of Incarcerated Parents*. New York: Lexington Books.

———. 1998. *Mothers and Children in Correctional Settings.* Pasadena, California: Pacific Oaks College, Center for Children of Incarcerated Parents.

Johnston, D. and M. Carlin.1996. Enduring Trauma in Children of Criminal Offenders. *Progress: Family Systems Research and Therapy.* 6: 22-39.

Johnston, D. and E. Michalak. Forthcoming. Mother-Child Correctional Programs in the United States. *Corrections Today.*

Kampfner, C. 1995. Post-traumatic Stress Reactions in Children of Imprisoned Mothers. In K. Gabel and D. Johnston, eds. *Children of Incarcerated Parents*. New York: Lexington Books.

Keay, I. 1989. *Children of Pain, Children of Joy*. Old Tappan, New Jersey: Fleming H. Revell Company.

Key, D. and G. Eyres. 2000. *A Child Serving Time on the Outside*. Fort Worth: Parents and Children Together.

Klein, N. C. C., J. F. Alexander, and B. V. Parsons. 1977. Impact of Family Systems Intervention on Recidivism and Sibling Delinquency. *Journal of Consulting and Clinical Psychology*. 45: 469-474.

Koban, L. A. 1983. Parents in Prison: A Comparative Analysis of the Effects of Incarceration on the Families of Men and Women. *Research in Law, Deviance and Social Control*. 5: 171-183.

Kolman, A. S. 1983. Support and Control Patterns of Inmate Mothers. *Prison Journal*. 632: 155-166.

Landreth, L. G. and A. F. Lobaugh. 1998. Filial Therapy with Incarcerated Fathers. *Journal of Counseling and Development*. 762: 157-165.

Lanier, C. S. 1987. November. Fathers in Prison: A Psychosocial Exploration. Presented at the annual meeting of the American Society of Criminology, Montreal, Canada.

———. 1993. Affective States of Fathers in Prison. *Justice Quarterly*. 10: 49-65.

LaPointe, V., M. O. Picker, and S. Harris. 1985. Enforced Family Separation: A Descriptive Analysis of Some Experiences of Children of Black Imprisoned Mothers. In A. Spencer, ed. *Beginnings: The Social and Affective Development of Black Children*. Hillsdale: Erlbaum.

Larson, C. P. 1980. Efficacy of Prenatal and Postpartum Home Visits on Child Health and Development. *Pediatrics*. 662: 191-197.

Leflore, L. and M. A. Holston. 1990. Perceived Importance of Parenting Behaviors as Reported by Inmate Mothers: An Exploratory Study. *Journal of Offender Counseling, Services and Rehabilitation*.141: 5-21.

Little, C. 1993. Heavy Price to Pay: Kids Suffer as Jail Numbers Rise. *Daily Southtown*.16221: 1,4.

Locey, T. 1999. Like Mother, Like Daughter. *U.S. News and World Report*. October 4: 18-21.

Loeber, R. and T. Dishion. 1983. Early Predictors of Male Delinquency. *Psychological Bulletin*. 94: 68-99.

Lundberg, D., A. Sheekley, and T. Voelker. 1975. An Exploration of Feelings and Attitudes of Women Separated from Their Children Due to Incarceration. Master's practicum, Portland State University, Oregon.

McCarthy, B. R. 1980. Inmate Mothers: The Problems of Separation and Reintegration. *Journal of Offender Counseling, Services and Rehabilitation*. 43: 199-212.

McCord, J. and N. McCord. 1959. The Effects of Parental Role Model of Criminality. *Journal of Social Issues*. 14: 66-75.

McGowan, B. and K. Blumenthal. 1978. *Why Punish the Children?* Hackensack, New Jersey: National Council on Crime and Delinquency.

Mihalic, S., K. Irwin, D. Elliott, A. Fagan, and D. Hansen. 2001. *Blueprints for Violence Prevention*. Bulletin. Washington, D.C.: U.S. Department of Justice, Office of Justice Programs, Office of Juvenile Justice and Delinquency Prevention.

Morris, P. 1965. *Prisoners and Their Families*. New York: Hart.

Olds, D. L, C. L. Henderson, R. Tatelbaum, and R. Chamberlain. 1986. Preventing Child Abuse and Neglect: A Randomized Trial of Nurse Home Visitation. *Pediatrics*. 781: 65-78.

Otterstrom, S. 1946. Juvenile Delinquency and Parental Criminality. ACTA *Pediatrica Scandinavica*. 33 Suppl. 5: 1-326.

Prison MATCH. 1984. *I Know How You Feel . . . Because This Happened To Me*. Berkeley, California: Prison MATCH.

Prison Visitation Project. 1993. *Needs Assessment of Children Whose Parents Are Incarcerated*. Richmond, Virginia: Department of Mental Health, Mental Retardation and Substance Abuse Services.

Project SEEK. 1997. Palmyra, Virginia: Family and Corrections Network.

Raine, A. 1993. *The Psychopathology of Crime*. San Diego: Academic Press.

Robins, L. N. 1979. Sturdy Predictors of Adult Outcomes: Replications from Longitudinal Studies. In J. E. Barratt, R. M. Rose, and G. L. Klerman, eds. *Stress and Mental Disorder*. New York: Raven Press.

Robins, L. N., P. A. West, and B. L. Herjanic. 1975. Arrests and Delinquency in Two Generations: A Study Of Black Urban Families and Their Children. *Journal of Child Psychology and Psychiatry*. 16: 125-140.

Rosenkrantz, L. and V. Joshua. 1982. Children of Incarcerated Parents: A Hidden Population. *Children Today*. 11: 2-6.

Sack, W. H. 1977. Children of Imprisoned Fathers. *Psychiatry*. 40: 163-174.

Sack, W. H., J. Seidler, and S. Thomas. 1976. Children of Imprisoned Parents: A Psychosocial Exploration. *American Journal of Orthopsychiatry*. 464: 618-628.

Schneller, D. P. 1978. *The Prisoner's Family*. San Francisco: R and E Research Associates.

Stanton, A. 1980. *When Mothers Go To Jail*. Lexington, Massachusetts: Lexington Books.

Swan, A. 1981. *Families of Black Prisoners: Survival and Progress*. Boston: GK Hall.

Task Force on the Female Offender. 1990. *The Female Offender: What Does the Future Hold?* Lanham, Maryland: American Correctional Association.

Tennessee Department of Corrections. 1995. The Children and Families of Incarcerated Felons. Planning and Research Section. Nashville, Tennessee.

U.S. Department of Justice. 1997. *Mentoring: A Proven Delinquency Prevention Strategy*. NCJ Publication 164834. Washington, D.C.: U.S. Department of Justice, Bureau of Justice Statistics.

———. 2000. *Incarcerated Parents and Their Children*. NCJ Publication 182335. Washington, D.C.: U.S. Department of Justice, Bureau of Justice Statistics.

U.S. Senate. 2001. FY2001, Department of Justice Appropriations Report 106-404. Washington, D.C.

Virginia Commission on Youth. 1992. *A Study of the Needs of Children Whose Parents Are in Prison*. Richmond, Virginia: Virginia Commission on Youth.

Wasserman, G. A., L. S. Miller, L. Cothern. 2000. *Prevention of Serious and Violent Juvenile Offending*. Bulletin. Washington, D.C.: U.S. Department of Justice, Office of Justice Programs, Office of Juvenile Justice and Delinquency Prevention.

Zalba, S. 1964. *Women Prisoners and Their Families*. Sacramento: California Department of Social Welfare and Department of Corrections.

Zeitz, D. 1963. Child Welfare Services in a Women's Correctional Institution. *Child Welfare*. 42: 185-190.

What Works in the Treatment of Family Violence in Correctional Populations: Issues and Directions

6

Lynn Stewart
Manager, Living Skills, Counter-Point and Family Violence Prevention Programs
Correctional Service of Canada
Ottawa, Canada

Natalie Gabora-Roth
Project Officer, Family Violence Prevention Programs
Correctional Service of Canada
Ottawa, Canada

Recent reviews and meta-analyses on the effectiveness of family violence treatment programs have not been encouraging. Within the past five years, researchers have found very weak or no treatment effects (Babcock, Green, and Robie, in press; Dunford, 2000; Levesque, 1998). Participants described as having the worst treatment outcomes are those with histories of criminal behavior and substance abuse and those with personality disorders; in short, men with profiles similar to those encountered in correctional settings. Gondolf (2000a), who recently completed a multi-site review of several domestic violence treatment programs, disagrees with the dim conclusions on their effectiveness.

Although he acknowledges evaluations as a whole do not provide unequivocal evidence for the efficacy of treatment for male perpetrators of family violence, he points out that in the past, serious methodological and conceptual problems made it difficult to draw conclusions. He is also critical of the more recent studies that employ a rigorous research design which he claims is not easy to implement appropriately in this field and may wash out contextual information that can contribute to a better understanding of the true impact of intervention on consumers (Gondolf, 2001).

It is also important to note that domestic violence treatment programs are not as theoretically sound or as empirically grounded as those in other areas such as substance abuse and sex offender treatment where there is a body of research and a treatment approach that provide more convincing outcomes. We can do a lot to improve on the development of family violence treatment programs, their implementation, the provision of community follow-up and risk management, and the training and supervision of facilitators. These factors could advance the field and launch an eventual cumulative body of knowledge on "what works" in the area.

This chapter begins with a review of the theoretical basis and the treatment models of family violence treatment programs. Next, it provides a recommended framework for intervening with offenders who perpetrate intimate violence. Given unconvincing treatment outcomes for programs applying the current treatment models, we argue for the establishment of a family violence program model for offenders based on effective corrections criteria rather than on political or ideological grounds. The point of departure, therefore, is to ensure that the interventions are designed according to the same principles as those of correctional programs that have demonstrated significant treatment effects, that is, they adhere to the risk, need, and responsivity principles prescribed by Andrews and Bonta (1998).

The chapter describes the application of the risk principle, detailing risk management strategies, including the use of risk assessment tools and appropriate referrals to programs of sufficient intensity and supervision; suggests how to adhere to the need principle, pointing to appropriate dynamic changeable targets for intervention that are directly linked to the offending behavior; and provides direction on how to address the responsivity principle by considering factors in the design of programs that promote the best outcomes for individual participants. Finally, the chapter provides an outline of a model program that respects these principles of effective corrections and a proposed assessment battery that would evaluate the effectiveness of the intervention.

Conceptual, Theoretical, and Practical Context
Definitions and Limitations of the Discussion

This chapter focuses on approaches and concepts aimed at addressing the problem of intimate violence and abuse of male offenders towards their female partners or ex-partners. In some cases, the abuse and violence are also indirectly aimed at the partner through assaults on the partner's family, children, friends, or new partner. Intimate same-sex violence has not been studied in large-scale surveys as it has for heterosexual couples, but reviews indicate that violence among lesbian and gay couples is also a significant problem, further complicated for the victims by their relative social marginalization and the threat of "outing" if they report the abuse (Renzetti, 1997). Papers based on profiles of individuals coming to individual counseling settings suggest that the dynamics of the abuse and the treatment targets may be like those of heterosexual couples in that perpetrators resort to threats and acts of violence to maintain a relationship that they perceive as increasingly insecure and unstable. Female-on-male intimate violence is also an issue that requires research and, in some cases, intervention, but it will not be addressed in this chapter.

Some advocates and researchers have broadly defined violence to include social policies that ignore issues of poverty and marginalization. For the purpose of this chapter, violence is defined conservatively as any act of deliberate physical, sexual, or threatened harm. Abuse, in the context of intimate relationships, refers to a range of behaviors, including emotional abuse and economic abuse. The goal of an effective treatment program would be the elimination of all forms of maltreatment.

Another important element of a wide-ranging project of intervention would be the provision of services to the women and children who are victims of violence and abuse. Addressing needs of victims, however, is not the mandate of most correctional settings. Working with the partners of male perpetrators, interviewing them sensitively and providing information or brokering services, if required, is usually the limit of interventions conducted with the family. This chapter, therefore, does not focus on the design of ancillary programs for the victims of the abusers. It is limited to an overview of directions we could take in treating and supervising male perpetrators of domestic violence. However, there is an argument for further development that could include the design of concurrent but separate programs for the partners of men in treatment, providing them also with training in skills that could enhance the treatment gains of the male perpetrators, particularly on those skills that require mutual support and cooperation.

Treatment Rationale

A generation ago, family violence was not "on the map" in public debate. There was very little discussion of the issue as an important social problem. It was viewed as a dark, private matter that was tolerated and, some argued, even incited by the victims. Since the 1970s, however, family violence has become an important social and political concern. Surveys across a number of countries have determined the rates to be significant with major costs to individuals and to society in general. In addition, policy development originally placed a priority on the provision of services for victims but, gradually, attention turned to the treatment of the perpetrators themselves.

It is difficult to compare the incidence of domestic violence across countries due to differences in survey methodology. However, broadly sampled American and Canadian surveys conducted by major research agencies have arrived at quite similar estimates. Twenty-nine percent of Canadian women who have ever been in a relationship report being physically abused by a partner (Statistics Canada, 1993). Straus et al. (1986) estimated rates of 27.8 percent based on a survey of American women. Rates of severe abuse causing injury are also roughly comparable between the two countries, at 5.4 percent in Canada and 7.2 percent in the United States.

The individual and societal cost of this level of domestic violence is now well documented. The national survey conducted in Canada on violence against women indicated that 45 percent of all women who had experienced violence had suffered an injury and, of these, 43 percent had required medical attention. Fifty-two percent had taken time off work as a result of injury (Statistics Canada, 1993). Victims of domestic violence demonstrate high rates of psychosomatic disease and drug and alcohol abuse. Statistics Canada estimates that health costs of injuries and chronic health problems caused by abuse amount to a billion dollars every year. A significant portion of police time is allocated to intervening in family violence situations (Levens and Dutton, 1980).

Moreover, there is a high co-occurrence of domestic violence against women and abuse of children in the home (Statistics Canada, 1999). In 28 percent of the cases of child homicide, there was a known history of domestic violence. Children are also indirect victims of domestic violence as witnesses to the abuse. Estimates are that in as many as 80 to 90 percent of cases of domestic violence, the children know about the violence even if they do not directly witness the attack. In an analysis comparing children who have witnessed violence often, sometimes, and seldom to those who have never witnessed violence, researchers found that child witnesses were more likely to exhibit behaviors such as conduct disorder, physical aggression, emotional disorder, indirect aggression, and property offenses.

In their review of the literature, Cunningham et al. (1998) noted that child witnesses often experience risk of injury as well as emotional trauma and reduced academic success. As adults, their own families are often characterized by poor parent/child communication. Suderman and Jaffe (1999) noted that, behaviorally, children who witness violence become aggressive, noncompliant, irritable, and easily angered. They also described psychological problems of anxiety, depression, withdrawal, low self-esteem, and an increase in somatic complaints. In their study of children in women's shelters, Suderman and Jaffe (1999) found that 56 percent of the children studied met the criteria for posttraumatic stress disorder, with most having some symptoms of the disorder.

Finally, Suderman and Jaffe (1999) also noted the occurrence of "subtle" symptoms, such as inappropriate attitudes regarding conflict resolution and violence against women, condoning relationship violence, and hypersensitivity about problems at home and self-blame. As adults, sons who are child witnesses of abuse are at an increased risk of becoming perpetrators of family violence and daughters are more likely to be victims. Straus, Gelles, and Steinmetz (1980) found that men who had witnessed wife assault in their families of origin had rates of battering three times greater than those who did not. Children in this study who were both witnesses and victims of abuse were twice as likely (one in three) to report an incident of spousal violence during the study year than those who did not. Saunders (1995) cites being a child witness to domestic violence is one of the three most important correlates of future spousal assault among male perpetrators.

There is evidence that offender populations in general have elevated incidences of being child witnesses or victims of child abuse. Robinson and Taylor (1995) found that 50 percent of federal Canadian offenders had been witness to or victims of abuse in their families of origin, suggesting that child abuse is a factor in adult criminality. Leyton (1986) and others, for example Hickey (1991), have proposed that childhood trauma, particularly being a child victim of domestic violence, contributes to the most extreme acts of adult violence, including acts of serial murder. Recent research on risk factors for future violence has confirmed that the seriousness of child abuse, along with psychopathology, are the two principal factors contributing to adult violence (Steadman, Silver, Monahan, Applebaum, Robbins, Mulvey, Grisso, Roth, and Banks, 2000). An effective intervention to reduce the incidence of family violence would have an enormously positive impact on families and on society in general.

Explanatory Models

A number of theoretical models have been proposed to explain the behavior of abusive men. Some models explain the abusive behavior in terms of individual pathology. Biophysical models have examined the predisposing impact of brain injury or biochemical disorder on some violent men, for example, Rosenbaum, Geffner, and Benjamin, (1997). Dutton (1995) has proposed that early negative parenting experiences that disrupt abusers' attachment to the earliest caregivers contribute to an insecure anxious adult attachment style typical of borderline personality disorders that is extremely sensitive to perceived relationship loss in adulthood.

The evolutionists' position in this regard is that men are subject to a biological imperative to secure their mates to ensure the transmittal of their genes to the next generation (Wilson and Daly, 1996). Thus, extreme sexual jealousy may be seen as an adapted response to perceived threats to a man's exclusive access to his sexual partner. Abusive and violent behaviors toward the partner and his sexual rivals are responses, albeit not socially accepted ones, that enforce his control over his partner's reproduction.

Social learning theory explains that perpetrators learn abusive and violent responses to situations through experiences such as receiving a reward or a benefit for the behavior, or through the modeling of respected others who are perceived as having received a positive consequence for their abusive behavior—in other words, getting what they want.

At different levels of explanation, each of these theories could account for aspects of men's abusive behaviors toward women. While there is evidence of brain damage among some individual male perpetrators and a history of being a child witness to violence in the home and disruption in early attachment patterns that are associated with elevated rates of adult violence, these theories cannot account for the abusive and violent behaviors of individuals who do not share these factors nor the nonabusive behavior of the majority of men who have experienced violent childhoods but establish nonviolent adult intimate relationships. Evolutionary theory has provided intriguing analysis for the deep-seated motivation of men's violence, but it has provided no convincing empirical evidence and cannot provide guidance for practitioners on what we should be doing to address violence toward women.

Since the late 1970s, the theoretical explanation that has had the most impact on the design of broadly based intervention programs for both male perpetrators and the victims of family violence is the feminist model. This approach points to the societal and political power imbalance between men and women as the key reason that men abuse women. The theory explains that the structure of patriarchal societies encourages the adoption of men's sense of entitlement to exert power and control over their families. This sense of entitlement justifies their use of a number of tactics such as the use of economic control, use of or threat of physical or sexual violence, and psychological abuse to maintain the power imbalance in their favor.

The Duluth model is the most influential proponent of the feminist theory in the treatment of abusive men (Pence and Paymar, 1993). The analysis of the attitudes that underlie the tactics of men who batter (the power and control wheel) and the program's emphasis on learning egalitarian nonviolent relationship strategies (the equality wheel) are now core components of most treatment programs for abusive men. In several states in the United States, it is a mandated treatment option. Evaluation studies, however, have not generally supported the treatment approach.

Indeed, even the theoretical basis for the approach has not been empirically established. In their meta-analytic review of twenty-nine studies of domestic violence, Sugarman and Frankle (1996) concluded that there was "limited support for the ideological component of the patriarchal theory of wife assault." They found that, contrary to feminist theory, violent husbands were more likely to have an "undifferentiated" general schema; that is, they did not adhere to rigid sex role stereotypes, and their attitudes toward women did not differ from nonviolent husbands.

Traditional households, where gender roles are sharply defined, are not necessarily violent, or even abusive, if both partners are satisfied with their respective roles.

Another criticism of the feminist explanation of family violence is that it cannot account for the high rates of violence among same sex relationships and evidence of female-on-male violence. In addition, feminist-focused treatment programs for male batterers that take an accusatory approach in working with participants may contribute to the high attrition rates reported in the field and to increases in hostility toward women. Yet, it cannot be argued that societally based attitudes that disparage women and policies and laws that expressly condone the abuse or economic repression of girls and women do not contribute to domestic violence. Similarly, it is not possible to say that a single-factor explanation fully accounts for complex social phenomena across all individuals or all societies. It is, therefore, not surprising that treatment programs derived from a single factor theory cannot point to clear evidence of effectiveness.

A complete and useful explanatory model should be multifaceted, recognizing that multiple factors contribute to family violence and providing an analysis of how factors interact to contribute to domestic violence and provide direction for intervention. Given that evidence points to multimodal treatment as being more effective in reducing criminal recidivism, it is reasonable to conclude that treatment programs to reduce relationship violence among criminal populations should also acknowledge the complexity of the origins of the problem by addressing multiple targets that are empirically shown to contribute to abusive behavior.

The theoretical treatment model adopted by Correctional Service of Canada, and shown in Figure 1, is influenced by a nested ecological model described by Dutton (1995) that explains domestic violence as multidetermined at a number of levels (*also see* Carr et al., this volume). The model, which is derived from the work of developmental psychologists and ethologists, provides a comprehensive explanation of intimacy violence that includes elements of most of the theories above. It considers the interactions between the broad social context that sanctions violence in general and violence toward women in particular (the macrosystem). It looks at the presence or absence of social structures such as prosocial supportive, or alternatively antisocial, peers and family members (the exosystem); the level of conflict in the couple, their communication pattern and each spouse's method of coping with conflict (the microsystem). Finally, it examines the perpetrator's intrapsychic features such as his history of being a victim or a witness to the violence, the pattern of

Figure 1. The Nested Model of Family Violence and Appropriate Interventions at Each Level (based on Dutton, 1995)

> **MACROSYSTEM**
> Society's broad cultural values and belief systems, the level of acceptance of violence in the society in general and violence toward women in particular.
> Intervention: Identify and challenge societal norms that influence perpetrator's beliefs and attitudes.

> **EXOSYSTEM**
> The influence of smaller groups like workplace peers, the level and type of social support the individual has.
> Intervention: Identify antisocial peer group and practice ways to respond; encourage association with prosocial support systems.

> **MICROSYSTEM**
> The couple's history of conflict and the way they deal with it.
> Intervention: Teaching communication skills, negotiation.

> **ONTOGENIC**
> The individual's thoughts, feelings and behaviors; his personal history of seeing violence as a child; his ability to cope with stress.
> Intervention: Work on skill development, problem solving, cognitive restructuring, emotion management, social skills

attachment to early caregivers, or individual differences related to problems in self-regulation, or in some cases even neurological impairment, or ontogenetic influences (the ontogenic level). Effective treatment would address relevant contributing factors at all levels of the model.

Intervening with Male Batterers: Applying Principles of Effective Treatment

Effective intervention begins with a comprehensive theoretical model which points to treatment targets that address the multiple factors that influence relationship violence. It should also be informed by the "what works" literature for the targeted population. In the case of abusive offenders, we believe that the intervention should be consistent with the broad features common to correctional programs that have the best outcomes in reducing recidivism. In other words, they should be broadly based on the principles of risk, need, and responsivity (Andrews and Bonta, 1998). This next section reviews details of these principles and processes that can be incorporated into the development and implementation of an intervention strategy for offenders with histories of violence against their partners.

Applying the Risk Principle

Effective corrections literature has noted that programs are more likely to be successful and more cost-effective if the level of service is congruent with the risk the offender poses to reoffend. Low-risk offenders should receive little or no intervention while more intensive treatment should be reserved for the higher-risk offenders. To respect this principle, an effective correctional program needs to select tools to assess reliably and validly the extent of the risk and design interventions sufficiently intensive to address the risk level. The range of correctional services to address higher-risk offenders should include direct treatment and informed case management that continuously monitors relevant risk factors when the offender is under community supervision.

Simple clinical judgment alone is no longer considered a professionally responsible risk assessment method. Without benefit of reliable anchors or the selection, and if possible weighting of risk factors, clinical judgment has been demonstrated to be unreliable and invalid. The debate about the selection of appropriate tools to assess risk for family violence, however, has not yet led to a consensus on what is most helpful to line staff who are responsible for monitoring risk. In considering the selection of appropriate tools, one needs to specify the criterion questions. For example, what kinds of recidivism are we interested in assessing and for what population? If we are looking at risk of lethality or serious harm to an intended victim as in the case of domestic violence, we may be assessing and monitoring different factors than in measuring abusiveness.

Application of actuarial measures that are psychometrically valid has been demonstrated to be more accurate than relying on clinical judgment alone (Quinsey, Harris, Rice, and Cormier, 1998), but there are limitations in applying these measures in clinical settings. Actuarial measures are useful in identifying membership in high-risk *groups* but need to be interpreted with care when applied to the *individual* clinical case. For this reason and for the purposes of case management, the most useful and dynamic approach may be a measure that isolates empirically validated risk factors, provides clear guidelines for rating each item, and allows for interpretation by case managers familiar with the case. There are now several well-established measures of risk for general dangerousness that have solid psychometric properties. For example, the Psychopathy Checklist PCL-R has been shown to have unique predictive value beyond that provided by general actuarial scales (Hare, 1991).

However, a recent study demonstrated that a more specific measure targeting risk for spousal assault would have better predictive power than the PCL (Kropp and Hart, 2000). Recent reviews have been optimistic regarding the development of theoretically and scientifically sound risk assessment instruments and procedures. In their extensive review of domestic violence risk assessments, Dutton and Kropp (2000) highlight reasons to expect greater success for assessing risk for spousal assault rather than for general violence. A brief review of the most widely used measures in the field follows.

Measures to Assess Lethality Risk

The most serious outcome of domestic violence is intimate femicide. Two lethality risk measures that have been used in the field are the Danger Assessment Scale (DA) and the Perpetrator Assessment Handbook (Sonkin, 1997). The DA (Campbell, 1995) provides a list of items derived from women's perception of the danger of being killed by their partners.[1] The instrument has some preliminary evidence of reliability and validity. Sonkin's measure outlines factors that discriminate lethal risk based on responses by women who have killed their partners, presumably because they felt they were responding to lethal violence by their partners. However, it is important to note that his risk marker list is a guide, not a psychometric test. Both measures include items such as the man's frequency of violence, severity of violence, frequency of intoxication, the man's drug use, the man's threat to kill, forced/threatened sexual acts, and the woman's suicide threats. Although these measures are composed of factors that have been associated with extreme violence for some populations retrospectively, and provide common-sense criteria for assessing risk, to date, little published research demonstrates the validity of these measures as risk prediction tools.

Research derived from police reports of spousal homicide cases describes the following features of the offender's behavior just prior to the event: for example, centrality of the victim obsessiveness about the partner; evidence of planning of the homicide; evidence of depression which, in a significant number of cases, results in the suicide or attempted suicide of the perpetrator; access to weapons; hostage-taking; threatening and stalking; escalation in drugs and alcohol use; violation of a no-contact order if it is in place; and, in general, presentation of a "man in crisis." However, the risk for lethality is not only determined by features of the perpetrators (Dutton and Kerry, 1999; Commission on Domestic Violence, 1997). The same police reports that compile a profile of intimate femicide cases also note the following features of the relationship between the perpetrator and the victim: for example, age discrepancy between the partners with the woman being younger than the perpetrator, the event happening in the context of a break-up or threatened break-up, and the relationship being common-law and in chronic turmoil.

There are also common features of the context or the situation at the time of the murder. These are, for example, that the death occurs in the home during the aftermath of an argument about a sexual indiscretion or a threat to leave the relationship; 90 percent of the victims had been killed within one year of the separation. These factors are features of the case that should signal to the case manager/probation or parole officer that close monitoring of the situation is required, particularly among those offenders who have already been assessed as at-risk for domestic violence.

Measures to Assess Spousal Assault Risk

Measures of spousal assault assess risk for a range of assaultive and dangerous behaviors, not just lethality. There appears to be an overlap among predictors of spousal assault or femicide. One measure of spousal assault that is becoming more broadly applied to the assessment of general risk for spousal abuse is the Spousal Assault Risk Assessment (SARA guide) (Kropp, Hart, Webster, and Eaves, 1995). This measure is designed as a dynamic assessment of general risk for relationship violence including that involving homosexual relationships. Through a review of the clinical and empirical literature, the authors identified twenty risk factors associated with spousal assault and provide clear criteria for rating the risk items.

The items sample four categories: (1) criminal history, (2) spousal assault history, (3) characteristics of the current offense, and (4) psychosocial adjustment. Generally speaking, the first three categories are relatively static, although there are some items, such as minimization or denial of spousal assault history that can change over time. Within the category of psychosocial assessment, many of the items focus on recent functioning, for example, recent relationship problems, while a few relate to historical issues, for example, childhood witness/victim of family violence.

The SARA allows for the identification of critical items whereby the assessor can note items that he or she sees as central to offenders' final risk rating. The overall score, based on the assessor's evaluation after consideration of the twenty items, is meant to govern the management of risk, with a high risk rating signaling that the individual needs more service and close supervision. The measure has been evaluated and determined to have good psychometric properties, but no studies have yet been completed to determine its validity as a risk predictor. The authors, however, point out that the measure is meant to be a guide for making decisions regarding risk and not as a risk-prediction measure; however, a recent version of the manual, published by Multi-Health Systems, provides cut-off scores for estimating risk. Preliminary results of a study examining the relative validity of the SARA and another popular measure, the Domestic Violence Screening Instrument (DVSI) used in Colorado, indicate that the SARA is superior to the DVSI in predicting future assaults, but both instruments predict reoffense above chance levels (Williams and Houghton, 1999 as cited in Dutton and Kropp, 2000). Unlike the PCL-R, the SARA does not require professional clinical qualifications to administer and interpret, although it does require training. It is currently the measure used throughout the Correctional Service of Canada to assess all new federal offenders at intake who meet criteria indicating a need for a more in-depth assessment of their histories of intimate violence. Another measure that might be considered is the Propensity for Abusiveness Scale (PAS). The PAS is a self-report measure that taps background factors such as parental treatment, attachment style, anger response, trauma symptoms, and stability of self-concept (Dutton, 1995). It does not appear to be influenced by social desirability and has been shown to be a good predictor of abusiveness across a variety of populations. It focuses primarily on emotional abuse and is recommended principally for noncriminal populations (Dutton and Kropp, 2000; Dutton, Landolt, Starzomski, and Bodnarchuk, 2001).

These measures, as intuitively useful as they appear to be, have yet to be well-researched. Unanswered in all cases is the extent to which the final rating, scores, or individual items have efficacy in predicting risk. Although the presence of more risk factors suggests greater risk, no research has been conducted on the interaction of individual risk factors, nor of the impact of "buffering" factors that may reduce risk despite the presence of risk factors. In most cases, the work is underway, but until the results are available, the measures, at least, provide a guide for case management by drawing attention to relevant factors to consider.

Identifying offenders at high risk is the first step in risk management. Following up with intensive service and monitoring of the risk factors are critical features. Accountable risk management of both lethality and general spousal assault would require that the parole officer/probation officer monitor relevant risk factors and take action if required and ensure the provision of treatment that targets these risk factors.

Risk Management

Informed, ongoing risk management focuses on the factors identified as risky for the client. It includes appropriate interviewing of the offender's partner. Such questioning, however, should not be attempted without training on issues related to family violence. Prior to each interview, the limits of confidentiality should be specified. The basis for the interview itself should be questions that are direct and specific to the range of abusive behavior that the woman may have experienced. In all cases, interviewers should avoid interviewing the woman when the perpetrator is in the room or even in the house, should not make assurances that information will be kept confidential if this is not possible, and should not advise her to leave without understanding the risk to her if she should do so or without providing her with a safety plan. For men of particularly high risk where there is concern about risk to a specific intended victim, risk management should include collateral contact with the partner's family, friends, or employers so that threatening, stalking, and other forms of abuse can be detected. For the offender who has completed treatment, ongoing self-monitoring through implementation of a relapse prevention plan puts the onus on the perpetrator to take responsibility for his relationship behavior. Ultimately, most offenders will be in the community without any safeguards or supervision. The benefit of well-designed interventions will assist them to adopt a violence-free relationship code independent of correctional supervision.

Applying the Need Principle

The need principle requires that correctional interventions be designed to target dynamic factors associated with criminal behavior. It follows that treatment programs for male batterers should address factors empirically related to spousal violence and abuse. Samples derived from referrals to community-based programs or to court-mandated probation orders are heterogeneous with respect to the offenders' education, social status, extent of criminal histories, and attitudes. These client characteristics contribute to differential outcomes following the initial assaultive incident. Recent research profiling batterers from community samples has identified at least three broadly defined typologies:

- Those who are generally violent and lacking in empathy—antisocial, estimated at about 25 percent of community samples.

- Those who are emotionally volatile, have a history of unstable relationships, self-defeating impulsivity, and fear of abandonment—borderline personality organization, estimated at another 25 percent of community samples.

- Those who experience discomfort dealing with intimacy but are not violent outside intimate relationships. This nonpathological group, sometimes referred to as the family-only group is estimated at about 50 percent of community samples (Dutton, 1995; Hamberger, Lohr, Bonge, and Tolin, 1996; Holtzworth-Monroe and Stuart, 1994; Saunders, 1992). Those in the family-only group restrict their violence to their spouses. Their violence is less severe. Members of the family-only group are often remorseful after the incidents. They have fewer drug and alcohol problems, have no substantial criminal histories, and are less likely to have histories of being abused as a child than perpetrators in the other two groups.

Offender populations, particularly incarcerated individuals with histories of violence against their partners, may be somewhat more homogenous than community samples. The Correctional Service of Canada, (Wexler, 2000) reviewed the files of all Aboriginal and non-Aboriginal federal offenders with histories of spousal violence admitted in 1997 (n=947). Of the test sample of non-Aboriginal men, only 13.5 percent[2] were classified in the family-only group. Virtually none (2 percent) of the Aboriginal spousal abusers were in the family-only group. Preliminary research suggests there may be two broad profiles of federal offenders with histories of spousal abuse: those offenders who are generally violent and assaultive and those offenders who have specific histories of problematic relationships marked by attachment anxiety, jealousy, and dependency (Kerry, 2000).

In addition to histories of violence against their partners, like most federally sentenced offenders, both groups have criminal histories and substantial problems with substance abuse. Addressing the criminogenic needs of offenders with histories of intimate violence that are also, broadly speaking, criminally oriented argues for the application of the principles of effective corrective matching for their interventions. However, for groups that are more clearly from the "family-only" group, interventions that are perhaps less intensive and less focused on skills development may be appropriate.

As pointed out above, risk factors associated with spousal violence are historic and static as well as dynamic. It is worth noting that factors found more frequently in abusers than nonabusers suggest a relationship to abuse in intimate relationships and point to promising targets to address in treatment. However these factors and targets may not be causally linked to spousal violence. For example, we have not yet established that addressing life history factors like witnessing abuse as a child will have an impact on reducing further offending among male batterers. Determining these causal links requires a program of research. For the purposes of case planning and risk assessment, both static and dynamic factors related to spousal assault are important to consider, but the targets of treatment generally will be the dynamic factors, that is, those amenable to change. Principal static factors noted in the profiles of abusive men and suggested methods to address them include those described below.

1. Violence in the family of origin, specifically witnessing the abuse of the man's mother (Saunders, 1995). Howell and Pugliesi (1998) found that men who witnessed family violence were three times more likely than those not observing family violence to become perpetrators, even when the effects of age, occupational status, and employment status were controlled. Hanson and Wallace-Capretta (2000) found that there was a significant relationship (phi = .35, $p<.0001$) between history of spousal violence among a group of Canadian men referred for treatment and being witness to violence in family of origin, but that this factor did not significantly predict recidivism. Among federal offenders, Robinson and Taylor (1995) found that being witness to violence in their family of origin is a significant correlate of spousal violence history. A history of early relationship problems beginning with problematic parent-child attachment has been associated with perpetrators with borderline personality features.

A method of addressing issues of childhood maltreatment is through participants' autobiographies. Incorporating an autobiographical component into a program for offenders is a sensitive endeavor. In our experience, facilitators must carefully circumscribe the group or individual work so that it is always clear that the goal in reviewing the life history is to assist the offender to address his perpetration of violence. This must be done sensitively and with empathy and attention to the participant's capacity to deal with what may be very traumatic events. If the program is a short one, it may be better not to use this approach.

If the approach is used, facilitators assist participants to understand how their personal histories, including their experience of being abused as a child, have contributed to the thinking process that underlie incidents of family violence. Exercises guide the participant to rethink the attitudes learned through exposure to violent models and help him use the emotion he feels about his childhood experience to understand the impact of his abuse on victims. Based on an understanding of the source of the participant's "worldview" and behavior patterns, he is encouraged to take responsibility for changes he can make to ensure that the patterns will not repeat themselves.

Little empirical evidence supports including an insight-based component in treatment with offenders. However, a recent study of desistance, the turning away from a pattern of criminality, suggests that "making good" is associated with offenders reconstructing their "script," their view of themselves and their aspirations (Maruna, 2001). The focus of this approach attends to changes in "identify, self-concept and the framework employed to judge oneself and others" (Shover, 1983). Among the elements of the process are the offender's acquisition of an altered perspective of his youthful self and activities and a revision of aspirations to include goals such as "contentment, peace, and harmonious interpersonal relationships" (Shover, 1983). We argue that including the development of an autobiography in treatment can mediate this maturation process. Moreover, participant feedback has consistently endorsed the autobiographical module as one of the most appreciated of the program. Using autobiographies consolidates the group as a unit and engages the offenders in the goals of treatment, providing a powerful tool to enhance responsivity.

2. Demographic factors—including being under forty years of age, having lower socioeconomic status, low education, and poor employment histories are correlates of intimate violence. Obviously, younger age and poverty cannot be addressed in treatment, but there is evidence that employment and education programs for offenders reduce recidivism (Boe,1998). While a family violence treatment program, in itself, cannot be expected to target educational upgrading or employment skills, a thorough correctional plan should look into linking perpetrators with histories of unemployment to educational upgrading or employment opportunities and encouraging employment stability.

Dynamic risk factors associated with abusers include attitudinal, health, personality, and lifestyle issues. We describe four of them.

1. Attitudes supportive of sexist roles and the abuse of women. The relationship of attitudes toward women and spousal assault is not straightforward. Hanson and Wallace-Capretta's (2000) study of factors related to recidivism in a population of Canadian men abusers found a moderate correlation between abusive behavior and sexist *and* pro-abuse attitudes. As cited earlier in this chapter, Sugarman and Frankel's (1996) meta-analysis of twenty-nine studies, however, concluded that abusers did not adhere to rigid sex role stereotypes and their attitudes toward women's roles did not differ from nonviolent husbands. Yllo and Straus' (1990) research found a curvilinear relationship between patriarchal structure and spousal violence. They found that American states with greater inequality for women and states with the most structural equality had the highest rates of spousal violence. Hanson and Wallace-Capretta's (2000) study of factors related to recidivism in a population of Canadian men abusers found a moderate correlation between abusive behavior and sexist *and* pro-abuse attitudes. In general, the evidence indicates that attitudes that endorse a patriarchal societal structure alone may not put women at heightened risk for violence unless the perpetrators also justify and endorse violence against women to enforce men's dominant roles.

Successful methods for addressing attitude change in other areas of correctional treatment are through cognitive restructuring techniques or the application of the ABC ➔ D ➔ E model. These techniques are similar to those employed in Rational Emotive Behavioral Therapy (Ellis, 1977) and other cognitive therapies (Beck, 1976, 1999). The basic principle is to have the offender identify an antecedent event that led to a violent incident (A); identify the "irrational beliefs," "self-talk," or "risky thinking" (B) at the time of the event; identify the consequences (C) or the emotions or behaviors that are the outcome of the thinking; and dispute (D) the thinking and replace it with more prosocial or less "risky" beliefs or thoughts (E). This process, repeated many times in the course of a program with practice through role play, allows the participant to take control of his life and behaviors by changing the way he thinks about a given situation. It is a cornerstone technique of any cognitive-behavioral intervention.

2. Substance abuse, especially alcohol consumption. Alcohol use, and, to a lesser extent, drug use, has been consistently associated with spousal abuse. Kantor Kaufman and Straus (1990) found that in more than 5,000 American couples, males' pattern of drinking was directly related to the extent and severity of spousal abuse, with the most severe drinkers being the most physically abusive. Statistics Canada's national survey of violence against women (Rogers, 1994) also found that men who drank regularly—minimally four times per week—assaulted their female partners at a rate that was triple the rate of assaultive men who never drank. The rate of wife assault increased to sixfold for women living with partners who consecutively drank five or more drinks.

Within the Correctional Service of Canada, Robinson and Taylor's (1995) survey of federal offenders with evidence of violence on file against a spouse found that alcohol abuse was one of the two most significant correlates of family violence for this group. Interestingly, drug abuse was not related. While the family violence program itself may not directly address substance abuse, the program material should assist the offender to make a link, where it exists, between substance abuse and family violence. In addition, parole officers should ensure that offenders who abuse substances are provided with the opportunity for treatment specific to this need, preferably in a program that shares a similar treatment approach to that of the family violence program.

3. Individual factors such as high levels of anger, problems with emotional self-management, use of cognitive distortions, lack of assertiveness, and poor communication skills. We have already referred to the research on typologies of batterers. This literature attests to batterers' profiles of one group—borderline—as having high levels of depression and anxiety and sensitivity to rejection (Hastings and Hamberger, 1988; Dutton and Kerry, 1999). Even when batterers who abused alcohol and those who did not were compared, Hastings and Hamberger found that the alcohol-abusing batterers had the most severe pathology. However, both groups shared high levels of personality pathology, aggressiveness, and passive-aggressiveness.

Moffitt, Krueger, Caspi, and Fagan (2000) found that negative emotionality, defined as irritability, proneness to suspiciousness, emotional volatility, and low thresholds for anger and hostility were risk factors for men in predicting abusiveness towards their partners. Maiuro and his colleagues (1986) compared spousal abusers to nonabusers on assertiveness and anger/hostility. They found that abusers were as able to refuse a demand or request as nonabusers, but abusers were not as able to initiate a request of a personal need in a direct and positive manner. There was also evidence of a significant and negative relationship between initiating behavior and covert anger/hostility which suggests that spouse abusers have difficulties in expressing their needs to others. When their needs are not met, they may become angry and frustrated.

Hanson and Wallace-Capretta (2000) confirmed that within their group of men in treatment, participants' reports of anger/hostility correlated significantly with having a history of partner assault (.37, p<.0001), and their partners' reports of men's anger/hostility correlated even higher (.65, p<.001). Problems in coping with extreme sexual jealousy and possessiveness is a particularly dangerous problem in abusive relationships. Reports on the circumstances of domestic homicide cite possessiveness and inability to accept relationship loss as the most common scenario preceding murder (Marzuk, Tardif, and Hirsh, 1992; Morton, Runyon, Moracco, and Butts, 1998; Wilson and Daly, 1996).

There is empirical support for the use of a number of cognitive-behavioral methods to address these problems. Cognitive therapies have been shown to be as effective as medication in addressing mild and moderate depression, anxiety, and other strong emotions (Beck, 1976; Hazaleus and Deffenbacher, 1986; Deffenbacher, Story, Brandon, Hogg, and Hazaleus, 1988; Hughes, 1993). Among juvenile clients, behavioral treatments focusing on the development of social skills for correctional clients have reduced aggressive acting out (Feindler, Ecton, Kingsley, and Dubey, 1986). A program that applied a number of cognitive and behavioral techniques to reduction of anger and aggression in federal offenders found strong reductions in general and violent offending, but only among high-risk offenders (Dowden, Blanchette, and Serin, 1999). The application of these techniques to adult spousal assaulters independent of other interventions has yet to be firmly established, but again the evidence from the effective corrections literature points in this direction.

4. Criminal lifestyle factors associated with problems in self-regulation. Offenders with histories of spousal assault commonly have backgrounds that are associated with other impulsive behaviors such as assault and impaired driving charges, problem gambling, inappropriate leisure patterns, substance abuse, frequent unemployment, and association with procriminal peers (Hanson et al., 1997). Spousal abusers share many of the characteristics of chronic criminals, which may be attributable to a similar failure in inhibition (Stewart and Rowe, 2001). Among populations of incarcerated and conditionally released spousal assaulters, the correlation with generalized antisocial orientation and behaviors associated with problems of self-regulation is strong. Over 31 percent of Robinson and Taylor's sample of federal offenders with histories of violence against an intimate partner had fifteen or more previous convictions. This factor of previous convictions was significantly related to spousal abuse (p<.05). Hanson and Wallace-Capretta (2000) found that association with criminal peers was correlated with a history of abusiveness and also with posttreatment recidivism, while association with abusive peers was related to a history of having been abusive but not to recidivism. In another study of Canadian federally sentenced men convicted of intimate femicide, Kerry (2000) found that these men were distinguished from other offenders and nonoffenders by the extent to which they associated with male peers during their leisure activities.

Given the cross-reference of the profiles of abusers with chronic offenders, those interventions proven to be effective in reducing criminal behavior should apply as well to federally sentenced spousal assaulters. Such effective interventions emphasize problem-solving, pause and delay responses to problem situations, and anticipation and rehearsal of prosocial responses to problem situations and relapse prevention. They also rely on an analysis of lifestyle to understand what components such as offenders' use of leisure time and their association with procriminal peers are "risky," in other words, set up the conditions for the next incident.

In addition to addressing factors that are problematic for the offender, a successful program should highlight and encourage protective factors that have been empirically demonstrated to be associated with desistance of offending. These may also be individual factors participants identify as strengths in their life. An example may be encouraging the exploration of a special talent or interest that puts the offender in touch with peers who have prosocial orientations and that replace rewards that were previously sought through violence and abuse. A complete relapse prevention plan would contain elements that highlight strengths and positive supports for the offender and detail effective coping responses to high-risk situations.

Methods to Address Criminogenic Needs

Meta-analytic and theoretical reviews have identified a cognitive-behavioral approach as the most effective treatment orientation in reducing criminal recidivism (Andrews and Bonta, 1998; Losel, 1996). There is limited research on the outcome of family violence treatment approaches with criminal populations, but one study found some support for a cognitive-behavioral approach over a process/psychodynamic approach with antisocial abusers (Saunders, 1996). The methods to address the treatment targets that were briefly discussed above are among those in the cognitive-behavioral repertoire.

Relatively little evidence is available to allow us to endorse one approach over another in the field of family violence treatment, unless one extrapolates from other populations. A cognitive-behavioral approach can address many of the multiple factors at the various levels of analysis identified in the nested model described earlier (*see* Figure 1). When appropriate, other forms of intervention could be used to address factors specific to a particular individual, the couple, or the family. For example, a percentage of perpetrators are identified as suffering from neurological disorders that could require a medically based intervention (Rosenbaum et al., 1997). Couples may wish to engage in couples' counseling after the initial treatment of the perpetrator is completed; families that wish to reconcile have benefited from a restorative justice model when a careful protocol is followed.

The treatment and risk management model we propose is launched by a basic core program that helps offenders change risky attitudes and learn basic skills associated with healthy relationships. Supplementing the initial intervention is likely to enhance the impact. A "one size fits all" approach driven by ideology or politics with no framework for detailed evaluation cannot advance progress toward effective methods of reducing intimate violence.

Applying the Responsivity Principle

Critical to the success of a program are practices that create opportunities for and increase the ability of the offender to respond to treatment issues. This approach of engaging the offender in the process of self-change and learning is referred to as the responsivity principle. It is not surprising that not every man who requires an intervention to address family violence is willing to attend a program in which he is required to admit publicly to the abuse of women and children. Thus, an effective program to address family violence needs to build in techniques that increase participants' motivation to change.

Although Andrews and Bonta (1998) highlight the importance of the responsivity principle in effective corrections, their discussion of how to apply it is limited to recommending that correctional programs use cognitive-behavioral techniques. They point out that programs are most effective if they are structured and focus on developing skills and use behavioral methods with reinforcements for clearly identified, overt behaviors, as opposed to nondirective counseling focusing on insight, self-esteem, or disclosure. The literature on adult learning observes that adults respond better when interventions employ active and participatory approaches such as role-playing rather than passive didactic instruction. Thus, the methodology of cognitive behavioral programs are more likely to conform to the cognitive and learning style of adult offenders. Maximizing responsivity would mean identifying ways to ensure that each program participant is able to meet the goals of the program.

Recent research has explored responsivity issues for participants in family violence programs. For instance, the majority of batterers exhibit narcissistic or avoidant traits that are well-suited to cognitive-behavioral group treatment approaches (White and Gondolf, 2000). High rates of attrition for family violence programs are also well-documented, and studies examining dropouts have determined that batterer program participants who report lower education, unemployment, and alcohol problems attend fewer program sessions (Daly, Power and Gondolf, 2001). Daly, Power, and Gondolf (2001) suggest that programs need to be sensitive to the social circumstances of their participants. The authors also suggest that approaches which focus on cognitive restructuring and men's responsibilities to women and the community may be challenging for men who are less educated.

Incompatibility between participants' abilities or expectations and the program approach may be most apparent for clients who are motivated by concrete outcomes—such as their partner returning if they complete the program—but they are required to focus on social and cognitive issues that involve considerable self-reflection. Rooney and Hanson (2001) demonstrated an interaction between verbal aptitude of participants and program structure; men with low verbal aptitude were more likely to remain in structured treatment programs that provide concrete examples and direct communication.

There are numerous other ways to engage participants by attending to their individual learning styles and histories. Programs can provide opportunities for individualized counseling in addition to group time to work out individual issues and problems with the material; those who have literacy problems can be paired with tutors or more advanced group members who can provide assistance. Even providing a physical environment that is conducive to learning such as a quiet room with adequate space, lighting, and privacy can be a factor in maximizing participant response to treatment. The literature also suggests that expanded orientation sessions and extensive follow-up with men who miss sessions are important (Daly, Power, and Gondolf, 2001).

Programs are also more effective if they provide for substantial, meaningful contact between the treatment personnel and the participants. A key component of effective treatment in all domains is a collaborative, supportive relationship between therapist and client that recognizes that personal change has to be self-motivated (Miller and Rollnick, 1991; Prochaska and DiClementi, 1983; Prochaska, DiClementi, and Norcross, 1992).

Figure 2 presents the FRAMES acronym representing factors that Miller and his colleagues identified as elements of successful psychological interventions. Many of these features are ensured through using a style of intervention consistent with motivational interviewing. Motivational interviewing is defined as a directive, client-centered counseling style for eliciting behavior change by helping clients to explore and resolve ambivalence. Compared with nondirective counseling, it is more focused and goal-directed. The examination and resolution of ambivalence is its central purpose, and the counselor is intentionally directive in pursuing this goal (Miller and Rollnick, 1991).

Prochaska and colleagues (1991) have also pointed out that insisting that individuals engage in an intervention that assumes a level of motivation to change if they are not "ready" is unlikely to be successful. They have isolated various change strategies or therapeutic methods that are appropriate to use at the different stages of readiness to change. We believe that there is promise in incorporating elements from these approaches into the design of domestic violence programs.

Figure 2. The FRAMES Elements

Elements of successful treatment interventions (Miller and Rollnick, 1991)

Feedback—provide feedback to increase awareness of his/her situation and the ways in which it is harmful.

Responsibility—emphasize that it is the individual's own decision to change.

Advice—provide advice to identify the problems and discuss the necessity for change.*

Menu—provide a choice of strategies for change.

Empathy—express acceptance and understanding of the person.

Self-efficacy—instill the client's perception that he or she can implement a change strategy.

*Advice giving in the spirit of motivational interviewing is done only when requested by the client.

For example, strategies for family violence perpetrators who are in the early stages of change, that is, are not yet sure they want to change (pre-contemplation and contemplation), would be predominately experiential while behavioral strategies would predominate for those in the later stages (action and maintenance) who are actively engaged in changing. An example of an experiential strategy is consciousness-raising through exposure to testimonials of men who have made changes, or review of results of evaluation tools assessing the extent of the participant's violence, or exposure to educational material detailing the kinds of abuse and the impact on victims and family violence. Examples of behavioral strategies are counterconditioning and stimulus control techniques, which train participants to be aware of the factors that are associated with their violence and to replace the violent behaviors with prosocial skills.

We strongly endorse training facilitators in the techniques of motivational interviewing so that they are skilled in using a collaborative, supportive approach to working with abusers. Interventions employing appropriate stage-based change strategies and a motivational interviewing style are antithetical to an accusatory or antagonistic approach in which men are allegedly held "accountable." We believe that shaming participants or addressing resistance head on is countertherapeutic and unlikely to contribute to treatment success.

Attention to Diversity

Another important element affecting responsivity is the extent to which the program content and the group facilitators are sensitive to issues of diversity in a multi-ethnic setting. Facilitators' cultural sensitivity, that is, their understanding of how culture can affect individual treatment response, is critical when facilitating groups composed of individuals from diverse ethnic backgrounds; however, so is the extent to which the program content can be relevant to the experience of the participants. This is a tall order in most large North American urban centers where individuals from multiple backgrounds could be participating in a single group. Some constituencies may be legally mandated to provide culturally specific programming for some groups. For example, the Correctional Service of Canada is required by law to provide culturally-specific programming to Aboriginal offenders.

An effective family violence program acknowledges the impact of race, racism, and immigration on the family lives of group participants. The vignettes, the videos, and the case studies in the program should represent a diverse ethnic population. We recommend development or, at least, input into development of program material by experts from diverse ethnic groups and hiring of program facilitators who reflect the multicultural backgrounds of the program participants. Other ways in which content or process could examine the impact of culture would be to have participants identify aspects of their cultures that endorse violence toward women always challenging the argument that any culture is based on the abuse of women and children and then call for participants to identify best practices within their culture that teach young men to respect women and nurture children.

In the Correctional Service of Canada, Aboriginal programs are developed with Aboriginal experts and input from respected community leaders. Where possible, they are delivered by Aboriginal facilitators. Aboriginal offenders are linked to an elder and participate in spiritual ceremonies if they wish. Facilitators who run programs with Aboriginal offenders in attendance are encouraged to establish a liaison with the Elders who can assist in making the material as relevant as possible. During training, facilitators and quality assurance officers are sensitized to cultural issues as they relate to family violence. The training provides an awareness of issues relevant to the experience of men and women who come from backgrounds other than that of the dominant culture and provides direction on handling of the excuse that an individual's culture condones his abusive behaviors.

Noting the higher dropout and reassault rates for African-American men participating in batterer programs compared to white men in the same programs, Gondolf and Williams (2001) recommend culturally focused counseling that includes a curriculum which identifies specific cultural topics, counselors who respond to emergent cultural issues, and racially homogenous groups that encourage disclosure. Some preliminary research suggests that African-American men are more comfortable and more engaged in culturally focused batterer counseling. These preliminary findings of the Gondolf and Williams (2001) study support clinical observations regarding the effectiveness of this approach. However, well-controlled outcome research on culturally focused batterer counseling is needed to substantiate their suggestion.

Appendix A provides an outline of the high and moderate intensity programs offered to federal offenders in Canada with histories of violence against their partners. A recent analysis of offenders' response to treatment in both the high and moderate programs demonstrated significant improvement on the intermediate variables, including improvement in skills application and prosocial attitude change, but we have yet to test the efficacy of the treatment in reducing recidivism.

Implementation of Effective Treatment for Offenders: Assessment and Evaluation

Procedural features that Gendreau (1996) and others have identified as common to effective programs highlight aspects of program implementation and ongoing quality assurance. These researchers have pointed out that successful programs ensure that treatment integrity is monitored to avoid program drift, service providers are adequately trained in the techniques of program delivery, graduates are provided with adequate maintenance and follow-up, and the effectiveness of the program are continuously monitored. The program, thus, becomes a continuous work in progress benefiting from the cumulative knowledge of facilitators and from the performance and feedback of the participants.

Methods of Ensuring Treatment Integrity

Treatment integrity implies that the program is run according to a set of approved standards that treatment providers and managers understand, and that compliance with the standards is assessed through, at least, annual reviews. Program integrity requires a curriculum guide or manual that lays out the goals of the sessions and the modules. This does not preclude stepping outside the manual content to address issues that come up in group, or exploring alternative methods to assist participants' understanding and learning, if necessary. However, it does call for the program to be recognizable across settings, each setting meeting the objectives of the program. Two methods of assessing the extent to which program objectives are met are through content quizzes and facilitator evaluations of participants' knowledge and skill development.

Facilitators who deliver the program should be selected based on qualities of individuals who are effective change agents. They should be articulate, humane, enthusiastic, prosocial role models. Cofacilitation with a male and female therapist can provide a demonstration of gender equality. Facilitators should be trained in the theoretical model the program has adopted and acquainted with the program content and the methods used to aid knowledge and skill acquisition. For example, program facilitators applying a cognitive-behavioral approach should be skilled in the structured learning approach including setting up role plays to aid skill acquisition.

Compliance with program standards, application of effective methods of facilitation, and delivery of program content can be monitored through videotaping of sessions or on-site reviews. In all cases, reviews should consist of feedback to the facilitators and their managers on what is working and what requires improvement. Management support is required to ensure that noncompliance is addressed with a plan for remediation that is honored.

The supervising parole or probation officers should review the offender's relapse prevention plan with him to bridge the move from the institution to the community. The relapse prevention plan contains a comprehensive identification of the factors related to the offender's offending pattern and the implementation of a strategy of self-management. This plan would address these factors as well as the identification of a realistic support network to assist in the case of relapse. The review and update of the relapse prevention plan can be completed in group or in the context of one-on-one supervision. Maintenance programs are usually based on the relapse plans that are completed at the end of the institutional program and therefore should use similar treatment and theoretical models as the intensive phase of treatment. Provision of, or referral to, additional services such as parenting programs or substance abuse programs, if warranted, would be part of any viable release and relapse prevention plan.

Finally, every program should be subject to regular evaluation of all aspects of its content and process of delivery, not only on the basis of its impact on recidivism. Information on what is working and what needs adjustment is a component of the critical feedback loop that contributes to continuous improvement of the intervention. Regular discussions with the consumers—the participants and their families—review of program content with facilitators, and examination of the data collected on measures of knowledge gained and skills acquisition should be fed back into regular manual and procedural revisions. Modifications and improvements to the program and its delivery do not have to hinge on or wait on information from large-scale evaluations.

As pointed out above, at this point we can say little about what definitively works in the treatment of family violence among male offenders. Most research has reported on community populations with only a portion of the caseload being described as "antisocial." Even in the evaluations based on noncriminal populations, individual components of the program have not been evaluated to assess their specific impact. The family violence treatment outcome literature in general does not help us draw any firm conclusions on effectiveness, being fraught with problems with research design and nonrepresentational treatment samples. A reading of the literature, however, does point to potentially profitable directions. The next section briefly reviews the recent outcome studies in the area of family violence treatment.

Evaluation Framework and Relevant Outcome Measures

Evaluation of program effectiveness can answer a number of important questions about treatment. First, and, most critically, does the program reduce the risk that participants will commit another incident of violence and abuse? Secondly, did the participant actually make changes on relevant treatment targets, for example, did he improve his attitude and did he learn any skills? Is there any evidence he could apply the skills in emotionally charged situations? Detailed analysis could also provide characteristics of participants who respond better to treatment than others, or conversely, those who do not respond. Strategic research can point to what elements of the program appeared to have the most impact on the outcome.

Very few treatment programs have the luxury of time to permit in-depth assessment. Assessment batteries, therefore, must be limited to the most relevant measures, that is, tools that evaluate change on the targets of treatment. For example, a relevant target for any cognitively based program is prosocial change in the participants' thinking process. Broadly speaking, we are looking for improvements in thinking that increase self-regulation, for example, thinking that is more systematic, slows down the reaction, provides a response pause and time to reflect, and considers consequences. In the case of family violence perpetrators, in addition to these process changes, we are looking for *content* changes toward thinking that critically analyzes beliefs and attitudes that endorse the abuse of women. Less "risky" thinking would be less sexist, less rigid, and more egalitarian, but most importantly, prosocial thinking would reject excuses and rationalizations for the abuse of women.

Several self-report attitudinal measures are used in the field. Typically, these measures focus on assessing the extent to which men endorse sexist attitudes toward women or endorse abusive and violent actions. Examples include the Attitudes Toward Women Scale (Spence, Helreich, and Strapp, 1972); the Hostility Toward Women Scale (Check, 1984); the

Abusive Beliefs Inventory (Shepard and Campbell, 1992); the Inventory of Beliefs about Wife Beating (Saunders, Lynch, Grayson, and Linz, 1987); and the Abusive Relationship Inventory (Boer, Kroner, Wong, and Cadsky, undated). Boer and his colleagues developed the Abusive Relationship Inventory for use with incarcerated or paroled offenders who may have a reading level that is below that required for other instruments.

A shortcoming of self-report measures is their susceptibility to impression management. To some extent, impression management can be statistically controlled through use of a measure of social desirability. However, even this precaution does not preclude respondents denying or minimizing their attitudes and behaviors. Many researchers opt for combining official records, interviews, and therapist rating methods with self-report and partner instruments to help increase the validity of their interpretations. A recent development in the assessment field is the use of standardized scenarios or vignettes to probe offenders' responses to hypothetical situations. Carefully constructed and scored, such measures can provide rich data, can better reflect actual competency, and can mitigate the extent to which social desirability contributes to their responses. Scenarios can tap various treatment targets at the same time. For example, thinking skills—how strategic and systematic is the thinking?; attitude—what interpretation does the offender make of the situation?; and skills application—is his response to the situation likely to provide a mutually satisfactory outcome, or will it increase the risk for violence and abuse?

Given that the primary goal of treatment is the cessation of violence against the partner, the principal treatment outcome variable of interest is a measure of repeated episodes of violence. Reliance on official records underestimates actual rates. As a result, base rates of recidivism that rely on these data are quite low. Most reports using official records have found that fewer than 20 percent reoffend after one to three years of follow-up. Dutton and his colleagues found a 20 percent reoffending rate after eleven years (Dutton, Bodnarchuk, Kropp, Hart, and Ogloff, 1997). Such low base rates will require large differences between treated and untreated groups or very large sample sizes to detect significant treatment effects. Some other researchers have found that with more detailed follow-up, including interviews with the partners, the base rates for reoffending are actually disturbingly high (Holtzworth-Munroe and Stuart, 1994). Follow-up interviews with the partner individually rather than conjointly, can supply information on the range, frequency, context, motivations, and consequences of abusive behaviors that official records lack.

However, evaluators must be aware of the tendency of both the victim and the perpetrator to minimize or deny abuse.

Standardized self-report questionnaires tend to elicit the highest reporting rates of abuse. They can provide a relatively quick and confidential screening of abuse (O'Leary and Murphy, 1999). The revised Conflict Tactics Scale (CTS2) (Straus, Hamby, Boney-McCoy, and Sugarman, 1996) is probably the most commonly used measure of behavioral indices of intimate violence and abuse. There are, however, several challenges in using these measures as well. Outcome data are limited to those abusers who continue to cohabit or, at least, maintain a relationship with the pretreatment partner. There are often difficulties tracking partners willing to participate in such follow-up interviews. Researchers have also noted that results of such surveys can be affected by the partners' and male participants' increased awareness of the range of behaviors that are abusive after treatment.

As a measure, critics of the Conflict Tactics Scale have noted that the instrument is limited to a focus on conflict-related violence, includes threats as violence, and equates different levels of violent acts. For example, use of a weapon or a threat are both counted as one incident. Other criticisms point out that the dynamics of family violence are ignored; one cannot ascertain the context of the violence or who initiates violence from the results. These issues become important in gaining a full understanding of the perpetrators. A measure that assesses the extent to which men psychologically abuse their partners is Tolman's Psychological Maltreatment of Women Scale. It assesses two forms of psychological abuse: emotional/verbal abuse and dominance/isolation (Tolman, 1999). The scale can be completed as a self-report by the offenders or by the women partners.

Best practice in pre- and posttreatment assessment batteries would seek out convergent sources of data that tap behaviors and attitudes that are the target of treatment. Rating scales completed by facilitators should systematically assess the observed progress of the offender in treatment against the program goals as, for example, an intervention-specific Goal Attainment Scale-Family Violence (GAS-FV).[3] Objective tests or quizzes assess the extent to which offenders have learned the knowledge content of the program. Participants' responses to scenarios or vignettes provide information on both skills development and attitude change and may not be as vulnerable to impression management as self-report measures. Profiling tools should provide information on the impact of factors related to criminal recidivism and spousal abuse, in particular, IQ, personality psychopathology, employment status at the time of offending, criminal history, age at time of offending, and extent of problem with substance abuse. A sample test battery for a family violence program that conforms to the principles of effective corrections is provided in Appendix A, page 191.

Treatment Effectiveness

Since in most correctional settings a group format is the most cost-efficient, this section will only review the outcome on group programs. In community settings, however, couples counseling, family counseling, and individual counseling are other formats for the delivery of interventions for relationship violence.

There are several problems that plague group treatment evaluation, and, therefore, limit any firm statement about what works. Group interventions vary in their treatment approach and degree of structure. Some are primarily educational, and some are unstructured self-help groups. More recently, court-mandated programs tend to combine a feminist analysis of power and control issues with a cognitive-behavioral approach. Nonrepresentative samples are created through screening in volunteers and through group attrition which in many community programs can be as much as 50 percent.

One problem of evaluation is that clinical studies have small samples, reducing statistical power. In addition, across studies there are different definitions of abuse or "relationship," as well as various outcome criteria, such as official conviction records, perpetrator self-reports, or partner reports. Most studies do not have a control group, although some use comparison groups. Quasi-experimental evaluations that compare treatment completers to dropouts tend to overestimate the effects of treatment because completers differ from dropouts on important characteristics and many studies do not correct for this. Other quasi-experimental evaluations that use matched groups may suffer from selection biases because the groups may differ in important ways. Apart from all these difficulties is the very real problem of accounting for the context in which the program participant lives, or in the case of incarcerated offenders, will return to. In Goldolf's (2002) words, "the system matters." The outcome of some programs could be enhanced by their participants graduating to communities with considerable access to services for victims, where the courts or policing policies are more lenient, and they are under long-term supervision orders; other programs' outcomes may be disadvantaged by graduating participants returning to isolated communities where there are few services for potential victims, high rates of interpersonal violence is the norm, and no supervision can be arranged. Generally, evaluations have determined that most abusers (53 to 85 percent) stop their violence after treatment in follow-up periods ranging up to fifty-four months (Dobash and Dobash, 1999; Edleson and Syers, 1990). However, it is harder to make a definitive assessment of whether treatment provides incremental improvement beyond the deterrent effect of arrest. Rosenfeld's 1992 review of mandatory treatment programs found that, on average, dropouts did just as well as those who attended treatment. He concluded that evidence to support the effectiveness of treatment was minimal.

Dutton (1995), on the other hand, cited strong treatment effects for court-mandated offenders. In a six-month follow-up, 16 percent of untreated abusers and 4 percent of treated offenders reoffended. Gains were maintained two and one-half years later when results indicated that 40 percent of untreated and 4 percent of treated men recidivated. The effects of treatment were also evident in samples of self-reports from men and of women partners from the treated group, which demonstrated that levels of violence and verbal aggression dropped after completion of the program. Dobash and Dobash (1999, 2000) evaluated nonequivalent criminal justice interventions with court-mandated abusers. They found that all the criminal justice interventions resulted in reductions in violence, but the treatment programs resulted in greater reductions in violence which were sustained after one year.

As in other areas of treatment, a major contribution to reducing the confusion in debates about the effectiveness of specialized programs has been meta-analyses. Meta-analytic techniques permit an evaluation of treatment effects across many studies. Levesque (1998) examined the spousal assault literature using the meta-analytic method. Only eleven studies were sufficiently well-designed to meet the inclusion criteria. She found moderately significant improvement in the treatment group (ES = .19; $p<.05$) using official records. She found no differences (ES = .06, ns) between treatment and comparison groups when using partner reports.

Babcock, Green, and Robie (in press) are completing their meta-analysis of the treatment literature in the area. At a recent conference, they reported that effect size due to group battering intervention on recidivism of domestic violence is in the "small" range; 52.5 percent of treated batterers were nonviolent, compared to 47.5 percent of the untreated batterers. There were no significant differences in the effect size between Duluth-type and cognitive-behavioral interventions. Studies that employed quasi-experimental methods *and* victim reports tended to generate the highest effect sizes. Davis and Taylor's (1999) review is more promising. Their review of quasi-experimental and experimental studies indicated what the authors described as a "fairly substantial" effect for batterer treatment, although they caution that the number of methodologically rigorous studies is still small and more are required before firm conclusions can be drawn.

A handful of well-controlled randomized evaluations have been conducted recently that did not find that treatment reduced recidivism beyond that of nontreatment controls (Taylor, Davis, and Maxwell, 1998; Dunford, 2000; Feder and Forde, 1999). However, as pointed out by Gondolf (2001), experimental evaluations have some major limitations of their own. He has challenged the conclusions and methodology of researchers using this design, arguing that an experimental research design is not a fair test of treatment because the assumptions underlying a rigorous research design are not easily met. He proposes the use of alternative analytical methods and research designs that can provide a broader and more meaningful view of the programs' impact such as community or systems analysis and consumer-based assessment. Dobash and Dobash (2000) are also critical of randomized evaluations of batterer interventions and argue for the use of more theoretically informed contextual evaluations.

Recent evaluations have addressed some of the limitations of earlier quasi-experimental studies. Statistically sophisticated evaluations that control for differences between completers and noncompleters have found substantial reductions for program completions. Jones and Gondolf (in press) used an instrumental variable analysis and found a reduction in reassault of 43 percent for program completers, suggesting a considerable deescalation of new reassaults. Preliminary findings from a subsequent analysis (Jones, D'Agostino, Gondolf, and Heckert, 2001) using propensity scores revealed that program completion reduces the probability of reassault by 26 to 34 percent. Their results showed that for men with risk factors such as severe psychopathology or drug use, the average effect of program completion on reassault is less than that of men without these risk factors. Conversely, a much higher program completion effect was found among men who were court-referred to batterer programs rather than those who voluntarily attended.

In addition to examining the question of program effectiveness, research has also investigated the relative effectiveness of various types of treatment programs. In general, this research design has employed stronger methodologies and has addressed the concern of administrations that are disinclined to permit studies where some offenders would receive some form of treatment over studies in which some offenders will not receive any treatment. To date, these studies have not found differences in program effectiveness according to treatment type or program length (Davis and Taylor, 1999; Gondolf, 1999).

Long-term effects of batterer treatment have also been a topic of recent research. A thirty-month follow-up of the same program participants confirmed the reassault trends observed at the fifteen-month follow-up (Gondolf, 2000b). There was no evidence of a threshold or escalation of new reassaults over the time studied, even after program participation and probation ended. Reassaults continued to decrease over time. Researchers and clinicians have recognized the heterogeneity of batterers, and research attention has also recently focused on the effectiveness of treatment interventions for various typologies of offenders. As noted in the responsivity section of this paper, this work has begun to guide program development.

Family violence treatment programs are not consistently well-developed and may not be intensive enough for higher risk perpetrators. Clearly, there is room for improvement in program design that could reasonably be expected to increase treatment effects. Moreover, many of the evaluated programs are short—around ten sessions; only a few are more than twenty sessions. Based on his meta-analysis of correctional treatment, Lipsey (1992) found that high intensity treatment, which he defined as those offering 100 hours of service, were more effective for high-risk offenders. None of the abuser programs we reviewed approached the recommended 100 hours of treatment.

Most interventions are not multimodal and they may continue to use confrontation instead of attempting to engage perpetrators collaboratively in treatment, which may be particularly ineffective with higher-risk criminal populations. Few, if any, of these programs provide formal descriptions of methods they use to engage poorly motivated clients, and there is a paucity of programs tailored for men from minority groups. It is not clear that any of the programs use a relapse prevention framework that ensures follow-up and maintenance for their graduates.

Conclusion

Effectively intervening to reduce family violence is not limited to the provision of programs for violent men. Since domestic violence was placed on the social agenda thirty years ago, advocacy has increased public awareness of the need for action to address this serious social problem. Valuable contributions have been made to the criminal justice system's response to cases of domestic violence. Shelters and other services for abused women have been established, and there has been a general consciousness-raising regarding the full impact of domestic violence on the direct victims and on the community as a whole. Perhaps as a result of these developments, the evidence is accumulating that the rate of intimate violence against women appears to have decreased over the last five years.

Intervention programs for men who are violent against their partners have been conducted since the 1970s, often by individuals with a deep commitment to social change. Their work, however, has not yet provided us with the solid foundation of evidence-based practice required to advance our knowledge of what works in treating these men. It is time to launch a systematic project of research and development into the area of family violence treatment. The need is established, and there is a lot of work to do. We suggest the work begin with an agreed-upon model of intervention that has merit, based on existing research and then systematically evaluate the impact of each element of the intervention. We require ongoing evaluation and monitoring of interventions based on sound standards of practice in order to accumulate the knowledge required to see the field evolve.

Appendix A

Family Violence Program Description

Treatment Targets

To increase offenders':

— Awareness of the consequences of their abusive behavior

— Ability to respond nonabusively

— Ability to change abusive beliefs and behaviors

— Ability to identify high-risk situations and to effectively manage these in the future

Treatment Primer

Candidates will be assessed for readiness to change. For offenders who are identified as appropriate for the program, but are not ready to change, for example, refusing treatment, a treatment primer will be offered to prepare them for engaging in the treatment process. Long-term offenders who are not prioritized for treatment for several years may also be offered the treatment primer.

The treatment primer consists of an information package or resource kit designed to raise awareness of family violence issues and to promote the value of addressing family violence concerns. The approach is collaborative and nonconfrontational. Resource materials will include fact sheets, books, videos, and testimonials and biographies of men who have changed. Offenders who use the resource materials will be given follow-up interviews with the program facilitators to discuss the materials.

Core Program Components: High Intensity Program

Module 1: Motivational Enhancement

Goals:

— Increase interest in the program and motivation to change.

— Develop group cohesion.

— Develop trust in the facilitators and the therapeutic process.

- Increase awareness of the extent and importance of the problem for each participant
- Develop personal goals.

Module 2: Psychoeducational Component

Goals:

- Increase awareness and provide definition of abusive behaviors.
- Develop understanding of the dynamics of family violence.
- Increase understanding of both healthy and unhealthy relationship patterns.
- Introduce relapse prevention and the ABC model for incorporation into autobiographies.
- Increase understanding of the link with substance use.

Module 3: Cultural Component

Goals:

- Examine cultural influences on the development of beliefs and attitudes supportive of family violence.
- Examine the impact of transitions such as immigration, and coping with racism on family dynamics.
- Identify positive values in the culture of origin that support and nurture healthy relationships.

Module 4: Autobiographies

Goals:

- Develop understanding of early abusive relationship patterns in family of origin and their impact on current behavior.
- Develop understanding of personal abusive relationship patterns.
- Identify personal risk factors and show how they contribute to abusive behavior.
- Develop understanding of personal dynamics of abuse and identify a personal abuse cycle.
- Develop an outline that will be the basis for the later presentation of relapse prevention material

Module 5: Skill Building

Goals:

- Identify specific change targets, including thinking patterns, attitudes and beliefs, and behaviors that underlie abuse, using the ABC model.
- Apply the ABC model to management of emotions.
- Develop skills to make targeted changes, for example, challenge thinking errors, irrational beliefs, and controlling behavior and replace with healthy prosocial alternatives.
- Develop social skills such as interpersonal problem solving, conflict resolution, and communication.
- Practice skills using role plays and exercises.
- Integrate skills into understanding of personal patterns.
- Link skills to empathy building and maintenance of healthy relationships.

Module 6: Parenting

Goals:

- Identify the range of abusive behaviors that constitute child abuse.
- Understand the impact of child abuse and being a child witness of abuse on children.
- Identify what abusers can do to assist child witnesses of abuse.
- Discuss some aspects of nonabusive nurturing parenting.
- Discuss how to manage high-risk situations that are triggered over coparenting issues.

Module 7: Relapse Prevention and Risk Management

Goals:

- Identify personal risk factors and high-risk situations for abusive behavior.
- Apply newly developed skills to coping with high-risk situations using role plays and exercises.
- Develop personal relapse prevention/risk management plans.

— Share plans with partners.

— Develop personal follow-up plans for the community, emphasizing the importance of continued treatment, maintenance, and support services.

Module 8: Healthy Relationships

Goals:

— Define healthy relationships.

— Integrate all previous program material under the common theme of healthy relationships.

— Apply program materials to the development of healthier relationships.

— Conduct review and gain closure.

Sample Assessment Battery*

TREATMENT TARGETS PRE AND POST	MEASURES PRE AND POST
Pro-abuse attitudes	Abusive relationships Inventory (Boer, Kroner, Wong, and Cadsky, undated)
Skills deficits and skills development	Vignettes tapping social skills, thinking skills and emotion management; Therapists' ratings on specific scales items on the GAS-FV
Relapse prevention knowledge and readiness	Vignettes tapping relapse prevention knowledge and skills; Therapists' ratings on specific scale items on the GAS-FV
Empathy/perspective taking	Vignettes tapping empathy and social perspective taking; Therapists' ratings on specific scale items on the GAS-FV
Responsivity measure	Treatment Readiness, Treatment Responsivity and Treatment Participation and Gain (Serin and Kennedy, 1997)
Knowledge content	Periodic quizzes on content
Jealousy	Interpersonal Relationship Scale (Hupka and Rusch, 1997)

*A copy of the sample assessment battery can be obtained from the second author. Note that a number of these measures are under copyright.

Mid and Post:
- Therapist rating scales (the GAS-FV)
- Consumer Feedback Form

Risk assessment tools:
- Spousal Assault Risk Assessment Guide general risk for assaultiveness (Kropp et al., 1995); lethality

Profiling tools:
- Extent of substance abuse: CLAI Computerized Lifestyle Assessment Instrument (Skinner, 1994) or the MAST Michigan Alcoholism Screening Test, (Selzer, 1971) and DAST Drug Abuse Screening Test (Skinner, 1992).
- Antisocial orientation/psychopathology: Antisocial Personality Disorder Checklist, Correctional Service of Canada measure based on DSM criteria, and the Psychopathy Checklist (Hare, 1991).
- Borderline Personality Organization (Oldham et al., 1985).
- Intellectual functioning: (for example, Shipley Institute of Living Scale, Zachery, 1986, Western Psychological Services).
- Antisocial Personality Questionnaire (Blackburn and Faecett, 1999).
- Relationship Style Questionnaire (Griffin and Bartholomew, 1994)

Social Desirability
- Paulhus Deception Scale (Paulhus, 1990).

Endnotes

[1] Factors on the DA include: access to/ownership of guns, use of weapons, threats with weapons, threats to kill, serious injury in prior abusive incidents, threats of suicide and alcohol or drug use and forced sex of female partner.

[2] Men with histories of violence against children or those whose race could not be identified were excluded from the study.

[3] Available through the Correctional Service of Canada.

References

Andrews, D. and J. Bonta. 1998. *The Psychology of Criminal Conduct, 2nd Edition*. Cincinnati, Ohio: Anderson Publishing Co.

Babcock. J., C. Green, and C. Robie. In press. Does Batterers' Treatment Work? A Meta-analytic Review of Domestic Violence Treatment. *Clinical Psychology Review.*

Beck, A. T. 1976. *Cognitive Therapy and Emotional Disorders*. New York: International Press.

———. 1999. *Prisoners of Hate: The Cognitive Basis of Anger, Hostility, and Violence*. New York: Harper-Collins.

Blackburn, R. and D. Fawcett. 1999. The Antisocial Personality Questionnaire: An Inventory for Assessing Personality Deviation in Offender Populations. *European Journal of Psychological Assessment.* 15: 14-24.

Boe, R. 1998. *A Two-Year Follow-Up of Federal Offenders Who Participated in the Adult Basic Education ABE Program*. Research Report, R-60, Ottawa: Ontario. Correctional Service of Canada.

Boer, D. P., D. G. Kroner, S. Wong, and O. Cadsky. Undated. Assessing the Dysfunctional Beliefs of Spouse Assaulters: Development and Validation of Abusive Relationships Inventory. Unpublished Manuscript.

Campbell, J. C. 1995. Prediction of Homicide of and by Battered Women. In J. C. Campbell, ed. *Assessing Dangerousness: Violence by Sexual Offenders, Batterers, and Child Abusers*. Thousand Oaks, California: Sage.

Check, J. V. P. 1984. *The Hostility Toward Women Scale*. Unpublished doctoral dissertation, University of Manitoba, Manitoba.

Cunningham, A., P. G. Jaffe, L. Baker, T. Dick, S. Malla, N. Mazaheri, and S. Poisson. 1998. Theory-Derived Explanations of Male Violence against Female Partners: Literature Update and Related Implications for Treatment and Evaluation. Paper presented for Reintegration Programs, Ottawa, Ontario: Correctional Service of Canada.

Daly, J., T. Power, and E. Gondolf. 2001. Predictors of Batterer Program Attendance. *Journal of Interpersonal Violence.* 16(10): 971-991.

Davis, R. C. and B. G.Taylor, 1999. Does Batterer Treatment Reduce Violence? A Synthesis of the Literature. *Women and Domestic Violence: An Interdisciplinary Approach.* 102: 69-93.

Deffenbacher, J. L., D. A. Story, A. D. Brandon, J. A. Hogg, and S. L. Hazaleus. 1988. Cognitive and Cognitive-Relaxation Treatments of Anger. *Cognitive Therapy and Research.* 12: 167-184.

Dobash, R. E. and R. P. Dobash. 1999. Criminal Justice Programmes for Men Who Assault Their Partners. In C. R. Hollin, ed. *Handbook of Offender Assessment and Treatment.* Chichester, England: John Wiley and Sons.

―――. 2000. Evaluating Criminal Justice Interventions for Domestic Violence. *Crime and Delinquency.* 462: 252-270.

Dowden, C., K. Blanchette, and R. Serin. 1999. *Anger Management Programming for Federal Male Inmates: An Effective Intervention.* Research Report R-82. Ottawa, Ontario: Correctional Service of Canada.

Dunford, F. 2000. The San Diego Navy Experiment: An Assessment of Interventions for Men Who Assault Their Wives. *Journal of Consulting and Clinical Psychology.* 683: 468-476.

Dutton, D. 1995a. A Scale for Measuring Propensity for Abusiveness. *Journal of Family Violence.* 102: 203-221.

Dutton, D. G. 1995b. *The Domestic Abuse of Women: Psychological and Criminal Justice Perspectives.* Vancouver, British Columbia: UBC Press.

Dutton, D. and P. R. Kropp. 2000. A Review of Domestic Violence Risk Instruments. *Trauma, Violence and Abuse.* 1(2): 171-181.

Dutton, D. G. and G. Kerry. 1999. Modus Operandi and Personality Disorders in Incarcerated Spousal Killers. *International Journal of Law and Psychiatry.* 223(4): 287-299.

Dutton, D. G., M. Bodnarchuk, R. Kropp, S. D. Hart, and J. R. P. Ogloff, 1997. Wife Assault Treatment and Criminal Recidivism: An 11-Year Follow-up. *International Journal of Offender Therapy and Comparative Criminology.* 411: 2-23.

Dutton, D. G., M. A. Landolt, A. Starzomski, and M. Bodnarchuk. 2001. Validation of the Propensity for Abusiveness Scale in Diverse Male Populations. *Journal of Family Violence.* 161: 59-73.

Edleson, J. L. and M. Syers. 1990. Relative Effectiveness of Group Treatments for Men Who Batter. *Social Work Research and Abstracts.* 26(2): 10-17.

Ellis, A. 1977. *Anger — How to Live with and without It.* Secaucus, New Jersey: Citadel Press.

Feindler, E. L., R. B. Ecton, D. Kingsley, and D. R. Dubey. 1986. Group Anger-control Training for Institutionalized Psychiatric Male Adolescents. *Behaviour Therapy.* 17(2): 109-123.

Gendreau, P. 1996. The Principles of Effective Intervention with Offenders. In A. T. Harland, ed. *Choosing Correctional Options that Work: Defining the Demand and Evaluating the Supply.* Thousand Oaks, California: Sage.

Gondolf, E. W. 1999. A Comparison of Reassault Rates in Four Batterer Programs: Do Court Referral, Program Length and Services Matter? *Journal of Interpersonal Violence.* 15: 428-437.

Gondolf, E. W. 2000. Reassault at 30 Months after Batterer Program Intake. *International Journal of Offender Therapy and Comparative Criminology.* 44: 111-128.

Gondolf, E. W. 2001. Limitations of Experimental Evaluation of Batterer Programs. *Trauma, Violence and Abuse.* 2(1): 79-88.

Gondolf, E. and O. Williams. 2001. Culturally Focused Batterer Counseling for African American Men. *Trauma, Violence and Abuse.* 2(4): 283-295.

Griffin, D. W. and K. Bartholomew. 1994. The Metaphysics of Measurement: The Case of Adult Attachment. In K. Bartholomew and D. Perlman, eds. *Advances in Personal Relationships*, Vol. 5. London: Jessica Kingsley.

Hanson, K. R., O. Cadsky, A. Harris, and C. Lalonde. 1997. Correlates of Battering among 997 Men: Family History, Adjustment, and Attitudinal Differences. *Violence and Victims.* 12(3): 191-208.

Hanson, K. R. and S. Wallace-Capretta. 2000. *Predicting Recidivism Among Male Batterers.* Report submitted to the Department of the Solicitor General Canada. Cat. No.: JS42-91/2000.

Hamberger, L. K., J. M. Lohr, D. Bonge and D. F. Tolin. 1996. A Large Sample Empirical Typology of Male Spouse Abusers and its Relationship to Dimensions of Abuse. *Violence and Victims.* 114: 277-292.

Hare, R. D. 1991. *The Hare Psychopathy Checklist-Revised.* Toronto: Multi-Health Systems.

Hastings, J. E. and L. K. Hamberger. 1988. Personality Characteristics of Spouse Abusers: A Controlled Comparison. *Violence and Victims.* 31: 31-48.

Hazaleus, S. and J. Deffenbacher. 1986. Relaxation and Cognitive Treatments of Anger. *Journal of Consulting and Clinical Psychology.* 54: 222-226.

Hickey, E. W. 1991. *Serial Murderers and Their Victims*. Belmont, California.: Wadsworth, Inc.

Holtzworth-Munroe, A. and G. L. Stuart. 1994. Typologies of Male Batterers: Three Sub-Types and Differences among Them. *Psychological Bulletin*. 1163: 476-497.

Howell, M. J. and K. L. Pugliesi. 1988. Husbands Who Harm: Predicting Spousal Violence by Men. *Journal of Family Violence*. 3: 15-27.

Hughes, G. V. 1993. Anger Management Program Outcomes. *Forum on Corrections Research*. 5: 1, 5-9.

Hupka, R. B. and P. A Rusch. 1977. The Interpersonal Relationship Scale. Paper presented at the annual meeting of the Western Psychological Association, Seattle, Washington.

Jones, A. and E. Gondolf. In press. Assessing the Effect of Batterer Program Completion on Reassault: An Instrumental Variables Analysis. *Journal of Quantitative Criminology*.

Kantor Kaufman, G. and M. A. Straus. 1990. The "Drunken Bum" Theory of Wife Beating. In M. A. Straus and R. J. Gelles, eds. *Physical Violence in American Families: Risk Factors and Adaptations to Violence in 8,145 Families*. New Brunswick, New Jersey: Transaction Publishers.

Kerry, G. 2000. Typologies of Federal Offenders Convicted of Intimate Femicide. Workshop Presentation, International Community Corrections Association Conference. Ottawa, Ontario.

Kropp, P. R. and S. D. Hart. 2000. The Spousal Assault Risk Assessment SARA Guide: Reliability and Validity in Adult Male Offenders. *Law and Human Behavior*. 24(1): 101-118.

Kropp, P. R., S. D. Hart, C. D. Webster, and D. Eaves. 1995. *Manual for the Spousal Assault Risk Assessment Guide, 2nd ed.* Vancouver, British Columbia: The British Columbia Institute on Family Violence.

Levens, B. R and D. G. Dutton. 1980. *The Social Service Role of the Police: Domestic Crisis Intervention*. Ottawa, Ontario: Solicitor General of Canada.

Levesque, D. A. 1998. Violence Desistance among Battering Men: Existing Interventions and the Application of the Transtheoretical Model of Change. Unpublished doctoral dissertation, University of Rhode Island, Kingston, Rhode Island.

Leyton, E. 1986. *Hunting Humans*. Toronto: McClelland and Stewart Ltd.

Lipsey, M. 1995. What Do We Learn from 400 Research Studies on the Effectiveness of Treatment with Juvenile Delinquents? In J. McGuire, ed. *What Works: Reducing Reoffending*. Chichester, England: John Wiley.

Losel, F. 1996. Effective Correctional Programming: What Empirical Research Tells Us and What it Doesn't. *Forum on Corrections Research*. 8: 33-36.

Maiuro, R. D., T. S. Cahn, and P. P. Vitaliano. 1986. Assertiveness Deficits and Hostility in Domestically Violent Men. *Violence and Victims*. 14: 279-289.

Maruna, S. 2001. *Making Good: How Ex-convicts Reform and Rebuild Their Lives*. Washington, D.C.: American Psychological Association.

Marzuk, P. M., K. Tardif, and C. S. Hirsch. 1992. The Epidemiology of Murder-Suicide. *Journal of American Medical Association*. 267(23): 3179-3183.

Moffitt, T. E., R. F. Krueger, A. Caspi, and J. Fagan. 2000. Partner Abuse and General Crime: How Are They the Same? How Are They Different? *Criminology*. 38(1): 199-232.

Morton, K., C. W. Runyan, K. E. Moracco, and J. Butts. 1998. Partner Homicide-Suicide Involving Female Homicide Victims: A Population-based Study in North Carolina, 1988-1992. *Violence and Victims*. 13: 91-106.

Miller, W. R. and S. Rollnick, S. 1991. *Motivational Interviewing: Preparing People to Change Addictive Behavior*. New York: The Guilford Press.

Oldham, J., J. Clarkin, A. Applebaum, A. Carr, P. Kernberg, A. Lottermen, and G. Haas. 1985. A Self-report Instrument for Borderline Personality Organization. In T. H. McGlashan, ed. *The Borderline: Current Empirical Research. The Progress in Psychiatry Series*. Washington, D.C.: American Psychiatric Press, Inc.

O'Leary, K. D. and C. Murphy. 1999. Clinical Issues in the Assessment of Partner Violence. In R. T. Ammerman and M. Hergen, eds. *Assessment of Family Violence: A Clinical and Legal Sourcebook, Second Edition*. Toronto: John Wiley Books.

Paulhus, D. L. 1990. Measurement and Control Response Bias. In J. P. Robinson, P. R. Shaver, and L. S. Wrightsman, eds. *Measurement of Personality and Social Psychological Attitudes*. San Diego: Academic Press.

Pence, E. and M. Paymar. 1993. *Education Groups for Men Who Batter: The Duluth Model*. New York: Springer.

Prochaska, J. O. and C. C. DiClemente. 1983. Stages and Processes of Self Change in Smoking: Toward an Integrative Model of Change. *Journal of Consulting and Clinical Psychology*. 5: 390-395.

Prochaska, J. O., C. C. DiClemente, and J. C. Norcross. 1992. In Search of How People Change: Application to Addictive Behaviors. *American Psychologist.* 47(9): 1102-1114.

Quinsey, V. L., G. T. Harris, M. E. Rice, and C. Cormier. 1998. *Violent Offenders: Appraising and Managing Risk.* Washington, D.C.: American Psychological Association.

Renzetti, C. M. 1997. Violence in Lesbian and Gay Relationships. In L. L. O'Toole and J. R. Schiffman, eds. *Gender Violence: Interdisciplinary Perspectives.* New York: New York University Press.

Robinson, D. and J. Taylor. 1995. *The Incidence of Family Violence Perpetrated by Federal Offenders: A File Review Study.* Ottawa, Ontario: Research Branch, Correctional Service of Canada.

Rooney, J. and K. Hanson. 2001. Predicting Attrition from Treatment Programs for Abusive Men. *Journal of Family Violence.*162: 131-149.

Rogers, K. 1994. Wife Assault: The Findings of a National Survey. *Juristat.* 14(9).

Rollnick S. and W. R. Miller. 1995. What Is Motivational Interviewing? *Behavioral and Cognitive Psychotherapy.* 23: 325-334.

Rosenfeld, B. D. 1992. Court-ordered Treatment of Spouse Abuse. *Clinical Psychology Review.* 12: 205-226.

Rosenbaum, A, R. Geffner, and S. Benjamin. 1997. A Biopsychological Model for Understanding Relationship Aggression. *Journal of Aggression, Maltreatment and Trauma Press.* 1(1): 57-79.

Saunders, D. G. 1992. A Typology of Men Who Batter: Three Types Derived from Cluster Analysis. *American Journal of Orthopsychiatry.* 62(2): 264-275.

———. 1995. Prediction of Wife Assault. In J. C. Campbell, ed. *Assessing the Risk of Dangerousness.* Newbury Park, California: Sage.

Saunders, D. G., A. B. Lynch, M. Grayson, and D. Linz. 1987. The Inventory of Beliefs about Wife Beating: The Construction and Initial Validation of a Measure of Beliefs and Attitudes. *Violence and Victims.* 21: 39-57.

Selzer, M. L. 1971. The Michigan Alcoholism Screening Test: The Quest for a New Diagnostic Instrument. *American Journal of Psychiatry.* 127: 89-94.

Shepard, M. F. and J. A. Campbell. 1992. The Abusive Behavior Inventory: A Measure of Psychological and Physical Abuse. *Journal of Interpersonal Violence.* 73: 291-305.

Shover, N. 1983. The Later Stages of Ordinary Offender Careers. *Social Problems.* 312: 208-218.

Skinner, H. A. 1992. The Drug Abuse Screening Test. *Addictive Behaviors.* 7: 363-371.

———. 1994. *Computerized Lifestyle Assessment.* Toronto: Multi-Health Systems.

Sonkin, D. G. 1997. *The Perpetrator Assessment Handbook.* Sausalito, California: Volcano.

Spence, J. T., R. Helrich, and J. Strapp. 1972. *A Short Version of the Attitudes Toward Women Scale.* Report No. TC007199. Princeton, New Jersey: Educational Testing Service ETS Test Collection Library. ETS Document Tracking No. TC007199.

Statistics Canada. 1993. *Highlights from The Violence Against Women Survey.* The Daily. Ottawa, Ontario: Statistics Canada.

Steadman, H., E. Silver, J. Monahan, P. Appelbaum, P. Robbins, E. Mulvey, T. Grisso, L. Roth, and S. Banks. 2000. A Classification Tree Approach to the Development of Actuarial Violence Risk Assessment Tools. *Law and Human Behavior.* 24: 83-100.

Stewart, L. and R. Rowe. 2001. Problems of Self Regulation among Adult Offenders. In L. L. Motiuk and R. C. Serin, eds. *Compendium 2000 on Effective Correctional Programming.* 1: 113-121.

Straus, M. A. and R. J. Gelles. 1986. Societal Change and Change in Family Violence from 1975 to 1985 as Revealed by Two National Surveys. *Journal of Marriage and the Family.* 48(August): 465-479.

Straus, M. A., R. J. Gelles, and S. K. Steinmetz. 1980. *Behind Closed Doors: Violence in the American Family.* New York: Doubleday.

Straus, M. A., S. L. Hamby, S. Boney-McCoy, and D. B. Sugarman. 1996. The Revised Conflict Tactics Scale CTS2: Development and Preliminary Psychometric Data. *Journal of Family Issues.* 173: 283-316.

Suderman, M. and P. G. Jaffe. 1999. Children and Adolescents who Witness Violence: New Directions in Intervention and Prevention. In R. D. Peters, R. McMahon, and D. A. Wolfe, eds. *Child Abuse: New Directions in Prevention and Treatment Across a Lifespan.* Thousand Oaks, California: Sage.

Sugarman, D. B. and S. L. Frankel. 1996. Patriarchal Ideology and Wide Assault: A Meta-analytic Review. *Journal of Family Violence.* 111: 13-40.

Taylor, B. G., R. C. Davis, and C. D. Maxwell. 2001. The Effects of a Group Batterer Treatment Program: A Randomized Experiment in Brooklyn. *Justice Quarterly.* 18(1): 171-201.

Tolman, R. M. 1999. The Validation of the Psychological Maltreatment of Women Inventory. *Violence and Victims.* 141: 25-37.

Wexler, A. 2000. Can Typologies of Male Batterers Be Generalized to Populations of Federal Inmates? Unpublished master's thesis. Carleton University.

White, R. and E. Gondolf. 2000. Implications of Personality Profiles for Batterer Treatment. *Journal of Interpersonal Violence.* 155: 467-488.

Wilson, M. I. and M. Daly. 1996. Male Sexual Proprietariness and Violence against Wives. *Current Directions in Psychological Science.* 51: 2-7.

Yllo, K. A. and M. Straus. 1990. Patriarchal Violence against Wives: The Impact of Structural and Normative Factors. In, M. A. Straus and R. J. Gelles, eds. *Physical Violence in American Families: Risk Factors and Adaptations to Violence in 8,145 Families.* New Brunswick, New Jersey: Transaction Publishers.

Zachary, R. A. 1986. *The Shipley Institute of Living Skills — Revised Manual.* Los Angeles: Western Psychological Services.

THE VIABILITY OF MENTORING AS A CORRECTIONAL STRATEGY: A LOOK AT WHAT WORKS

7

Betsy A. Matthews
  Assistant Professor, Department of Correctional and
    Juvenile Justice Studies
  Eastern Kentucky University
  Richmond, Kentucky

Over time, informal relationships between learned advisors and younger, less experienced proteges have served as a vehicle for transmitting wisdom, expertise, and support from one generation to the next. It was not until the early 1900s, however, that an organized mentoring movement emerged whereby social service organizations used programmatically created relationships between adult volunteers and at-risk youths as a mechanism for fostering personal growth and keeping kids out of trouble (Beiswinger, 1985). Today, mentoring programs for youths are found in a variety of settings including schools, churches, local community organizations (for example, YMCA), and specialized mentoring organizations (for example, Big Brothers/Big Sisters and Boys and Girls Clubs) (National Mentoring Partnership, 1998). Additionally, many businesses and other professional organizations are using mentors to help adults develop various career-related competencies (American Correctional Association, 1996; Haensly and Parsons, 1993).

Mentoring has received substantial support from key policymakers. It was a favored initiative of the first Bush administration's Points of Light Foundation (Freedman, 1991). More recently, the Juvenile Mentoring Program (JUMP) was established as part of the 1992 amendments to the Juvenile Justice and Delinquency Prevention Act of 1974 (Office of Juvenile Justice and Delinquency Prevention, 1998). In recent years, there has been a growing interest in mentoring programs within both adult and juvenile justice systems. This broad support for mentoring programs is largely due to anecdotal success stories. Mentoring is a feel-good concept and, as such, it appeals to many audiences. Recent studies that have provided evidence of mentoring's potential for preventing crime and other antisocial behaviors give teeth to these emotional reasons for adopting mentoring as a key correctional strategy.

Before correctional and juvenile justice agencies adopt mentoring programs as the new panacea, however, they must somehow marry this feel-good approach with the growing body of knowledge about what works to change the behavior of offenders, and more specifically, to reduce recidivism. This chapter is designed to facilitate this marriage by focusing on two key questions: (1) what evidence exists to suggest that mentoring is a viable correctional strategy, and (2) what factors are associated with the development of effective mentoring relationships? The author hopes that this information will help agencies objectively assess mentoring's value as a correctional strategy and provide some guidance for developing theory and research-driven programs.

Mentoring Within the Justice Context: Is it Viable?

This section of the chapter addresses the viability of mentoring programs within the justice context by discussing how they support organizational needs and philosophies, assessing their empirical and theoretical relevance as a crime control strategy, and reporting results of available outcome studies.

Organizational Needs and Philosophies

The unprecedented increase in criminal justice populations over the past twenty-five years has stretched resources to the limit. Many state prisons are operating at 15 percent of their rated capacity (Bureau of

Justice Statistics, 2001), and the national average for probation and parole caseloads has reached 124 and 67, respectively (Camp and Camp, 2000). Overburdened correctional staff have succumbed to the pressures of large caseloads by routinizing their approach to working with offenders. Thus, the helping role of corrections has been subverted to activities and strategies designed to control an offender within the correctional program. Recognizing the limitations of this routinized and control-oriented approach, correctional agencies are trying new ways to enhance services for offenders, many of which involve the use of volunteers. For example, recognizing the limits of traditional probation services, Michigan's 36th District Court in Detroit instituted a program called Partners Against Crime that was designed to enhance traditional probation through a volunteer-probationer friendship (Frentz, 1996). Volunteers provided offenders with a one-to-one relationship with a positive role model who could offer support and assistance and help offenders to resolve problems in a law-abiding, productive way. Advocates of mentoring within the justice system believe these types of volunteer services fill an important void in probation services by interjecting a more humanistic approach to working with offenders (Frentz, 1996; Leenhouts, 2000).

Mentors may be an invaluable resource by enhancing basic correctional services or by providing specific types of services that have been lacking historically. One specific area in which mentoring programs are beginning to emerge is as part of the reentry phase of corrections. In response to the high failure rates within the first few months of release from correctional institutions, the New York City Jail and the departments of corrections in Massachusetts, Delaware, Oklahoma, and Georgia have instituted mentoring programs to facilitate the reintegration process (Chandler, 1996; Connelly, 1995; Justice Research and Statistics Association, 1998; Knight and Heliotis, 1996; Lisante and Navon, 2000). Mentors assist offenders in developing a reentry plan prior to their release and in providing consistent support for carrying out the plan in the community.

In addition to the more obvious resource benefits, mentoring and other volunteer programs can enhance the public image of corrections. Noting that the credibility of corrections has been threatened by high failure rates, Terry (2000) states that volunteer "efforts have helped make court [and correctional] processes more accessible, understandable, and visible" (p. 17). Citizens who have served as mentors to adult or juvenile offenders report a greater understanding of the problems experienced by offenders and the challenges facing the criminal and juvenile justice systems (Connelly, 1995; Mecartney, Styles, and Morrow, 1994). As a result of this increased exposure and understanding, mentors have the potential to become correction's best advocates.

The appeal of mentoring is as philosophical as it is pragmatic. One of the most persistent trends in corrections is to shift from an offender-focused model of justice to a model of community and restorative justice that "places the community and victims at the center of justice activities and efforts" (Barajas, 1998, p. 2). Advocates of restorative justice view crime as a violation of individuals and interpersonal relationships (Zehr and Mika, 1997). As such, they seek to repair these relationships in three ways: (1) by providing victims with support, opportunities for input, and restitution; (2) by holding offenders accountable for the harm they caused; and (3) by empowering communities to develop constructive responses to crime that recognize our mutual responsibilities to one another (Pranis, 1998). Toward these ends, correctional agencies are seeking community input and developing opportunities for citizen involvement. Mentoring programs meet this need by engaging community members in the justice process in a way that encourages the development of positive relationships between offenders and community members and promotes healing and reintegration.

Despite the apparent organizational fit between corrections and mentoring, there are several barriers to incorporating mentoring programs into correctional strategies. First, regardless of their volunteer nature, mentoring programs have attached costs for the program structure needed to recruit, screen, train, and match volunteers to offenders (Sherman, 1997). These costs fall far below the cost of other types of correctional programs, however, and if, as early studies are indicating, mentoring programs are effective in reducing substance abuse and delinquency, they have the potential to produce long-term cost savings. A study of Big Brothers/Big Sisters programs estimated the cost to be about $1,000 per match (Tierney, Grossman, and Resch, 1995). The cost of a Women's Mentoring Program at a Massachusetts Correctional Institution was less than $2,000 per inmate (Knight and Heliotis, 1996). Yet, the actual cost-benefits of mentoring are not yet clear. What is clear is that a failure to recognize program costs may undermine a program's effectiveness. Two juvenile justice agencies that attempted to institute mentoring programs without allocating additional resources were unsuccessful, with less than one-fourth of the matches meeting regularly enough to sustain meaningful relationships (Mecartney, Styles, and Morrow, 1994).

Correctional personnel working with a mentoring program for adult offenders in Oklahoma indicated that agency administrators underestimated the amount of time it takes to prepare mentors and offenders for the relationship and to monitor the interactions between the pairs. Because of this miscalculation, or oversight, no additional human resources were allocated, and correctional staff felt burdened by the extra duties associated with the program (Connelly, 1995).

Second, experience suggests that engaging citizens as volunteers for justice- and crime-related initiatives is a challenge. Recruiting and sustaining citizen involvement were the most difficult aspects of community policing and crime prevention programs (Grinc, 1994; Skogan, 1990). Mentoring programs for delinquent youths have encountered similar problems. Survey findings reveal that citizens favor early intervention programs over prisons as a solution to crime (Cullen, Wright, Brown, Moon, Blankenship, and Applegate, 1998). However, when citizens were approached about serving as mentors for youths in two juvenile justice agencies, they cited fear of the youth as an impediment to their involvement (Mecartney, Styles, and Morrow, 1994). Thus, although survey findings reveal that citizens favor prevention and early intervention programs over prisons as a solution to crime (Cullen, Wright, Brown, Moon, Blankenship, and Applegate, 1998), the willingness of citizens to participate in such programs is mixed.

Overcoming the negative perceptions of offenders is only part of the problem in recruiting volunteers for mentoring programs. More basic is the problem of demographics of who needs mentors and who volunteers. Although males and minority groups are overrepresented among the offender population, they are underrepresented among volunteers (Fisher and Cole, 1993). This is particularly problematic for mentoring programs whose success is dependent upon matching people with volunteers with whom they can identify. Third, mentoring may be an appropriate intervention for youths, but how receptive are adult offenders to the idea of being paired with a volunteer in a "mentoring" relationship? Although this issue has not been explored fully in research, some anecdotal evidence suggests that adults may resist the concept of mentoring.[1] In addition, women offenders who were questioned about their interest in participating in a mentoring program focus groups with women offenders were offended by the idea. It seems that, for these women, the term "mentoring" was associated with programs for children. As such, the suggestion that they might need a mentor evoked feelings of inferiority and was perceived as an insult. The women were much more receptive to the concept of mentoring when it was couched in terms of a "probation aid" or "friend" who would be available for support and assistance in times of need.

A review of organizational needs and philosophies suggests that volunteer mentoring programs have the capacity to supplement existing correctional services and enhance the public's image of corrections. Moreover, there is a clear link between mentoring programs and community and restorative justice initiatives that have gained momentum across the United States. Until correctional agencies can overcome recruitment obstacles and negative offender perceptions, however, the long-term organizational benefits of mentoring will remain elusive.

Empirical and Theoretical Relevance

A review of the empirical literature on resiliency and protective factors suggests that mentoring programs have merit as a strategy for reducing a youth's likelihood of delinquency. Resiliency refers to the capacity for successful adaptation to disruptive, stressful, or challenging circumstances (Richardson, Neiger, Jensen, and Kumpfer, 1990; Cicchetti and Garmezy, 1993). Protective factors are what moderate the effects of adversity and enhance resilient responses to risk (Hawkins, Catalano, and Miller, 1992). Three categories of protective factors have been identified in the literature:

- positive personality and social orientation
- warm and supportive relationships with family members or other adults
- prosocial family and community norms (Garmezy, 1985; Howell, 1997)

A supportive relationship with a caring adult has consistently emerged in research as an important protective factor (Garmezy, 1985; Hawkins, Catalano, and Miller, 1992; Rutter, 1987; Werner and Smith, 1992). Researchers have found that supportive relationships with adults mitigate the effects of high-risk environments by providing a youth with a sense of "felt-security" (Bretherton, 1985; Mecartney et al., 1994), by improving a youth's self-concept (Unger and Wandersman, 1985), and by promoting self-efficacy (Werner, 1993). Sadly, however, high rates of poverty, increased divorce rates, and the need for both parents to work outside the home have left many youths without this much needed supervision, support, and affection (Howell, 1997; Office of Juvenile Justice and Delinquency Prevention,

1998). It is these youths that are most vulnerable to delinquency (Werner, 1993) and for whom mentoring programs may prove to be most beneficial.

In addition to this, the empirical support for mentoring programs also have theoretical relevance. Social learning theorists argue that most of our learning occurs vicariously, by observing and imitating others (Akers, 1985; Bandura, 1986). Thus, the concept of modeling becomes important when trying to promote positive behavioral change. A mentor can serve as a positive role model for offenders to imitate. One example is the Positive Role Model Program in Newport, Rhode Island (Bureau of Justice Assistance, 1997). The program uses female college students to model positive behaviors for delinquent girls in a group home. The college students expose the girls to positive leisure activities and educational and career opportunities and, by example, teach the girls how to establish personal boundaries and resist peer pressure.

Several meta-analyses have revealed that delinquency programs that employ social learning strategies are effective in reducing delinquency (Andrews, Zinger, Hoge, Bonta, Gendreau, and Cullen, 1990; Lipsey and Wilson, 1998). Other empirical support for social learning approaches comes from studies on the correlates of crime which have found that having antisocial peers and criminal parents substantially increases a youth's likelihood of engaging in delinquent behavior (Elliot, Huizinga, and Ageton, 1985; Farrington, 1995; Patterson and Dishion, 1985). As will be discussed later in this chapter, the success of programs rooted in social learning theory is dependent on the characteristics of the models.

Within the literature on mentoring programs for youths, the concept of mentoring is most clearly linked to control theory, a prominent criminological paradigm. The primary theoretical assumption of control theory is that people conform because of the presence of social constraints. This idea has been advanced by a number of control theorists (Nye, 1958; Reckless, 1967; Reiss, 1951). It was Hirschi (1969), however, that conceptualized these constraints as a "social bond" that forms between an individual and society.

In his social bond theory, Hirschi (1969) identified four key elements of the social bond including attachment, commitment, involvement, and belief. Attachment refers to feelings of closeness, admiration, and positive identification with others. The stronger the attachments, the more sensitive a person is to the opinions and expectations of others and the more a person is bound by societal norms. Commitment reflects a person's "stakes in conformity." That is, an individual who has an investment in conventionality (for example, education and work) will not endanger this investment by engaging in deviant activities. Involvement refers to the amount of time spent in conventional activities such as studying or extracurricular activities. An individual engrossed in these activities will not have time to engage in deviant acts. Belief is defined as a person's views regarding the moral validity of society's rules. Those who do not hold strong beliefs in society's rules are more likely to violate them.

Attachment is viewed as the most important element of the social bond and is typically examined in the context of youths' relationships to parents, teachers, and peers (Curran and Renzetti, 1994). Although research on the effects of attachment to teachers (Gottfredson, 1986; Liska and Reed, 1985) and peers (LaGrange and White, 1985) is equivocal, research is generally supportive of an inverse relationship between attachment to parents and delinquency (Agnew, 1985; Krohn and Massey, 1980; Hirschi, 1969; Rankin and Wells, 1990; Wiatrowski, Griswold, and Roberts, 1981; Witchcoff, Knight, and Tripodi, 1996). In a reanalysis of Glueck and Glueck's data, Sampson and Laub (1993) found that the concept of attachment played an important role in crime desistance for adults. Adults who were attached to their spouses and had stable jobs had stakes in conformity and, as such, were less likely to engage in crime and other antisocial behavior that could damage their reputation and relationships (Sampson and Laub, 1993). Mentoring programs are perhaps the best example of programs that are designed to develop a social bond and, thus, bolster peoples' stake in conformity.

Some criminologists would argue that, rather than social constraint, the real benefit of mentoring comes from the social support that a mentoring relationship can provide (Cullen, 1994; Currie, 1985). These authors have argued that the deterrent and incapacitative natures of current criminal justice policies are inherently nonsupportive and that they erode community life. What is needed, they suggest, are policies that promote the development of supportive social networks that are characterized by reciprocity and trustworthiness and that insulate people from the effects of negative environments and circumstances. On a small scale, mentoring programs offer a strategy for providing people with this much needed social support.

Lin (1986, p. 18) defines social support as "the perceived or actual instrumental and/or expressive provisions supplied by the community, social networks, and confiding partners." Instrumental provisions refer to any type of assistance that is provided to facilitate the achievement of a goal including more tangible assistance, such as transportation to a job interview or money for rent, or less tangible assistance in the form of advice or guidance on important issues such as parenting or money management (Lin, 1986; Vaux, 1988). The expressive provisions of social support refer to the emotional support, affection, and sense of belonging that can be attained from a relationship with an individual or a larger social network (Vaux, 1988). Both the instrumental and expressive functions of social support are reflected in mentoring programs. Mentoring programs for adults, for example, typically focus on the provision of instrumental support that is designed to facilitate the development of a specific competency (for example, reading, parenting, or job seeking skills).

Mentoring programs for youths, whose overriding purpose is to provide youths with a one-to-one friendship with a caring adult (Grossman and Garry, 1997), seem to be more reflective of the expressive function of social support. Although the provision of social support has not been directly tested as a correctional strategy, there are reasons to believe that it may be a viable approach to reducing recidivism. Drawing on the work of Hagan (1993) and Sullivan (1989), Cullen (1994) argues that differential levels of social support affect the amount of "social capital" youths have available to them for mobilizing resources on their behalf. For example, youths with high levels of social support are able to use these social relationships, or personal connections, to gain access to the legitimate labor market and, in that way, may be able to avoid a criminal lifestyle. Cullen (1994) also argues that the stress-reducing effects of social support help people to cope with adverse circumstances and, in turn, avoid crime and delinquency.

All three of these theories have fairly substantial empirical support. It is unclear, however, which theoretical constructs account for the recent success that mentoring programs are having in reducing delinquent and other antisocial behaviors. Is it the learning that takes place? Is it the stake in conformity that a caring relationship provides, or is it the social support offered during times of stress? These questions cannot be answered until mentoring programs are studied with more theoretical specificity. Chances are that each of these theoretical constructs contributes to the success of mentoring, and that their importance varies according to the needs of the offender. Certainly, it can be argued that mentoring programs are theoretically relevant and, therefore, that they offer promise as a crime-reduction strategy.

Results of Mentoring Evaluations

A 1997 review of mentoring evaluations led researchers from the University of Maryland to conclude that mentoring programs were "promising enough to merit further replication and evaluation" (Sherman, 1997, p. 33). Since that review, more studies have been conducted that provide additional support for mentoring's potential as a delinquency prevention strategy. Less evidence is available to support mentoring's application to adult offender populations.

Programs for Youth

Table 1 (page 216) provides a brief overview of the methodologies, program descriptions, and outcomes of five studies that used an experimental design to study the effectiveness of mentoring programs for youth. Each of these studies involved the random assignment of cases to either a treatment group in which the youth was assigned to a mentor or to a no-treatment control group. The results are mixed. Early studies by Goodman (1972) and Dicken, Bryson, and Kass (1977) reported no significant improvements in various attitudes and behaviors of mentored youths as compared to youths in the control group. Fo and O'Donnell's (1975) evaluation of the "buddy system" found that study outcomes varied depending on the youths' past history of delinquency. For those youths who had committed a major offense in the year prior to the study, participation in a buddy system contributed to less involvement in delinquency during the one-year follow-up period than youths in the no-treatment group. The opposite was true for youths who had no history of major offenses. For these youths, participation in the buddy system contributed to significantly greater involvement in delinquency.

Two recent evaluations revealed more favorable results for the effects of mentoring. First, a study of eight Big Brothers/Big Sisters programs found that youths who participated in the mentoring program were significantly less likely than youths in the control group to start using drugs or to skip school, earned slightly higher grades, and had improved relationships with parents and peers (Tierney, Grossman, and Resch, 1995). Second, a study of a multimodal drug prevention program for middle school students provided additional support for the preventive capacity of mentoring programs. In this study, the researchers compared the outcomes of three randomly assigned study groups: (1) a no-treatment group; (2) a group who participated in life skills training, attended a parent workshop, and performed community service; and (3) a group who, in addition to these three program components described in number 2, received mentoring from older adults (LoSciuto, Rajala, Townsend, and Taylor et al., 1996). The results revealed significantly better outcomes for both of the groups participating in the drug prevention program as compared to the no-treatment group. The group who received mentoring, however, fared the best with better attitudes toward school, better school attendance, and lower rates of substance abuse than the group who participated in the other components of the drug prevention program but did not have the benefit of mentoring.

One can only speculate as to the reasons for the differences in outcomes among these studies. In his review of the mentoring literature, Sherman (1997) suggested that these contrasting results between studies could be a reflection of the differences between programs in the early stages of development, (Dickens, Bryson, and Kass, 1977; Fo and O'Donnell, 1975; Goodman, 1972) and stable, standardized programs such as Big Brothers/Big Sisters. Perhaps, it is a matter of who served as the mentors that is at issue. For example, college students served as mentors in two of the studies that revealed no significant differences between treatment groups (Dicken, Bryson, and Kass, 1977; Goodman, 1972), while the other programs that were evaluated used either elders or volunteers with a broad spectrum of characteristics. Although colleges and universities are often good resources for volunteers, research has found that student's academic schedules interfere with the demands of a mentoring relationship (Tierney and Branch, 1992; Sipe, 2001). However, the fact that the study of Dickens et al. and his colleagues (1977) found no relationship between participation in mentoring and improved attitudes or behavior of youths may be a function of the follow-up period of sixteen weeks, a period too short to determine whether change has occurred. Research conducted by Morrow and Styles (1995) suggests that it takes at least four months for programmatically created mentoring relationships to develop fully and become more than a paper match.

Other, less scientifically rigorous studies, offer additional evidence of mentoring's capacity for producing positive changes in youths (*see* Table 2, page 220). Through the use of repeated measures at intake to the mentoring program and again at the end of a one-year follow-up period, two studies (Mecartney et al., 1994; Tierney and Branch, 1992) found that youths felt more in control of their personal lives, and one study found a decreased frequency in self-reported delinquency, alcohol use, and marijuana use (Mecartney et al., 1994). None of these studies, however, revealed

Table 1. Results of Mentoring Program Evaluations Using Experimental Designs

Authors	Study Methods	Follow-up Period	Target Population	Program Description	Program Outcomes
Goodman (1972)	Boys randomly assigned to a companionship (n=88) or rejection status (n=74)	2 years	Fifth and sixth grade moderately troubled boys	Companionship therapy between college students and boys. 2 one-hour visits per week	No significant differences were found in the level of change in key problem areas (for example, self-esteem or aggression) between companioned boys and control boys
Fo and O'Donnell (1975)	Youth were randomly assigned to an adult buddy (n=264) or a no-treatment group (n=178). Pre and post measures included parent and teacher ratings of youth's quiet and/or aggressive behavior and their sense of competence and self-esteem.	1 year	Multi-ethnic youth, ages 10-17, referred by the schools, police, courts, social welfare agencies, and community residents.	Community-based program. Trained indigenous nonprofessionals who served as "buddies" for youths. Weekly contacts	For youth who had committed major offenses in the year prior to the study: Participation in the Buddy System resulted in reduced involvement in delinquency as compared to youth in the no-treatment group ($p<.04$). For youth with no record of major offenses in the year prior to the study: Participation in the Buddy System resulted in a significant increase in delinquent behavior ($p<.02$)
Dicken, Bryson, and Kass (1977)	Random assignment to companion (n=43) and control (n=23) conditions.	16 weeks	Underprivileged, caucasion, boys and girls, ages 6-13.	Volunteers in a university psychology program served as one-to-one companions to youth.	Teacher ratings - no differences between companioned children and control group; perceived little change in either group.
Tierney, Grossman, and Resch (1995)	Random assignment of youth to either treatment group (mentoring program, n=481) or control group (waiting list, n=472). Pre- and post measures on parent and peer relationships and self-concept.	18 months	At-risk boys and girls, ages 10-16	8 geographically diverse Big Brothers/Big Sisters programs. Average duration of match was 12 months. Mentors spent an average of 3 hours weekly with youth.	The treatment group: • was 46% less likely to start using illegal drugs; • was 27% less likely to skip school; • was 37% less likely to skip a class; • earned slightly higher grades; • felt better about how they could perform; • had improved relationship with parents; • felt more emotionally supported by peers

(Cont. on next page)

Table 1. Results of Mentoring Program Evaluations Using Experimental Designs (cont.)

Authors	Study Methods	Follow-Up Period	Target Population	Program Description	Program Outcomes
LoSciuto, Rajala, Townsend, and Taylor (1996)	Randomized pre and post test control group design. Students were randomly selected from pool of sixth grade classes and assigned to one of 3 study groups: 1) a no treatment group (n=189) 2) a group that participated in the life skills curriculum, performed community service, and had a parent workshop (n=193) 3) a group that participated in the above components and received mentoring from older adults (n=180)	1 academic year	Middle school male and female students at high risk of drug abuse.	Older adult volunteers serve as mentors to youth as part of drug prevention program. Spent 4 hours a week with mentee. Additional program components include community service, a classroom-based life skills curriculum, and parent workshops.	Results favoring the mentoring group over the no treatment group include: • attitudes toward school, future, and elders as seen on the Rand well-being scale; • attitudes and knowledge about older people; • reactions to situations involving drug use; • school attendance; and • community service. Results favoring the mentoring group over the 2nd group include: • attitudes toward school, future, and elders; • school attendance; and • frequency of substance use.

significant changes in school-related variables such as feelings toward school or perceptions of scholastic competence.

Preliminary results of the first ninety-three juvenile mentoring programs that were funded by the Office of Juvenile Justice and Delinquency Prevention suggests that a high percentage of youths and mentors felt that the mentor had helped the youths to get better grades, attend all classes, avoid antisocial behaviors and friends, and get along with their family. Although too subjective to serve as a measure of program effectiveness (Office of Juvenile Justice and Delinquency Prevention, 1998), youth and mentor perceptions of benefits provide insight into the type of improvements that might be achieved through mentoring relationships.

Programs for Adults

Although there are anecdotal reports about the effectiveness of mentoring programs for adults offenders (*see*, for example, Knight and Heliotis, 1996; Withey, Anderson, and Lauderdale, 1980), only two published outcome studies could be located (*see* Table 3, page 222). The first is a study of the Partners Against Crime Program, in Michigan's 36th District Court which provides strong support for mentoring as a strategy for reducing the recidivism of adult offenders (Martin, 1995). The study involved an experimental design in which offenders were randomly assigned to either a control group that received traditional probation only or to a treatment group that received probation plus a one-to-one mentoring relationship. After a one-year follow-up period, only 14.3 percent of the treatment group had been arrested for a new offense compared to 25 percent of the control group.

A study by the National Institutes of Health provides additional support for mentoring with adult offenders (National Institutes of Health as cited in Leenhouts, 2000). This study used a nonequivalent control group design to examine rates of recidivism for offenders in two misdemeanor courts in comparable cities. In one of the courts, offenders were assigned to a volunteer mentor who conducted a detailed presentence investigation and spent six-to-twelve hours per month with the offender. In the other court, offenders were assigned to probation that entailed a routinized monthly visit of approximately five minutes. A five-year follow-up study revealed that for every 100 probationers on routine probation, there were 270 repeat misdemeanor convictions. In the court that used volunteer mentors, the number of subsequent misdemeanor convictions was twenty-three. The

National Institutes of Health study also revealed improved attitudes of offenders participating in the volunteer mentoring program.

Summary of the Viability of Mentoring in the Justice Context

Three major conclusions can be drawn about the viability of mentoring in the justice context. First, if done correctly, mentoring has the potential to address practical organizational needs. Whether volunteers are an asset to the organization or an additional burden for already overworked staff will be determined by the level of financial and human resources allocated to the program.

Second, the value of mentoring as a correctional strategy with adult offenders is not yet known. At present, there is only one study that provides a strong scientific basis for believing that mentoring relationships will reduce adult criminality. Considering this study, the National Institutes of Health study, and the research identifying the importance of adult social bonds in crime desistance (Sampson and Laub, 1993), the benefits of the social capital that can evolve from a mentoring relationship (Hagan, 1993; Sullivan, 1989), and the stress-reducing qualities of social support (Vaux, 1988), it may be worth putting mentoring programs to the test as a method for reducing the recidivism of adult offenders. Agencies must first, however, overcome recruitment obstacles and the negative perceptions that adult offenders have expressed about mentoring programs.

Third, there appears to be a strong theoretical and empirical basis for implementing mentoring programs as a strategy for reducing the recidivism of juvenile delinquents. In addition to the resiliency literature that clearly demonstrates the protective function of a caring relationship with a supportive adult, there now exists a fairly substantial body of research that directly tests mentoring's capacity for producing attitudinal and behavioral changes in youths. Most notable are the two, well-controlled studies that showed that mentoring was effective in reducing truancy and substance abuse (Tierney et al., 1995; and LoSciuto et al., 1996). It should be noted, however, that most of the studies reviewed in this chapter tested mentoring's potential as a primary prevention strategy with "at-risk" or "troubled" youths rather than as a secondary prevention strategy with youths already involved in the justice system (Anderson, 1994). Despite this, there are two reasons to believe that mentoring programs may be a viable secondary prevention strategy. First, Fo and

Table 2. Results of Mentoring Program Evaluations Using a Nonexperimental Design

AUTHORS	STUDY METHODS	FOLLOW-UP PERIOD	TARGET POPULATION	PROGRAM DESCRIPTION	PROGRAM OUTCOMES
Freedman (1988)	One-group post-test only 47 pairs	Variable	Teenage mothers, jail-bound young offenders, students in danger of dropping out of school	Five programs in which elders and youth were paired in mentoring relationships.	Youth reported improvement in quality of day-to-day lives and described learning a variety of functional skills.
Tierney and Branch (1992)	One-group post-test only 65 pairs	1 year	4th to 9th grade youth who were recruited from schools or housing projects.	Three Campus Partners in Learning Programs College students were paired with youth Program activities varied and included one-to-one interaction, group meetings, and an academic component.	Mentees reported increased exposure to social, cultural and recreational opportunities. No significant changes in global self-worth, social acceptance, scholastic competence, or social support scales. Significant change in locus of control scale: mentees felt more in control of their personal lives.
Mecartney, Styles, and Morrow (1994)	One-group pre and post-test Original sample was 161 youth. Pre and post measures were only available for 71 youth.	1 year	Delinquent boys and girls, ages 11-18.	Mentoring relationships between elders and youth Programs were implemented as component within 1 institutional and 1 community-based juvenile justice program.	Significant improvements in feelings of self-worth, self reliance, and family support. Youth experienced a more internal locus of control. Decreased frequency in self-reported delinquency, alcohol use, and marijuana use. No change in their feelings toward school.

(Cont. on next page)

Table 2. Results of Mentoring Program Evaluations Using a Nonexperimental Design (cont.)

Authors	Study Methods	Follow-up Period	Target Population	Program Description	Program Outcomes
OJJDP (1998)	One-group post-test only 93 JUMP projects 3,080 youths	Variable	5-18 year old boys and girls	Juvenile Mentoring Program (JUMP) established as part of the 1992 amendments to the 1974 Juvenile Justice and Delinquency Prevention Act JUMP projects may operate as a component of a larger agency, or may stand alone to provide only mentoring services.	% of youth perceiving the mentoring relationship as helping them to: • get better grades (92.1%) • attend all classes (87.6%) • stay away from alcohol (83.1%) • stay away from drugs (83.2%) • avoid fights (84.7%) • stay away from gangs (83.2%) • stay away from knives or guns (79.1%) • avoid friends who start trouble (77.5%) • get along with family (85.0%)

Table 3. Studies of Adult Mentoring Programs

Authors	Study Methods	Follow-up Period	Target Population	Program Description	Program Outcomes
Wayne State University (1995)	Probationers were randomly assigned to either a treatment group receiving traditional probation plus a volunteer mentor (n=100) or a control group receiving traditional probation only (n=100).	1 year	Adult offenders convicted of a misdemeanor offense	Community volunteers are assigned to offenders for one-to-one relationships. Designed as probation enhancement. 1 hour of contact per week.	The probation-only group had an arrest rate of 25 percent compared to 14.3 percent for the treatment group.
National Institutes of Health (2000)	Nonequivalent control group design Control group - adult probationers assigned to routine probation (n=?) Treatment group - adult probationers assigned to a volunteer mentor (n=?)	5 years	Male and female adults convicted of misdemeanor offenses.	Volunteer had 6-12 hours of contact per month.	The treatment group had: • reduced rates of recidivism; and • Improved the attitudes of offenders.

O'Donnell (1975) found that mentoring contributed to reduced involvement in delinquency for youths with a history of major delinquency. Second, many studies have demonstrated that mentoring programs can have an impact on factors that are known correlates of delinquency such as negative attitudes towards school, truancy, substance abuse, relationship with parents, and feelings of control over their lives.

Given the potential of mentoring as a correctional strategy, what is now needed is a basis for program development. The remainder of this chapter will focus on identifying factors that are associated with the development of effective mentoring relationships.

Developing Effective Mentoring Relationships

The promise of mentoring is being impeded by an insufficient number of mentors and a high rate of attrition in mentoring relationships. According to the National Mentoring Partnership (1998), only one out of seven people recruited by established mentoring programs turns out to be a suitable mentor. Furthermore, research on mentoring programs suggests that of the mentor and youth pairs that are initiated, only one-fourth to two-thirds form sustainable relationships (Morrow and Styles, 1995). What then, is the best way to formulate effective mentoring relationships? Recent research on mentoring programs for youths has been devoted to answering this question. Other helpful sources of information include the counseling literature, the literature on the principles of effective correctional intervention, and research on volunteerism. Drawing upon all of these sources, this section of the chapter identifies the youth, the mentor, the match, and the organizational characteristics that have been found to (or are likely to be based upon literature on other helping relationships) that contribute to effective mentoring relationships.

Youth Characteristics[2]

Several demographic characteristics appear to influence youths' capacity to develop a social bond and their behavioral responses to mentoring programs. Developmental theorists, for example, have argued that youths between the ages of ten and fourteen who are on the "cusp of delinquency" are promising targets for mentoring and other prevention programs (Sherman, Gottfredson, MacKenzie, Eck, Reuter, and Bushway, 1997). It has also been argued that relationships with unrelated adults may be most beneficial for older children who have more control over their protective systems and are able to seek protective relationships outside of their immediate environments.

Several studies have found that minority youths gained more positive benefits from mentoring relationships (Goodman, 1972; Tierney, Grossman, and Resch, 1995). This differential response to mentoring may reflect the greater need among minority youths for a range of supportive adults in their lives. According to McLoyd (1990), the poverty and economic hardship among a disproportionate number of minority children diminishes the capacity for supportive, consistent, and involved parents and impedes the establishment of other supportive social networks. Mentoring programs appear to address this void which exists for many minority youths and serves as a protective factor that deflects the consequences of adverse economic situations. This finding supports the "needs principle" of effective correctional interventions which suggests that programs are more effective with clients who demonstrate a clear need for the specific services provided (Andrews, Bonta, and Hoge, 1990).

Although the impact of gender on mentoring relationships has not been explored fully, it is likely that males and females respond differently to the mentoring relationship, given the significant role that gender plays in shaping youths' life experiences. Maccoby (1990) suggests that boys prefer relationships that are characterized by well-defined roles and a directive, interactive style while girls value a more intimate and integrated relationship. Initial results of an ongoing study of Big Brothers/Big Sisters of the Bluegrass suggests that the value of a mentoring relationship for girls lies in having someone to talk to while for boys the most prized aspect is the fun activities they engage in with their mentor.[3]

Two studies revealed that mentoring programs contributed to greater attitudinal and behavioral gains among the more troubled youths (Fo and O'Donnell, 1975; Goodman, 1972). This latter finding concurs with research on delinquency programs that report better outcomes for high-risk youths (Lipsey and Wilson, 1998), and suggests that mentoring programs may be appropriate for a higher risk population than that typically targeted for participation.

Mentor Characteristics

Available research suggests that the characteristics and style of the mentor can affect the degree to which the relationship is satisfying and helpful for the youth. For example, several studies have found that mentors in successful relationships allowed the relationships to be youth-driven—that is, mentors based their activities and approach on the youth's interests and developmental needs and focused on providing support to youth rather than on changing the youth (Morrow and Styles, 1995; Styles and Morrow, 1992; Tierney and Branch, 1992; Tierney et al., 1995). Morrow and Styles (1995) contrast these youth-driven, "developmental" relationships with "prescriptive" relationships described as those in which the adult mentor set the goals, pace, and groundrules of the relationship with little consideration of the youth's interests or desires. Morrow and Styles (1995) found that these "prescriptive" relationships contributed to mutual dissatisfaction among mentors and mentees.

The consistent use of positive reinforcement also is important to the mentoring relationship. Hawkins (1995), for example, suggests that for bonding to occur, the significant adult must be consistent in the use of positive reinforcement for the demonstration of prosocial attitudes and behaviors. In addition to promoting bonding between the mentor and the youth, evidence suggests that consistent reinforcement is a necessary ingredient for promoting positive behavioral change among mentored youths. An early study by Fo and O'Donnell (1974) found that youths who were rewarded through social and material reinforcement by their mentor showed more reductions in the problem behaviors of truancy and fighting than a control group of youths in mentoring relationships with no contingency conditions.

Several studies have identified a mentor's capacity for empathy as critical to the success of the relationship (Dicken, Bryson, and Kass, 1977; Goodman, 1972). These findings regarding effective mentor characteristics concurs with the counseling literature which reports that . . . counselors' level of empathy and acceptance of the client are two characteristics that consistently are correlated with the strength of the therapeutic alliance and client improvement (Cooley and Lajoy, 1980; Lorr, 1965; Traux and Mitchell, 1971). Goodman (1972) asserts that Carl Roger's client-centered theory provides a good basis for assessing a mentor's helping skills since each of the necessary and sufficient conditions for change (in other words, empathy, acceptance, and genuineness) are seen in everyday behavior and are not dependent on professional training.

Emotional outgoingness is another mentor characteristic that contributes to mutually satisfying and helpful relationships. Two studies of mentoring pairs (Dicken, Bryson, and Kass, 1977; Goodman, 1972) revealed that the attitudinal and behavioral outcomes of youths who were paired with outgoing mentors were better than the outcomes for youths who were paired with the quiet, more reserved mentors.

A study by Andrews (1980) on volunteer and professional probation officers suggests that good interpersonal skills, while important, are not sufficient for promoting positive behavioral changes. What is also necessary is the ability to demonstrate anticriminal values, attitudes, and behaviors. Andrews found that, regardless of their professional or volunteer status, officers who were empathic but demonstrated antisocial values contributed to high rates of recidivism among offenders. Thus, volunteers' attitudes toward authority and laws and their ability to demonstrate anticriminal values and behaviors are important considerations for mentoring programs with adult and juvenile offenders.

Matching Characteristics

Although literature on mentoring often refers to the importance of matching youths and mentors on key characteristics, the research on this issue is limited in scope. One study found that although the objective factors of age, race, and gender were commonly considered when making matches, they were not strongly correlated with frequency of meetings, the length of the match, or its effectiveness (Grossman and Garry, 1997). Other early studies have suggested the importance of considering the "emotional outgoingness" of youths and mentors when making matches. Among the mentoring dyads included in the studies, those that paired quiet or outgoing children with outgoing mentors resulted in the most improvement in self-concept and other key problem areas while the "double-quiet dyads" resulted in the least improvements (Dicken et al., 1977; Goodman, 1972). Aside from these studies, there is limited information upon which to base matching decisions.

Past studies on delinquency programs have found that matching youths to the appropriate staff and treatment environment is critical to the success of a program (Palmer, 1974; Reitsma-Street and Leschied, 1988; Warren, 1971, 1983). Thus, treatment matching, or the "responsivity principle" has been identified as a principle of effective correctional intervention (Andrews, Bonta, and Hoge, 1990; Gendreau, 1996). The responsivity principle suggests that clients should be matched to programs and counselors, based on their interests, personal characteristics, and learning styles (Andrews, Bonta, and Hoge, 1990; *also see* Stewart et al., this volume). For example, according to research on modeling theory, people are more likely to imitate the behavior of those who are similar to them (Bandura, 1986). It may be that pairing youths and mentors with similar life experiences and interests will increase the likelihood of developing a successful relationship in which effective modeling can take place.

The conceptual level matching model is another example of how the responsivity principle could be applied to mentoring relationships. The Conceptual Level Matching Model describes interactions between a person's conceptual level and the level of structure provided in an environment or relationship (Reitsma-Street and Leschied, 1988). Conceptual level refers to "how individuals think, differentiate information, integrate and evaluate clues, and arrive at solutions" (Reitsma-Street and Leschied, 1988, p. 93). Individuals at lower levels of conceptual maturity have not internalized culturally accepted norms and values; they depend on simple, concrete rules to guide their evaluation of information and interpersonal interactions. Individuals at higher levels of conceptual maturity are more flexible, less reliant on authority, and capable of developing their own solutions based on internalized standards of behavior. Youths at a low level of conceptual maturity are often frustrated by a lack of structure and rules within relationships or treatment environments, while youths at medium to high levels of conceptual maturity are often frustrated by too much structure (Brill, 1978; Reitsma-Street and Leschied, 1988). Considering this differential response to structure, it may be that youths with a low level of conceptual maturity would respond well to some aspects of the mentor-driven "prescriptive" relationships that were described by Morrow and Styles (1995) as being mentor-driven and goal-oriented, and as having explicit rules and expectations for youths. It is certainly an issue worthy of further exploration.

Organizational Characteristics

Several studies have identified the screening, training, and supervision of pairs as important factors in the success of a mentoring program (Furano, Roaf, Styles, and Branch, 1993; Morrow and Styles, 1995; Tierney et al., 1995). Morrow and Styles (1995) found that mentors who received prematch training were more likely to be involved in the "developmental" relationships (in other words, relationships that accommodate youths' developmental needs and interests) that are associated with more success. These mentors were also found to have more contact with the caseworker. According to Furano and his colleagues (1993), it is the regular contact between mentoring pairs and caseworkers at Big Brothers/Big Sisters that leads to the high rate of interaction among pairs and distinguishes Big Brothers/Big Sisters from other mentoring programs.

The literature on volunteerism provides three important insights for mentoring programs. First, the primary motivations for volunteering include satisfying altruistic needs, gaining career-related experience, socializing, gaining satisfaction from work, and feeling needed (Brown and Zahrly, 1989 as cited in Fisher and Cole, 1993; Independent Sector, 1992). The successful recruitment of volunteers is dependent on an agency's ability to address these diverse motivations. Second, training has been found to add significantly to the rewards of volunteer work. Fisher and Cole (1993) suggest that volunteers need initial and periodic training to learn about the organization; acquire the skills and knowledge necessary to undertake a particular job; be updated about changes in the position, the organization, or the clients; and promote personal growth and enrichment. Training is particularly important for volunteers working with offenders—"it should include 'be wary' guidelines and discussions about realistic expectations" (Arnold, 1993, p. 122).

Third, ongoing supervision and recognition have been found to sustain volunteers' interests and involvement (Gidron, 1983). One person, designated as the volunteer coordinator, should assume primary responsibility for the supervision and recognition of volunteers, but all agency staff who are working with volunteers should receive training on the type of guidance, support, and recognition that contribute to volunteer satisfaction. In sum, the volunteer literature suggests that attending to volunteer needs will lead to mutual benefits for the agency and the volunteers.

Summary of the Elements of Effective Mentoring Relationships

Based on available research, it appears that:

- Minority, female, and more troubled youths may gain the most positive benefits from mentoring relationships.

- Mutually satisfying relationships are associated with developmental relationships in which mentors emphasize the provision of support to youths over attempts to change youths, and base their approach to the relationship on the youths' interests and needs.

- Mentors who are empathic, emotionally outgoing, and consistent in their use of positive reinforcement , are more effective in promoting positive behavioral change in youths.

- Mutually satisfying mentoring relationships are associated with consistent screening, training, and supervision practices.

Although this previous research on mentoring programs has made significant contributions to the state of knowledge on the formulation of effective relationships, it has some limitations. First, small sample sizes have limited the generalizability of the findings (*see*, for example, Freedman 1988; Morrow and Styles 1995; Tierney and Branch 1992). Second, much of the research has been exploratory and limited to descriptive analytical techniques (*see*, for example, Mecartney, Styles, and Morrow 1994; Morrow and Styles 1995; Tierney and Branch 1992) which makes it difficult to ascertain the strength of the association between specific factors (for example, youth, mentor, matching, and organizational characteristics) and the success of the relationship. It also precludes the ability to determine the independent effects of each factor. Third, most of the research has been conducted on programs designed for troubled, or at-risk, youths. Thus, caution should be exercised when applying the findings to higher risk, delinquent youths or to adult offenders who are likely to have very different characteristics and needs.

Given these limitations, future research should include, where possible, larger samples and more quantitative data to allow for more sophisticated analysis. It also should build on the responsivity principle by examining the outcomes of various dyad types. For example, does matching mentors and mentees based on similar life experiences facilitate the development of successful relationships? Does pairing a youth who has a low level of conceptual maturity with a mentor who provides a high level of structure in the relationship contribute to positive behavioral change? Lastly, and perhaps most importantly, given the context of this chapter, future research should also be devoted to discovering what factors contribute to the development of effective mentoring relationships for juvenile and adult offenders.

The obvious and more immediate benefits of the proposed future research include improved screening, training, and matching procedures for mentoring programs, and increased satisfaction and friendship among mentoring pairs. The implications, however, are more far-reaching. First, in the counseling profession, the "working alliance" (in other words, the quality of the therapeutic relationship) has long been viewed as an intermediate criterion of counseling effectiveness—stronger alliances contribute to better outcomes (Frieswyk, Allen, Colson, and Coyne, 1986; Horvath and Symonds, 1991; Stiles, Agnew-Davies, Hardy, Barkham, and

Shapiro, 1998). Extrapolating from this literature, it could be argued that improved mentoring relationships will contribute to more positive attitudinal and behavioral change among the youths or adults who are targeted for participation. Second, the findings from further relationship-formation studies could be used to help guide the development of helping relationships in other offender-serving institutions.

General Conclusions

The information presented in this chapter points to several guidelines for the development of mentoring programs within the justice context:

1. A sufficient level of human and financial resources must be invested in the program to support the program's infrastructure necessary for recruiting, screening, training, and supervising mentors.

2. Mentoring programs should target those offenders with an identified need for a supportive relationship (in other words, the need principle).

3. Mentoring programs should accommodate, through good matching procedures, the personal characteristics of offenders that may influence their response to the program (in other words, the responsivity principle).

4. Agencies should ensure, through screening and/or training, that mentors possess the following competencies:
   - knowledge of general and specific youth needs
   - effective and consistent use of positive reinforcement
   - good interpersonal skills including a high level of empathy and emotional outgoingness

Before mentoring programs can be considered a viable, large-scale correctional strategy, however, their effectiveness in reducing the recidivism of juvenile and adult offenders must be demonstrated. Future outcome studies are needed to provide additional evidence of mentoring's effectiveness with adult populations; test its effectiveness with more serious delinquent/criminal populations; determine its impact on important criminogenic needs; and incorporate official measures of delinquency.

Given the initial evidence of effectiveness, its theoretical relevance, and the other more systemic benefits of mentoring, it appears that sufficient support exists for cautious, small-scale implementation of mentoring programs within the correctional and juvenile justice context. Past relationship-formation studies on mentoring programs, as well as research on counseling and correctional interventions, provide a solid basis for program development. The biggest challenge may be in garnering the public support needed to sustain such a program.

The idea of using a caring relationship as a mechanisms for promoting behavioral change in offenders reflects a return to a more humanistic approach to corrections that is long overdue. It is now up to correctional and juvenile justice agencies to develop theory and research-based mentoring programs that can demonstrate their viability as a key correctional strategy.

Endnotes

[1] These anecdotes regarding adult offenders' resistance to having a mentor were gleaned from audience responses to this paper at the ICCA conference in Philadelphia, Pennsylvania in September, 2001.

[2] The author of this paper is currently conducting an evaluation of the mentoring program operated by Big Brothers/Big Sisters of the Bluegrass. Results of this revaluation research will be available in August 2002. To this author's knowledge, relationship-formation studies are not available on adult mentoring programs.

[3] This finding has been referred to as the "needs principle" in the literature on "what works" in correctional intervention.

[4] The author of this paper is currently conducting an evaluation of the mentoring program operated by Big Brothers/Big Sisters of the Bluegrass. Results of this research will be available in August 2002.

References

Akers, R. L. 1985. *Deviant Behavior: A Social Learning Approach, 3rd Edition.* Belmont, California: Wadsworth.

American Correctional Association. 1996. *Mentoring in Corrections.* VHS. Lanham, Maryland: American Correctional Association.

Agnew, R. 1985. Social Control Theory and Delinquency: A Longitudinal Test. *Criminology.* 23(1): 47-61.

Anderson, M. L. C. 1994. High Juvenile Crime Rate: A Look at Mentoring as a Preventive Strategy. *Criminal Law Bulletin.* 30(1): 54-75.

Andrews, D. A. 1980. Some Experimental Investigations of the Principles of Differential Association through Deliberate Manipulations of the Structure of Services Systems. *American Sociological Review.* 45: 448-462.

Andrews, D. A., J. Bonta, and R. D. Hoge. 1990. Classification for Effective Rehabilitation: Rediscovering Psychology. *Criminal Justice and Behavior.* 17(1): 19-52.

Andrews, D. A., I. Zinger, R. D. Hoge, J. Bonta, P. Gendreau, and F. T. Cullen. 1990. Does Correctional Treatment Work? Clinically Relevant and Psychologically Informed Meta-analysis. *Criminology.* 28: 369-404.

Arnold, C. S. 1993. Respect, Recognition Are Keys to Effective Volunteer Programs. *Corrections Today.* 55(5): 118-122.

Bandura, A. 1986. *Social Foundation of Thought and Action: A Social Cognitive Theory.* Englewood Cliffs, New Jersey: Prentice-Hall.

Barajas, E. Jr. 1998. Community Justice: An Emerging Concept and Practice. In American Probation and Parole Association, ed. *Community Justice: Concepts and Strategies.* Lexington, Kentucky: American Probation and Parole Association.

Beiswinger, G. L. 1985. *One To One: The Story of the Big Brothers/Big Sisters Movement in America.* Philadelphia, Pennsylvania: Big Brothers/Big Sisters of America.

Bretherton, I. 1985. Attachment Theory: Retrospect and Prospect. In I. Bretherton and E. Waters, eds. *Growing Points of Attachment Theory and Research.* Chicago: University of Chicago Press.

Brill, R. 1978. Implications of the Conceptual Level Matching Model for Treatment of Delinquency. *Journal of Research in Crime and Delinquency.* (15)2: 229-246.

Bureau of Justice Assistance. 1997. Revitalizing Communities: Innovative State and Local Programs. Publication No. NCJ-165360. Washington, D.C.: U.S. Department of Justice, Bureau of Justice Assistance.

Bureau of Justice Statistics. October 2001. *Nation's State Prison Population Falls in Second Half of 2001; First Such Decline Since 1972.* http://ojp.usdoj.gov/bjs/abstract/p00.htm.

Camp, C. G., and G. M. Camp. 2000. *The Corrections Yearbook 1999: Adult Corrections.* Middletown, Connecticut: Criminal Justice Institute, Inc.

Chandler, R. 1996. The Georgia Department of Corrections' Volunteer Mentoring Program. In B. Fulton, ed. *Restoring Hope through Community Partnerships: The Real Deal in Crime Control.* Lexington, Kentucky: American Probation and Parole Association.

Cicchetti, D. and N. Garmezy. 1993. Prospects and Promises in the Study of Resilience. *Development and Psychopathology.* 5: 497-502.

Connelly, J. 1995. Mentors and Tutors: An Overview of Two Volunteer Programs in Oklahoma Corrections. *Journal of the Oklahoma Criminal Justice Research Consortium.* 2: 80-88.

Cooley, E. J., and R. LaJoy. 1980. Therapeutic Relationship and Improvement as Perceived by Clients and Therapists. *Journal of Clinical Psychology.* 36: 562-570.

Cullen, F. T. 1994. Social Support as an Organizing Concept for Criminology: Presidential Address to the Academy of Criminal Justice Sciences. *Justice Quarterly.* 11(4): 527-555.

Cullen, F. T., J. P Wright, S. Brown, M. Moon, M. B. Blankenship, and B. K. Applegate. 1998. Public Support for Early Intervention Programs: Implications for a Progressive Policy Agenda. *Crime and Delinquency.* 44: 187-204.

Curran, D. J. and C. M. Renzetti. 1994. *Theories of Crime.* Needham Heights, Massachusetts: Allyn and Bacon.

Currie, E. 1985. *Confronting Crime: An American Challenge.* New York: Pantheon Books.

Dicken, C., R. Bryson, and N. Kass. 1977. Companionship Therapy: A Replication in Experimental Community Psychology. *Journal of Consulting and Clinical Psychology.* 45(4): 637-646.

Elliott, D. S., D. H. Huizinga, and S. S. Ageton. 1985. *Explaining Delinquency and Drug Use.* Beverly Hills, California: Sage.

Farrington, D. P. 1995. The Development of Offending and Antisocial Behaviour from Childhood: Key Findings from the Cambridge Study in Delinquent Development. *Journal of Child Psychology and Psychiatry.* 36: 929-964.

Fisher, J. C. and K. M. Cole. 1993. *Leadership and Management of Volunteer Programs.* San Francisco, California: Jossey-Bass, Inc.

Fo, W. and C. O'Donnell. 1974. The Buddy System: Relationship and Contingency Conditions in a Community Intervention Program for Youth with Nonprofessionals as Behavior Change Agents. *Journal of Consulting and Clinical Psychology.* 42(2): 163-169.

———. 1975. The Buddy System: Effect of Community Intervention on Delinquent Offenses. *Behavior Therapy.* 6: 522-524.

Freedman, M. 1988. *Partners in Growth: Elder Mentors and At-Risk Youth.* Philadelphia, Pennsylvania: Public/Private Ventures.

———. 1991. *The Kindness of Strangers: Reflection of the Mentoring Movement.* Philadelphia, Pennsylvania: Public/Private Ventures.

Frentz, K. 1996. Partners against Crime. In B. Fulton, ed. *Restoring Hope through Community Partnerships: The Real Deal in Crime Control.* Lexington, Kentucky: American Probation and Parole Association.

Frieswyk, S., J. Allen, D. Colson, and L. Coyne. 1986. Therapeutic Alliance: Its Place as a Process and Outcome Variable in Dynamic Psychotherapy Research. *Journal of Consulting and Clinical Psychology.* 54: 483-489.

Furano, K. P., A. Roaf, M. B. Styles, and A. Y. Branch. 1993. *Big Brothers/Sisters: A Study of Program Practices.* Philadelphia, Pennyslvania: Public/ Private Ventures.

Garmezy, N. 1985. Stress Resistant Children: The Search for Protective Factors. In J. E. Stevenson, ed. *Recent Research in Developmental Psychopathology; Journal of Child Psychology and Psychiatry, Book Supplement No. 4.* Oxford: Pergamon.

Gendreau, P. 1996. The Principles of Effective Intervention with Offenders. In A. T. Harland, ed. *Choosing Correctional Options That Work.* Thousand Oaks, California: Sage Publications.

Gidron, B. 1983. Sources of Job Satisfaction among Service Volunteers. *Journal of Voluntary Action Research.* 12(1): 20-35.

Goodman, G. 1972. *Companionship Therapy: Studies of Structured Intimacy.* San Francisco: Jossey-Bass.

Gottfredson, D. C. 1986. An Empirical Test of School-based Environmental and Individual Interventions to Reduce the Risk of Delinquent Behavior. *Criminology.* 24: 705-731.

Grinc, R. M. 1994. Angels in Marble: Problems in Stimulating Community Involvement in Community Policing. *Crime and Delinquency.* 40: 437-468.

Grossman, J. B. and E. M. Garry. 1997. Mentoring: A Proven Delinquency Prevention Strategy. *Juvenile Offender.* 13: 18-21.

Haensly, P. A. and J. L. Parsons. 1993. Creative, Intellectual, and Psychosocial Development through Mentorship: Relationships and Stages. *Youth and Society.* 25(2): 202-221.

Hagan, J. 1993. The Social Embeddedness of Crime and Unemployment. *Criminology.* 31: 465-491.

Hawkins, D. J. 1995. Controlling Crime Before it Happens: Risk-focused Prevention. *National Institute of Justice Journal.* 229: 10-18.

Hawkins, D. J., R. F. Catalano, and J. M. Miller. 1992. Risk and Protective Factors for Alcohol and Other Drug Problems in Adolescence and Early Childhood: Implications for Substance Abuse Prevention. *Psychological Bulletin.* 112: 64-105.

Hirschi, T. 1969. *Causes of Delinquency.* Berkeley: University of California.

Horvath, A. O. and D. B. Symonds. 1991. Relationship between Working Alliance and Outcome in Psychotherapy: A Meta-analysis. *Journal of Counseling Psychology.* 38: 139-149.

Howell, J. 1997. *Juvenile Justice and Youth Violence.* Thousand Oaks, California: Sage.

Independent Sector. 1992. *Giving and Volunteering, 1992.* Washington, D.C.: Independent Sector.

Justice Research and Statistics Association. 1998. *Programs in Correctional Settings: Innovative State and Local Programs.* Washington, D.C.: U.S. Department of Justice, Bureau of Justice Assistance.

Knight, J. W. and H. Heliotis. 1996. *A Process Evaluation of the Women's Mentoring Program at Hodder House/MCI Framingham.* Boston: Massachusetts Department of Corrections.

Knight, K. W. and T. Tripodil. 1996. Societal Bonding and Delinquency: An Empirical Test of Hirschi's Theory of Control. *Journal of Offender Rehabilitation.* 23: 117-129.

Krohn, M. D. and J. L. Massey. 1980. Social Control and Delinquent Behavior: An Examination of the Elements of the Social Bond. *The Sociological Quarterly.* 21: 529-543.

LaGrange, R. L. and H. R. White. 1985. Age Differences in Delinquency: A Test of Theory. *Criminology.* 23: 19-45.

Leenhouts, K. L. 2000. *Misdemeanor Courts, Hope for Crime Weary America: Volunteer Mentoring in Misdemeanor Courts.* Reno, Nevada: National Judicial College.

Lin, N. 1986. Conceptualizing Social Support. In N. Lin, A. Dean, and W. Edsel, eds. *Social Support, Life Events, and Depression.* Orlando, Florida: Academic Press.

Lipsey, M. W. and D. B. Wilson. 1998. Effective Intervention for Serious Juvenile Offenders: A Synthesis of Research. In R. Loeber and D. P. Farrington, eds. *Serious and Violent Juvenile Offenders: Risk Factors and Successful Interventions.* Thousand Oaks, California: Sage Publications.

Lisante, T. F. and B. Navon. 2000. A New York City Jail-Community Re-entry Collaboration. *Journal of Correctional Education.* 5(2): 237-240.

Liska, A. E., and M. D. Reed. 1985. Ties to Conventional Institutions and Delinquency: Estimating Reciprocal Effects. *American Sociological Review.* 50: 547-560.

Lorr, M. 1965. Client Perceptions of Therapists: A Study of the Therapeutic Relation. *Journal of Consulting Psychology.* 29(2): 146-149.

LoSciuto, L., A. K. Rajala, T. N. Townsend, and A. S. Taylor. 1996. Outcome Evaluation of Across Ages: An Intergenerational Mentoring Approach to Drug Prevention. *Journal of Adolescent Research.* 11(1): 116-129.

Maccoby, E. 1990. Gender and Relationships: A Developmental Account. *American Psychologist.* 45(4): 513-520.

Martin, D. 1995. *Impact Evaluation of Partners against Crime (PAC) in Detroit, Michigan.* Detroit, Michigan: Wayne State University, Urban Safety Program.

McLloyd, V. C. 1990. The Impact of Economic Hardship on Black Families and Children: Psychological Distress, Parenting and Socioemotional Development. *Child Development.* 61: 311-346.

Mecartney, C. A., M. B. Styles, and, K. V. Morrow. 1994. *Mentoring in the Juvenile Justice System: Findings from Two Pilot Programs.* Philadelphia, Pennsylvania: Public/Private Ventures.

Morrow, K. V. and M. B. Styles. 1995. *Building Relationships with Youth in Program Settings: A Study of Big Brothers/Big Sisters.* Philadelphia, Pennsylvania: Public/Private Ventures.

National Mentoring Partnership.1998. *Mentoring: Elements of Effective Practice.* Washington, D.C.: National Mentoring Partnership.

Nye, F. I. 1958. *Family Relationships and Delinquent Behavior.* New York: John Wiley and Sons.

Office of Juvenile Justice and Delinquency Prevention. 1998. *Juvenile Mentoring Program: 1998 Report to Congress.* Washington, D.C.: U.S. Department of Justice, Office of Juvenile Justice and Delinquency Prevention.

Palmer, T. 1974. The Youth Authority's Community Treatment Project. *Federal Probation.* 38(1): 3-13.

Patterson, G. R. and T. R. Dishion. 1988. Multilevel Family Process Models: Traits, Interactions and Relationships. In R. Hinde and J. Stevenson-Hinde, eds. *Relationships within Families: Mutual Influences.* Oxford, United Kingdom: Clarendon.

Pranis. K. 1998. Promising Practices in Community Justice: Restorative Justice. In American Probation and Parole Association, ed. *Community Justice: Concepts and Strategies.* Lexington, Kentucky: American Probation and Parole Association.

Rankin, J. H. and L. E. Wells. 1990. The Effect of Parental Attachments and Direct Controls on Delinquency. *Journal of Research in Crime and Delinquency.* 23(2): 140-165.

Reckless, W. C. 1967. *The Crime Problem, 4th Edition.* New York: Appleton-Century-Crofts.

Reiss, A. J., Jr. 1951. Delinquency as the Failure of Personal and Social Controls. *American Sociological Review.* 16: 196-207.

Reitsma-Street, M. and A. W. Leschied. 1988. The Conceptual-level Matching Model in Corrections. *Criminal Justice and Behavior.* 15(1): 92-108.

Richardson, G. E., B. L. Neiger, S. Jensen, and K. L. Kumpfer. 1990. The Resiliency Model. *Health Education.* 21(6): 33-39.

Rutter, M. 1987. Resilience in the Face of Adversity: Protective Factors and Resistance to Psychiatric Disorder. *British Journal of Psychiatry.* 14(7): 598-611.

Sampson, R. J. and J. H. Laub.1993. *Crime in the Making: Pathways and Turning Points Through Life.* Cambridge, Massachusetts: Harvard University Press.

Sherman, L. W. 1997. Communities and Crime Prevention. In L. W. Sherman, D. Gottfredson, D. MacKenzie, J. Eck, P. Reuter, and S. Bushway, eds. *Preventing Crime: What Works, What Doesn't, What's Promising: A Report to the Attorney General of the United States.* Chapter 3. Publication No. NCJ-165366. Washington, D.C.: U.S. Department of Justice, National Institute of Justice.

Sherman, L. W., D. Gottfredson, D. MacKenzie, J. Eck, P. Reuter, and S. Bushway. 1997. *Preventing Crime: What Works, What Doesn't, What's Promising: A Report to the Attorney General of the United States.* Publication No. NCJ-165366. Washington, D.C.: U.S. Department of Justice, National Institute of Justice.

Skogan, W. G. 1990. *Disorder and Decline: Crime and the Spiral of Decay in Urban Neighborhoods.* Berkeley: University of California Press.

Stiles, W. B., R. Agnew-Davies, G. E. Hardy, M. Barkham, and D. A. Shapiro. 1998. Relations of the Alliance with Psychotherapy Outcome: Findings in the Second Sheffield Psychotherapy Project. *Journal of Consulting and Clinical Psychology.* 66: 791-802.

Styles, M. B. and K. V. Morrow. 1992. *Understanding How Youth and Elders Form Relationships: A Study of Four Linking Lifetimes Programs.* Philadelphia, Pennsylvania: Public/Private Ventures.

Sullivan, M. L. 1989. *Getting Paid: Youth Crime and Work in the Inner City.* Ithaca, New York: Cornell University Press.

Terry, C. W. III. 2000. Opening the Courts to the Community: Volunteers in Wisconsin's Courts. *Bureau of Justice Assistance Bulletin.* Publication No. NCJ-178935. Washington, D.C.: U.S. Department of Justice, Bureau of Justice Assistance.

Tierney, J. P. and A.Y. Branch. 1992. *College Students as Mentors for At-Risk Youth: A Study of Six Campus Partners in Learning Programs.* Philadelphia, Pennsylvania: Public/Private Ventures.

Tierney, J. P., J. B. Grossman, and N. L. Resch. 1995. *Making a Difference: An Impact Study of Big Brothers/Big Sisters.* Philadelphia, Pennsylvania: Public/Private Ventures.

Traux, C. and K. Mitchell. 1971. Research on Certain Therapist Interpersonal Skills in Relation to Process and Outcomes. In A. Bergin and S. Garfield, eds. *Handbook on Psychotherapy and Behavior Change.* New York: Wiley.

Unger, D. G. and A. Wandersman. 1985. The Importance of Neighbors: The Social, Cognitive, and Affective Components of Neighboring. *American Journal of Community Psychology.* 13: 139-169.

Vaux, A. 1988. *Social Support: Theory, Research, and Intervention.* New York: Praeger.

Warren, M. Q. 1971. Classification of Offenders as an Aid to Efficient Management and Effective Treatment. *Journal of Criminal Law, Criminology, and Police Science.* 62(2): 239-258.

———. 1983. Applications of Interpersonal-Maturity Theory to Offender Populations. In W. S. Laufer and J. M. Day, eds. *Personality Theory, Moral Development, and Criminal Behavior.* Lexington, Massachusetts: Lexington Books.

Werner, E. E. 1993. Risk, Resilience, and Recovery: Perspectives from the Kauai Longitudinal Study. *Development and Psychopathology.* 5: 503-515.

Werner, E. E. and R. S. Smith. 1992. *Overcoming the Odds: High Risk Children from Birth to Adulthood.* New York: Cornell University.

Wiatrowski, M. D., D. Griswold, and M. Roberts. 1981. Social Control Theory and Delinquency. *American Sociological Review.* 46: 525-541.

Withey, V., R. Anderson, and M. Lauderdale. 1980. Volunteers as Mentors for Abusing Parents: A Natural Helping Relationship. *Child Welfare*. 59(10): 637-644.

Zehr, H. and H. Mika. 1997. *Restorative Justice Signposts*. Akron, Pennsylvania: Mennonite Central Committee.

WHAT WORKS IN FAITH-BASED PROGRAMMING

8

Chris Carr
Director General of Chaplaincy Division
Correctional Service of Canada
Ottawa, Canada

Dwight Cuff
Senior Project Officer Performance Assurance
Chaplaincy Division, Correctional Service of Canada
Abbotsford, British Columbia

David Molzahn
Special Advisor to the Director General (Community Ministries)
Chaplaincy Division, Correctional Service of Canada
Ottawa, Ontario

Grandfather, look at our brokenness. We know that in all Creation only the human family has strayed from the Sacred Way, We know that we are the ones who are divided and the ones who must come back together to walk in the Sacred Way. Grandfather, Sacred One. Teach us love, compassion, honor that we may heal the earth and heal each other.
— **An Ojibway Prayer**

It is an honor to be able to include this chapter in this volume. It is with great humility that we approach this topic. We hope that it will be helpful in clarifying some of the issues involved in this ongoing dialog. We draw heavily on our experience of a "living tradition" of faith-based ministry in the Canadian criminal justice system and in the community at-large.

We begin with a discussion of the historical relationship between the criminal justice system and the faith communities. We then outline some principles that offer clarity to the current issues and challenges of the "faith-based" dynamic. Next, we discuss faith-based programming through the "What Works" lens, followed by a review of the literature on faith-based programming, and a description of three faith-based programs from Canada that are examples of spiritual programming that works. Then, we provide our closing reflections.

Historical Perspectives

In matters of justice, the concerns of faith communities and those of the state often overlap. Both are deeply concerned with just relationships. All people must live by the laws of the state to help them live together as best they can. Justice is to be considered not only in its relationship to the laws of the state but also in its relationship to God, who in many traditions, is in a covenant relationship with his people.

Given the similarity of concerns for just relationships, and the complexity of human history, the relationship between faith communities and the criminal justice system has varied greatly. Letters in the New Testament and early Christian documents urged adherents to settle their differences outside of the public courts. However, those in prison were to be visited as a sacred duty. The Christian community was challenged by Jesus to see a simple prison visitation as an encounter with divinity. Although the meaning of Matthew 25:31-46 is subject to interpretation, many who have engaged in prison ministry have experienced the deep truth of the statement "I was in prison and you visited me" (Matthew 25:36).

On the conceptual side, some fundamental teachings in the Christian community came to influence the way criminal offenses were viewed:

- Offenses must not be ignored; yet, offenders must not be condemned.
- The concept of personal morality and its independent free will are cherished; yet, individual responsibility is demanded.

- The spiritual implications of offenses against the community are weighed, not only their social and monetary costs.

- The spiritual and pastoral care of offenders is essential, but with an emphasis on reconciliation with the community and with God.

The relationship between the Christian community and the state has moved back and forth between and among outright separation, cautious dialog, and formal alliance.

The alliance has a long history, first moving forward with the emperor Constantine, who granted Christianity a powerful position in the Roman Empire (313 A.D.). Some of the more distinctive characteristics of his reign occurred within the field of criminal law (McHugh, 1978, citing Cochrane, p.16). He authorized Episcopal courts to engage in civil litigation (McHugh, 1978, citing Cochrane, p. 16). Emperor Theodosius went much further, using legal sanctions against the "enemies" of Christendom (McHugh, 1978, p. 17). Today, this alliance is interpreted as an abduction of the Christian community to prop up a dying political and social order. What happened was not so much an effort to "christianize civilization as (an effort) to civilize Christianity" (McHugh, 1978, citing Cochrane, p. 17).

In the Middle Ages, "law" in the contemporary sense was largely unknown, with some practices slowly evolving and gaining widespread acceptance. The "ordeal" tested people about their guilt, and there was an evolving interest in the model of monastic prisons. Canon Law, introduced around 1140 A.D., permeated all of life, not just ecclesiastical matters. Thomas Aquinas felt heresy merited death (McHugh, 1978, p. 26). The spirit of compassion was seriously damaged.

In the Reformation period, Luther developed a distinction between private and public morality, which removed followers' reason to question brutal treatment by the state. By contrast, Calvin promoted a view that the state and the law could "promote the religious purpose of the maintenance of true religion" (McHugh, 1989, citing Cochrane, p. 25). He believed that the state had an important role in enforcing the moral order.

In the eighteenth century, the Quakers were instrumental in the development of the "penitentiary" as a type of prison. The Quakers believed that prisons could assist inmates with issues of the soul such as repentance and conversion. Prisons were places where offenders could be penitent for their behavior and make fresh commitments to a change of thinking and behavior. As such, the penitentiary was a faith-based initiative. However, times have changed. Today, the Quakers are in the forefront of the prison abolition movement.

The dialog about the role of organized religion in prisons and on behalf of prisoners continues, as witnessed by President Bush's initiative and a decision by organizations such as the International Community Corrections Associations to explore this issue. It is certainly a vital debate in Canada, where several church organizations now face bankruptcy, the result of past problems and misunderstanding. Some churches, including Catholic, United (Methodists), and Anglican (Episcopal), entered into a contract with the government of Canada to provide residentially based education to the Aboriginal community during the first half of the twentieth century. Later, it became known that some of the employees of these schools inflicted physical and sexual abuse on the residents. The former residents brought lawsuits against the government-funded schools. Although only a few named the churches in their lawsuits, the government of Canada insisted that the churches be included in the litigation. Although few have been settled, some churches are now in the process of selling their assets to pay for their portion of the liability. Yet, faith-based groups and individuals continue their compassionate involvement with those in conflict with the law. The Salvation Army, the inner-city missions, the millions of volunteer visitors, and creative reconciliation work demonstrates that it is in "the doing" that faith communities live out and incarnate their spirituality.

The historical relationship between the faith communities and the state continues to be complex. We now ask the question, "What is faith?"

The Significance of Faith in Faith-based Efforts

"Faith-based" is a very inclusive concept:

- It is used to justify capital punishment (for example, an eye for an eye) and to condemn it (respect for life).

- It is used to justify punishment generally (for example, the moral code, systems of penitence) and to condemn the very concept of punishment (per some proponents of restorative justice).

- It is used to promote some political positions and to condemn the same positions (for example, abortion and capital punishment).

Many people "have faith." Faith is applied in life as it is understood and integrated. It has an impact on all of life, or it is not faith. This is the nature of faith and its logical conclusion. Without addressing questions of content, faith has two foci: the individual and the community.

The Individual Focus: Stages of Faith Development

Fowler's (1981) work on the stages of faith development is very helpful. He identified seven stages:

1) Primal faith (infancy, *God is like Mommy and Daddy*).

2) Intuitive-projective faith (early childhood—*what's fair is fair*).

3) Mythic-literal faith (childhood and beyond—beginnings of order in the world).

4) Synthetic-conventional faith (adolescence and beyond—*I believe what the Church believes*).

5) Individuative-reflective faith (young adulthood and beyond—*as I see it God is . . .*).

6) Conjunctive faith (early mid-life and beyond, if at all—*More than just words*).

7) Universalizing faith (mid-life and beyond, very rare—*I have a dream*).

It is not clear what leads a person to change faith levels; indeed, it may be somewhat unconscious. Recognition of stages leads to a more tolerant approach to the ways in which people live their faith and provides a framework to understand growth. Some stages are more suited to religious structures and organizations than others. For instance, many organizations easily embrace stage four (noted above) but struggle with stage five. People differ in terms of their genetics, family of origin, and personality, and they also differ in terms of their faith formation. All are on a "journey," but all are at different points on that journey. Thus, a "cookie cutter" approach to faith is not appropriate. Individuals respond to faith in their own personal way.

The Communal Focus: Social Thought in the Church

Faith is not only a personal act but also an expression of the community. "No one can believe alone, just as no one can live alone" (Catechism of the Catholic Church, #166). "The human person needs to live in society . . . through the exchange with others, mutual service and dialogue . . . man (sic) develops his (sic) potential; he (sic) thus responds to his (sic) vocation" (Catechism of the Catholic Church, # 1879). An important doctrine, developed in the nineteenth century, has grown to emphasize a fundamental respect for human dignity. It has consequences for how the community is organized and recognizes that some social systems are incompatible with human dignity. Faith-based programming, from this perspective, focuses on building a healthy community, on modeling just and caring societies, and on improving family ties. The spiritual caregiver will be seen as a representative of a faith-based community into which the condemned person is invited and welcomed, thus bringing dignity to the offender. Quality faith-based programming must touch both the personal and the communal dimensions of faith.

Defining Faith-based Programming

What exactly does faith-based programming mean? What particular characteristics make a program faith-based? This is a challenging question. Is it the curriculum? Is it the spirit in which the curriculum is presented? Is it that a program is overtly religious? Does the faith of a clinician make a program faith-based? Do references to sacred texts or prayers make a program faith-based? These are difficult questions and a reductionistic approach inherent in these questions complicates the discussion. In considering the question, several cautions should be considered.

The first caution is to avoid reductionism. For example, many correctional workers are people of a faith or connected to a faith group. As stated earlier, well-integrated faith influences all of life. Thus, a question that practitioners might ask of themselves is, "What role does faith play in my life and occupation?" When a clinician, belonging to a particular faith group, delivers a program, it is reasonable to assume that faith, because of its impact on the clinician, will influence the delivery of that program. This would be true if the program were overtly faith-based or not. The argument is that since faith permeates all of life, then it will influence the delivery of a program. This is certainly the case in other fields as well, we believe. For example, a psychology class is taught from a different perspective if the teacher is an atheist, a practicing Muslim, or a fundamentalist Christian.

In addition, the term "faith," in faith-based programming, is often set within a medical or clinical framework, placing it in an all-or-nothing context. However, faith is personally practiced and is much more fluid in experience. Faith is rarely fully apprehended or experienced. The journey of faith may include getting lost, changing the way, getting sidetracked, and sometimes even denying one's faith. This and much more belongs to the journey of faith. The question then is, "At what point is a program faith-based?" The response is largely directly tied to the definitions of faith-based programming.

If the definition of faith-based programming includes people of faith who deliver programs, then it could be argued that many programs delivered by psychologists, social workers, nurses, and therapists are faith-based programs. If not faith-based, they would certainly be faith-influenced. However, if the definition of faith-based programming does not include the faith of individuals, but focuses more on faith practices, then it could be argued that Alcoholics Anonymous (AA) is a faith-based program. Twelve-step meetings usually begin with a prayer and include rituals, some of which are rooted in faith traditions. Is AA a faith-based program? If it is, then the question of whether faith-based programs work is a moot point, given that AA, a faith-based program (though not "religion-based" program), is one of the most successful alcohol rehabilitation programs of the twentieth century. The reductionist approach does not lend itself to understanding or describing adequately the impact of faith upon correctional programming. The definition of faith-based programming could, in large measure, determine the answer to the question of whether faith-based programming works.

A second caution concerns the ambiguity surrounding the term "program." McGuire (2000) states: "It is difficult to arrive at a single, clear-cut, unassailable definition of correctional programs that will firmly demarcate them from other forms of activity conducted with individuals sentenced by criminal courts." (p. 5). McGuire goes on to state that correctional programming has similarities with other programs in that they usually include aspects of education, training, therapy, or the alleviation of emotional distress—instilling new modes of thinking and problem-solving. Programs often have a healing component in them, as well. He concludes by saying: "Each of these domains [is] virtually impossible to define in any simple, satisfactory and mutually exclusive way" (McGuire, 2000, p. 5).

McGuire (2000) also offers a general description of a program: "a circumscribed set of activities, with an appointed objective, and consisting of a number of elements that are mutually inter-connected" (p. 7). Two more specific definitions follow. The first defines correctional programs as "planned sequences of learning opportunities delivered to adjudicated offenders with the general objective of reducing their subsequent criminal recidivism" (McGuire, 2000, p. 7). McGuire's (2000) second definition fits more closely with the many programs delivered in community ministry settings. The second definition is also wider in scope and more inclusive. It includes mentoring schemes for young offenders or therapeutic communities for substance-abusing offenders (McGuire, 2000, p. 6). If we use McGuire's first definition, the term "program" is a misnomer when applied to faith-based programming. Because of the mentoring nature of many faith-based programs, it is difficult to replicate planned sequences of learning opportunities. These sequences are highly individualized and become difficult to study from a social research perspective. Lesson plans can be developed, but the praxis of those lessons is individualized. General teaching principles, however, are comparable to most other programs. The goal of assisting offenders to reintegrate successfully into society is at the heart of most chaplaincy and faith-based programs.

An added difficulty in defining the term "program" is that most of what the faith communities offer fits within a larger integrated context. An offender may approach a spiritual care provider for food, housing, transportation, or employment assistance. A chaplain or volunteer may assist the offender with these practical needs, but also offer supportive advice, some counsel, and a prayer. Few chaplains or faith-based volunteers would refer to the prayer or spiritual advice as a program. Yet, many offenders and their families meet with the spiritual care provider to receive service within a spiritual context. The spiritual context is more about "being" than it is about "doing," and "being" is difficult to study empirically.

Defining faith-based programming is challenging. Faith-based programs frequently meet program definitions but include characteristics that are difficult to study empirically. The aspects of faith-based programming that connect with the mystery of faith and those that have a personal application make the issues more challenging. Developing studies that will capture the full impact of these programs adequately is, in part, the challenge. In Canada and the United States, we are now conducting such studies.

Faith and What Works: Measuring Impact

For many in the faith community, the "What Works" paradigm is a new approach. Including "faith" with impact studies is not only new to faith communities but also new to corrections. It is bringing a psychological methodology to bear on theology and spirituality. Some find this difficult while others believe it to be essential and necessary.

Institutional and community chaplains share in the corrections mandate of wanting safer communities and helping offenders stay out of prison by successfully reentering society. That is the goal of the "What Works" paradigm. The desire is to find the best ways of helping offenders not commit further criminal acts and to reduce recidivism. The question of "What Works" raises important issues and seeks to identify and assess areas where more attention should be focused. Intrinsic to the question are additional questions of how programs should be evaluated and what efforts should be made to bring about greater results, thereby reducing the risk to society for further criminal activity. Posing and responding to these and related questions will provide the kinds of information and impetus to improve programs and interventions, and contribute to reductions of risk of further criminal behavior.

Criteria for determining what works have come out of a number of meta-analytic projects that have endorsed efforts to develop criteria for successful correctional programs. Andrews and Bonta (1995) have classified risk factors into static and dynamic categories. Static risk factors such as age, previous criminal history, and early family setting reflect the offender's history. Dynamic risk factors, described later in this chapter, deal with the offender's present situation and are considered to be changeable with effort. The Level of Service Inventory, Revised (LSI-R), created by Andrews and Bonta (1995), seeks to address these factors of risk through an evaluation process.

Until recently, there were few systematic studies published on the relationship between recidivism and religious programming. In 1998, O'Connor, Ryan, and Parikh published a study entitled "A Model Program for Churches and Ex-offenders." This study examined the impact of faith-based programming that mobilized, trained, and equipped church-based volunteers to help offenders successfully reintegrate into their communities. The impact of the programs was assessed with the LSI-R instrument. Pre- and post-LSI-R tests were conducted as was a six-month assessment. These assessments helped indicate future areas of need for program attention. The results were very favorable, but the population studied was small. A few other studies have been conducted regarding the role of religion and recidivism. The Center for Social Research in Salem, Oregon was involved in these studies. The outcomes have been promising in both producing lower levels of in-prison infractions and lowering recidivism rates (O'Conner, Brooks, and Sprauer, 1999). These will be discussed below in the literature review.

Similar to the "What Works" criteria is the Correctional Service of Canada's Offender Intake Assessment and Correctional Planning process. This tool refers to a set of dynamic risk factors that are similar to those listed in the LSI-R. They are dynamic in the sense that they can change, or be influenced to change. They are not static like historical factors. The seven factor domains include the following:

1) Employment: The value placed on work and the role of work in one's life.

2) Marital/family: The value placed on being with family and the support one derives from family members.

3) Associates/social interaction: The value placed on noncriminal associates and the opportunity for positive social interaction.

4) Substance abuse: The value placed on living without reliance on alcohol and/or drugs.

5) Community functioning: The value placed on having the knowledge and necessary skills for daily living.

6) Personal/emotional orientation: The value placed on being in control of one's life.

7) Attitude: The value placed on living in law-abiding ways.

Faith-based programming could significantly affect every one of these factors. Its effectiveness could be measured, in part, by the extent to which it influences these seven dynamic factors. It is significant to note that chaplaincy interventions, within the Canadian context and especially in the community, address these seven dynamic factors in many ways. For example, community chaplains assist offenders with employment reentry. They support and assist with the reintegration of families where appropriate and link offenders with communities that provide a healthy social network.

Further, chaplains bring many resources such as contact with individuals and groups of people who are not criminals and with whom ex-offenders can have positive social interactions. Many chaplains also sponsor substance abuse programs in their facilities and are often trained in substance abuse programming. Chaplains also assist offenders with implementing daily living skills and frequently provide supportive counsel. Chaplains are well-connected with the resources in the community and often sit on community boards and committees. They contribute to offenders living in law-abiding ways.

As we discuss in the literature review, the literature on "What Works" is silent regarding the "faith factor." This a surprising omission, given that many offenders both in and out of prison relate to their faith communities, chaplains, and faith-based volunteers. An offender survey conducted by the Correctional Service of Canada (1996) indicated that 50 percent of inmates were very satisfied with chaplaincy services. One-third of inmates said that they access chaplaincy services at least once a month. This included attending worship services, Bible studies, or other forms of religious practice. Such participation is common in most prisons, making religious and faith-based programming one of the most common "programs." In addition, there is considerable anecdotal evidence that supports the positive correlation between faith and offender rehabilitation; however, limited empirical evidence exists.

A Canadian study completed in the fall of 2001 discovered that more than 10,000 individuals, including offenders and their families, accessed community ministries across Canada. Quite simply, many offenders and their families appreciate and value the service they receive from faith-based agencies or ministries. In all cases, the services are accessed on a voluntary, noncompulsory basis. Other studies (for example, Cesaroni, 2001; Molzahn, 2001) have shown that the spiritual care provider's availability and interventions, based upon offenders' self-reports, resulted in offenders not continuing to commit violent crimes. The point is that there does not seem to be provision in the "What Works" literature to examine or account for these impacts of faith. Nowhere are interventions by or with the faith community mentioned. Perhaps in the future more attention will be focused in this area.

Literature Review[1]

The health care system was the first to recognize the impact of spirituality on health and wellness. During the past twenty years, a body of research has been assessing the impact of spirituality on health. Many studies are establishing a positive correlation between spirituality and health. In May 2001, the Universary of Calgary Faculty of Medicine sponsored a North American Multidisciplinary Conference on Spirituality and Health with more than 300 healthcare professionals to share research and explore this topic. Similar interest has emerged to examine religion/spirituality in prisons. In fact, some corrections specialists have documented the role of faith groups in offender rehabilitation and in the very creation of the prison system in the United States and Canada (Colson, 1979; Colson and Van Ness, 1988; O'Connor and Parikh, 1998; Skotnicki, 1992).

The practice of religion in prison is widespread. The United Nations affirms the right of every prisoner to receive religious services. A chaplain, elder, volunteer, or a person authorized by his or her faith community usually delivers spiritual service/care to prisoners. In Canada, the ratio of full-time chaplains to inmates is 1 to 150-200. In addition, the Correctional Service of Canada has contracts with representatives from such faith traditions as Muslim, Buddhist, Judaism, Sikh, Aboriginal, and Wiccan who provide spiritual/religious services to incarcerated persons. Many inmates are involved in worship services, bible studies, pastoral care groups, religious education, mentoring programs, and other programs of a spiritual nature. These activities are delivered in small groups, large groups, one-to-one, or pursued by the inmate in the confines of his or her cell through correspondence, videotape, audiotape, or computer.

Given the increasing attention to faith and faith-based programming in corrections, there is relatively little written, raising the questions: Is there any research that demonstrates religious involvement contributes to offender rehabilitation? Is there a positive correlation between offender involvement in spiritual and religious activities and reduced recidivism? Is all of this religious and spiritual activity making a difference in the lives and behaviors of offenders?

Sadly, the data are limited. O'Connor, Brooks, and Sprauer (1999) observe that the field of correctional research and offender rehabilitation has usually overlooked the impact of religious and spiritual programs on inmates (*see also* Andrews et al., 1990). Gendreau (1995) and Gartner, et al. (1990) reinforce the idea that the "faith factor" is being overlooked. This omission has led Bainbridge (1989) to call religion the "forgotten variable."

Although there has been a dearth of research concerning the impact of spirituality on offender rehabilitation, there has been a growing interest in the topic since the 1980s. In one study of 782 men in a minimum-security prison who were serving their first term of incarceration, Johnson (1984) found no significant correlation between self-reported religiosity, church attendance, or prison chaplain's rating of inmate religiosity and amount of time spent in confinement for disciplinary infractions. Young and colleagues, however, did find a significant long-term impact of a prison program sponsored and run by Prison Fellowship Ministries, entitled "Discipleship Seminars" on adult criminal recidivism. They assembled two groups of women and men: one group consisted of 180 federal inmates who participated in the Prison Fellowship program; the other was a matched control group of 185 inmates from a cohort of 2,289 inmates who were released around the same time as the Prison Fellowship inmates. The study examined the re-arrest patterns of the two groups over a period of eight to fourteen years. The research demonstrated that the Prison Fellowship group had a significantly lower rate of recidivism than the other group.

Clear and colleagues (1992) found a significant relationship between religiosity and rehabilitation. They asked whether an inmate's religiosity had an impact on in-prison adjustment and in-prison infractions. The researchers studied 760 men in 20 prisons throughout 12 states representing different regions of the country as well as different security levels. The "Hunt and King," a set of statements about a person's religious beliefs attempting to measure a person's mythological symbolic religious commitment, was used to assess religiosity. The subjects were also asked questions about depression, self-mastery, self-esteem, demographics, and criminal histories. The Wright Adjustment Scale measured in-prison adjustment (Wright, 1985). Infractions were measured by the self-reported number of disciplinary infractions.

Clear and colleagues, after controlling for demographics and criminal history, demonstrated that high religiosity directly predicted fewer infractions and indirectly predicted better adjustment. Religiosity was one of the strongest predictors of the number of infractions along with variables such as the number of prior prison arrests and age at time of arrest. Religiosity fell out of the regression equation on adjustment when the control variables were introduced but was indirectly related to better adjustment when depression was considered. The findings of the study were "prison-specific." That is, the religious effects on adjustment and infractions were found in some but not in all of the prisons. The two effects also were not found together; instead, there was either a religious effect on adjustment or a religious effect on infractions.

Clear (1992) also discovered that there might be a positive correlation between an offender's commitment to religion and his or her outlook on life. He found that religious inmates showed a reduced sense of personal threat and aimlessness during incarceration, and were less subject to depression and feeling threatened. Their commitment to religious expression seemed to give them more optimism and a feeling of being more comfortable than those inmates who were less religious.

O'Connor and colleagues (1994) found that religious involvement had no relationship to in-prison infractions but had some relationship to recidivism. After controlling for self-selection bias, prison misconduct, and level of risk for recidivism, the study found that there was a significant difference in recidivism when those who had high rates of ministry participation were compared to those who had low or no ministry participation (O'Connor, 1995). However, O'Connor (2002), reflecting on a weakness of the research, stated that the study had no way of determining the level of religious activity practiced by those in the comparison group. In fact, he wonders whether the research might have been comparing religiously involved inmates to other religiously involved inmates.

A secondary analysis of O'Connor's data by a different team of researchers confirmed that there was no significant overall difference between the religious participants and their "non-religious" comparison group on in-prison infractions or re-arrest within one year. Nonetheless, they did find that there was evidence of a significant relationship between high religious attendance and lower rates of recidivism. O'Connor (1995), reflecting on the level of participation in religious programming as a significant factor, offers the following: "Conversion theory views conversion, and the accompanying behavioral changes, as an ongoing process." He continues by stating, "Attendance at a couple of Bible study classes cannot be expected to create lasting conversion and, as a result, reduced recidivism" (1996, p. 18).

O'Connor and Perryclear (2001) considered the impact of prison religion on offender rehabilitation at a large medium/maximum-security prison in South Carolina. During the year of the study, 779 out of 1,579 inmates had attended, at least, one religious service or program. Religion/spirituality played an important role in this prison. More than 800 religious meetings were held during the year, along with a support staff of two prison chaplains, four inmate clerks, and 232 volunteers. The estimated cost of these religious services was a remarkable $150 to $200 per inmate. O'Connor and Perryclear, after controlling for a number of demographic and criminal history factors, found an inverse relationship between the intensity of religious involvement and the presence or absence of in-prison infractions. As religious involvement increased, the number of inmates with infractions decreased.

In summary, this emerging research on the role that religious practice plays in offender rehabilitation is insightful. The Chaplaincy Division of the Correctional Service of Canada is now embarking on a two-year project to assess the impact of chaplaincy and faith-based programming on offenders and ex-offenders both inside and outside prison. For many years, there has been a great deal of anecdotal evidence that the faith factor is significant. Now, through planned, careful research, a body of literature must be created that addresses this issue.

Three Faith-based Initiatives

In Canada, and many other countries, there are numerous faith-based initiatives that are making positive contributions to offender rehabilitation (*see* the Appendix, beginning on page 264). Three faith-based programs, different along several dimensions, will be presented in this section: (1) Circles of Support and Accountability, (2) Community Chaplaincy, and (3) Healing Lodges, which are located in the Aboriginal community.

Circles of Support and Accountability

Circles of Support and Accountability (CSA) is a faith-based program that seeks to reintegrate warrant-expiry sexual offenders into communities (*see* Molzahn). The program began in 1994 after new detention legislation was created in Canada. Offenders detained to the last day of their sentence (warrant expiry date or WED) left the institution with little or no community support and no monitoring mechanisms in place to assist with their safe reentry to the community of residence. Many communities became alarmed when they heard that a sex offender was moving into their community. As a result, the offender usually had to face a fear-based, emotionally charged, vigilante reception provided by the community.

Circles of Support and Accountability began with a local church's response to the return of an offender to a community. The pastor had visited the offender while he was in prison and built a relationship. Now that the offender was out of prison, the pastor felt compelled to continue the support. Out of that support emerged this faith-based program. Since those early days, there have been at least fifty Circles of Support and Accountability throughout Canada. Ministries, churches, and agencies that were well established in their communities responded to the need. All of them have the goal of preventing further victimization and promoting a safer community.

Circles of Support and Accountability volunteers receive extensive training and essentially provide a mentoring-type relationship with the offender. Professionals including police representatives, psychologists, and physicians support the Circles of Support and Accountability initiative. They offer volunteers and advice as they support the offender who is referred to as the "core member" and hold him or her accountable. They also advocate, confront, mediate, and celebrate achievements, when appropriate. In short, volunteers walk with the core member and help him or her reenter the community of residence by becoming a community of support. For many core members, it is the first time they have experienced a wholesome community.

Volunteers stated that they find the experience enriching and deeply fulfilling. They are also highly motivated and approach their work with a sense of "call" and "mission" (Molzahn, 2001, p. 24). Some want to "give back" to their community. This sense of "call" was a major motivating factor for volunteers and helped them transcend many challenges. Thus, directing this sense of call or mission is of paramount importance. The volunteers' faith is an important reason they give for being involved in the Circles of Support and Accountability program.

Most core members experienced a great deal of success with the Circles of Support and Accountability program. Some have remained in the community for more than two years and some much longer. Given the short time since the establishment of the program, this is a great achievement. When interviewed, core members expressed thanks to the volunteers for their help and support. All core members stated that if it were not for volunteers, "they would not be [t]here," meaning that they would have been back in prison. The reason for the statement is noteworthy, however. Most core members stated that they had feelings of bitterness toward the "system" which detained them; thus, they left the institutions feeling bitter and angry. They also stated that since being out of prison there were occasions when they had been angry enough to consider acting out aggressively and even committing another sexual crime (Ceasoroni, 2001; Molzahn, 2001). The core members said that the volunteers helped them process their anger in a positive manner so that they did not victimize anyone else. The benefits to the community are immense, and the interventions of volunteers have had a major impact on reducing victimization.

Recidivism studies have been conducted on this program and found that there has been a 50 percent reduction in recidivism when compared with those warrant expiry sex offenders who were not in a circle (Wilson, Stewart, Stirpe, Barret, and Cripps, 2000). The Wilson et al. study also found that when considering the program in terms of harm reduction, each incident where recidivism occurred was less invasive than the incident for which the offender had been incarcerated originally.

Circles of Support and Accountability is a complex program blending faith, theology, psychology, criminology, and restorative justice principles together. It both complements and challenges the definitions of our common understanding of a program. In a sense, it is a support and mentoring initiative that encompasses all of life. It helps individuals realize their full potential and models what it means to be a full citizen of society. Yet, at some point, this program also helps to affirm human dignity and allows the volunteer to be a friend.

Community Chaplaincy

Community Chaplaincy is a diverse faith-based program with the long-term goal of having safer communities and reducing criminal recidivism. Community chaplains typically are people who have a vision and aptitude for community ministry. The ministry has a contract with the Correctional Service of Canada to provide services to offenders and their families. These contractors usually provide Community Chaplaincy as part of a larger ministry to their community and thus have additional resources to those provided by the Correctional Service of Canada.

Community Chaplaincy ministries are accountable to many stakeholders, the Correctional Service of Canada being one of many. Other groups are the faith community, community agencies, municipalities, the local police, and professional groups, among others. Each group is concerned about and committed to having safe and healthy communities. Most programs and services offered fall within the definition of correctional programs provided by James McGuire (2000), cited in earlier sections of this chapter. As with most chaplaincy programs, there is a mentorship component.

Community Chaplaincy focuses much of its attention on the reintegration needs of offenders. These needs fall into seven dynamic domains that contribute towards the successful reintegration of offenders into society (Correctional Service of Canada, Offender Intake Assessment and Correctional Planning). More than 10,000 individuals are served through Community Chaplaincy ministries in a given year. Many offenders and their family members have longstanding relationships with the community ministry that provides them with daily living support. Others have short-term relationships that end after a certain need is met. Some community ministries have a "drop in" component where offenders, family members, or community members may drop in and receive or offer support to others who are there. For some, it has become their supportive community. Most often, faith-based volunteers staff these sites. Experiencing supportive community, having a warm place to rest, having a meal or a coffee, and staying off the street are just some of the benefits of the drop-in center. In some cases, lower functioning individuals spend more time in the drop-in center where they find a safe place. Mental health challenges are numerous at most Community Chaplaincy ministries.

The average age of offenders working with community chaplains is estimated to be thirty-four. This is compared to the average age of volunteers, which is forty-two. As mentorship is frequently a model that community ministries use, the relatively small age difference is an advantage for a beneficial relationship. Chaplains and volunteers spend 52 percent of their time with offenders, 14 percent with offender-families, 21 percent making prison contacts, and 12 percent in the "other" category. The offender group consists of offenders on day parole, full parole, statutory release, and WED (warrant expiry date) offenders. The high risk and high needs offenders demand more ministry time by both chaplains and volunteers. Critical to the relationship that chaplains have with offenders are the contacts they make in the institution. Contact is made with offenders and Correctional Service of Canada staff regarding discharge planning for an offender.

Families are central to helping offenders move back into society. However, they need support and guidance. In addition, families frequently experience financial hardship when the wage earner goes to prison. As a result, most community chaplains and faith-based volunteers provide or create a network with agencies that provide food, clothing, and furniture to these families.

The "other group" (12 percent) refers to those no longer serving time, youth and young offenders, and victims. The "parish" of most community chaplains includes not only the offenders and their families but also the wider community. The pastoral identity of community chaplains does not restrict their involvement to only offenders or their families. Community ministries have an early intervention strategy. The first six weeks are often most critical for reintegration. As a result, 80 percent of the offenders are contacted within thirty days of the offender coming into the community. Contact occurs at the halfway house, community corrections center, at the chaplain's office or other places in the community. Parole officers are usually supportive and refer offenders to the community chaplain.

Offenders have many specialized needs. Some have supervision challenges and others have daily living challenges. The challenges include:

- Peace bonds or strict release conditions: Seventeen percent of offenders have such conditions when released from the institution. These offenders need a great deal of support.

- Rage interventions: Chaplains and volunteers occasionally deal with angry offenders. Studies have indicated that these interventions are very effective in reducing victimization (Ceasoroni 2001, Molzahn 2001); 34 percent of the offenders dealt with substantial anger issues with the chaplain or with a volunteer.

- Grief: Twenty-nine percent of the offenders dealt with grief and loss issues. These losses included the death of family members or friends, loss of family, loss of job, loss of community, plus many other issues. Many chaplains also noted that they frequently supported offenders who were dealing with childhood traumatic events such as being victims of sexual abuse.

- Mental health: Thirty-nine percent of the offenders had mental health issues. They included those with psychiatric needs who needed to take medication continuously, plus those with anxiety and bipolar disorders, depression, and schizophrenia. Suicide prevention support was also provided. Many referrals were made to community agencies.

- Addictions: Thirty-three percent of the offenders received support for their addiction problems from the community ministry. Alcohol, drugs, sex, and gambling were some of the addictions noted. Some ministries provided faith-based support programs, and others hosted support programs like AA or NA in their facilities.

- Food: Twenty-two percent of the individuals relating to the community ministry requested assistance for food. Some of the contacts came through institutional contacts when offenders in prison reported to the community chaplain that their families needed food. Many individuals were also directed to community food banks.

- Older offenders: Thirteen percent (mostly older offenders) required assistance in restarting their lives. Frequently, they arrive in the community lonely, not having had many relationships.

- Medical care: Thirteen percent of the offenders reportedly had medical needs, for example, HIV, Hepatitis C, sexually transmitted diseases, cancer, or other medical and dental needs. One chaplain stated that 70 percent of all the offenders that he worked with had Hepatitis C or were infected with HIV.

- Housing: Fifty-two percent of the offenders received assistance to improve their housing.

- Other: Many other areas of support were indicated, for example, support to lifers and support for transportation, telephone assistance, job-hunting, court appearances, hosting and planning spiritual retreats, Christmas gifts for children, and spiritual reading and video materials.

Community ministries are well-connected with many resources in the communities and are full community partners. Strong community relationships are essential for healthy community ministries. Community Chaplaincies reported having more than 1,200 active volunteers. Volunteers receive extensive training and are full partners in the ministry. They provided approximately 217,000 hours of service with a dollar value of $3.4 million dollars per year. On average, each community ministry received more than 7,000 volunteer hours per year or the equivalent of $110,000 in labor hours.

One unique form of support that is deeply appreciated is prayer support. Many chaplains and people of faith often state that prayer support is the most important support they receive in their ministry. Prayer is difficult to quantify and measure. It simply is. Many volunteers pray for their communities and for the community ministries. It is a unique part of chaplaincy and one area where volunteering is most directly linked with the faith community. It also adds to the debate of what faith-based programming is. Most of what is mentioned above is practical support; yet, prayer is spiritual support. Chaplains would argue that both are important and the unique contribution of the Community Chaplaincy ministry is that it is offered within a spiritual context.

Community ministries also receive over $1.6 million per year as "in kind" support such as office space, training and meeting rooms, food, clothing, and transportation. The National Community Chaplaincy budget in 2000/2001 was $758,538. The average expenditure for each community ministry was approximately $24,000. For this investment, Correctional Service of Canada chaplaincy partners with ministries that generate more than $5 million worth of value. It is a large investment in offenders, families, and communities.

Perhaps the greatest area where the impact of faith is evident in Community Chaplaincy is in the area of motivation. Community chaplains were polled as to why they chose to be chaplains. They reported that they were motivated by several factors, for example: a sense of call (99 percent); work with the poor (79 percent); concern about justice issues (84 percent); restorative justice (90 percent), desire for healthy communities (85 percent), desire to get involved in healing work (83 percent), academic interest (40 percent), intrigue about the "street culture" (38 percent), a desire to give back to their community (57 percent), search for a place to volunteer (28 percent), need for a job (30 percent), a similar previous experience with the clientele (50 percent); past experience of friends (47 percent); and other reasons (8 percent). Community chaplains indicated that spirituality is a major reason that they choose this form of ministry. Calling, caring for the poor, justice, and healing are typically aspects that belong to a sense of call. Personal experiences also seem to motivate chaplains to be involved in the ministry.

Finally, Community Chaplaincy fulfills a broad mandate. It serves many individuals, is fully engaged in the community, and mobilizes many volunteers. Where recidivism data are minimally available, other mandates are being fulfilled. Corrections is concerned with community engagement, strong community partners, and volunteer mobilization. It is concerned with families and offender reintegration and having safe communities. Community chaplaincy delivers in each of these areas.

Aboriginal Healing Lodges[2]

Over the past ten years, the Correctional Service of Canada has introduced a new way of delivering corrections for Aboriginal offenders serving a federal sentence. The Supreme Court of Canada joined the Royal Commission on Aboriginal Peoples and the auditor general in a call to stop filling Canadian prisons with Aboriginal peoples. The Commissioner of Corrections in Canada also stated that there are too many First Nation, Inuit, and Metis offenders in the Canadian correctional system. While forming only 3 percent of the general Canadian population, Aboriginal offenders make up 17 percent of the federal penitentiary inmates and represent an even greater percentage in the provincial institutions. In the Canadian Prairie provinces, Aboriginal people make up more than 60 percent of the inmate population in some penitentiaries.

The Solicitor General's office was determined to address this challenge and introduced a strategy to deal with the large numbers of Aboriginal people in the corrections system. It included legislation, programming, and the building of healing lodges designed and operated by Aboriginal people from Aboriginal communities. This strategy included Correctional Service of Canada developing a working relationship with Aboriginal elders and also with some aboriginal communities.

Aboriginal elders provide a variety of programs for Aboriginal offenders in the Correctional Service of Canada facilities. Opportunities are presented to address criminogenic factors from an aboriginal perspective. Included are programs that address educational upgrading, substance abuse, violent behavior, sex offending behavior, and spiritual teachings. The elders provide an Aboriginal identity for many offenders who are searching for such an identity. Their approaches incorporate healing, reconciliation, spirituality, respect, accountability, balance, and restoration.

Most Aboriginal offenders choose to participate in the Aboriginal programs. Prior to the Aboriginal option, many Aboriginal offenders did not complete programs at the same rate as that of other offenders. The need to provide Aboriginal alternatives to core programs was recognized. These alternative programs use innovative approaches to programming in contrast to the cognitive-behavioral model favored for standard programs.

The relationship with the Aboriginal community continues after an offender is released from the institution. Offenders who wish to continue on their healing journey from an Aboriginal perspective can find the tools and resources in their own communities and with their own people. Having these culturally appropriate programs after release is most important, as is the space in which the program is conducted.

The healing lodges are a key part of the strategy for providing culturally-sensitive programs. Healing lodges reflect the physical space and the programs of the Aboriginal culture. The spiritual programs and ceremonies often include offenders, staff, volunteers and/or family and friends. Lodges are designed to accommodate small groups and are built in a circular manner, which enhances the Aboriginal celebrations and rituals.

In a follow-up study by the Correctional Service of Canada with 412 Aboriginal offenders admitted to some of the healing lodges:

- 286 or 69.4 percent completed the program.
- Of those completing, 16 or 6 percent had been returned to federal custody for committing a new offense while on conditional release.

- In contrast, the national federal recidivism rate was 11 percent in 1997-98 (for full parole and statutory release).

The indication is that the Aboriginal healing lodge participants had a 5 percent lower federal recidivism rate. The early indication is that Aboriginal healing lodges were having a positive impact and that more Aboriginal offenders were being safely and successfully reintegrated to the community. More studies are being conducted.

Conclusion

In this chapter, we have offered some insights concerning faith-based programming and its impact on offender rehabilitation both inside and outside of prisons. We began the chapter by offering a brief historical sketch of the relationship between the faith community and the state system of criminal justice. However, we cautioned against a simplistic understanding of terms like "faith," presenting principles to see faith as inclusive, personal, and communal and a narrow perspective which views faith-based through too small a lens. We also offered a discussion of the question, "Does faith-based programming work?" We then presented a brief overview of the small but growing body of literature that has been addressing this question over the past decade. The chapter moved from the philosophical and theoretical to the practical by portraying three diverse faith-based programs in Canada: Circles of Support and Accountability, Community Chaplaincy, and Aboriginal healing lodges.

As the authors embark on a two-year study of the impacts of chaplaincy and faith-based programming both in prison and in the community, they are confident that they will learn more about the significance of the "faith factor" in the field of criminal justice. Evidence-based research in the faith communities is viewed with some degree of skepticism. How does one measure faith? As noted above, "faith" is complex and sometimes illusive. It is important to continue the path established in the 1980s in healthcare and the 1990s in corrections. This path applies good research practices that combine quantitative and qualitative research methods in evaluating faith and spirituality. If faith really does "work" let's not be afraid to answer the question, "How is it working?"

Endnotes

[1] Thanks to Tom O'Connor for graciously providing us with a literature review on this subject in an article entitled "Prison Religion in Action and its Influence on Offender Rehabilitation," *Journal of Offender Rehabilitation*, 2002.

[2] Adapted from a paper by Gina Wilson (2000), entitled "Enhancing the Role of Aboriginal Communities in Federal Corrections."

Appendix

Examples of Faith-based Programs in Canada

- Forgiveness Group (Regional Psychiatric Center-Prairies). This is an interdenominational initiative that explores forgiveness from a spiritual and treatment perspective.

- Drama (Regional Psychiatric Center-Prairies). The Saskatoon Christian Centre, in cooperation with Prison Fellowship, uses drama (with full costumes and props) once a month to promote spiritual awareness.

- Person to Person Program (Saskatoon). An Interfaith Visitation program that pairs inmates without family or friends in the area with volunteers from the local area.

- M2W2 (British Columbia). A prison visitation program which has grown out of the Mennonite community. It matches inmates with a community volunteer.

- Alpha (throughout Canada). A fourteen-week Christian education program that operates in prison, as well as in the community for offenders, ex-offenders, and their families.

- Kairos Marathons (Atlantic Canada). An encounter group that brings inmates and volunteers together for an intensive time of self- and spiritual exploration and renewal.

- St. Luke's Renewal Center (Springhill, Nova Scotia). An initiative that is sponsored by the Christian Council for Reconciliation in Atlantic Canada. The Center, built and operated by the local faith communities, is located on the prison grounds. It is designed to offer spiritual programming, reflection, and renewal to both individuals and groups.

- Prison Pause (throughout Canada). This is sponsored by Prison Fellowship. It is designed to help inmates make plans for their release. It uses the biblical story of the patriarch Joseph to illustrate how he kept the faith, dreamed his dreams, and overcame obstacles to move from despair to success.

- Life Recovery Groups (Stony Mountain Institution). These groups use materials published by InterVarsity Press to help participants address issues such as family dysfunction, distorted images of God, shame, bitterness, abuse, loss, addictions, and codependency.

- Parenting Group (Regional Psychiatric Center-Prairies). This group attempts to address parenting issues from a Christian and Aboriginal point of view.

- Forgiveness Group (Regional Psychiatric Center-Prairies). This is a group designed to explore issues of forgiveness. The members are encouraged to use their own spirituality to approach issues dealing with forgiveness.

- Overnight Family Accommodation (Grand Cache Institution). A church has opened up a suite in the basement of its parish to help spouses of inmates with accommodation while visiting from out of town.

- Circles of Support and Accountability (throughout Canada). A program of support and accountability for warrant-expiry sexual offenders.

- Bars None. A community support program for ex-offenders.

- Alternatives to Violence Program (throughout Canada). A program that explores alternatives to violence sponsored by the Quakers.

- Project Art Lab. An experience in the arts with children of prisoners through faith-based volunteers.

- Gambling Addiction Reflection Group. This faith-based group works with those struggling with a gambling addiction.

- Clothing Depot. Sponsored by a faith-based group that provides clothes to offenders, ex-offenders, and their families.

- Overcomers Twelve Step Program. This program is designed for offenders, ex-offenders, and their families to assist them with addictions and compulsive behaviors.

- Steps to Security (Drumheller Institution). A faith-based group for twelve step recovery. Its goal is to assist the individual in addressing addictions and compulsion, and bringing a healthy balance and perspective to one's life.

- Community Chaplaincy (throughout Canada). A grassroots initiative created to support offenders, ex-offenders, and their families in the community reintegration process.

- Sounding the Depths (Stony Mountain, Manitoba). This program is designed to facilitate self-examination of the inner life through eight consecutive weekly sessions. Its goal is to help participants understand why some life responses have negative effects and others produce wholeness and healing.

- Grief Recovery Group (Mission/Ferndale, British Columbia). This group is designed to assist inmates with grief and trauma issues.

References

Andrews, D. A. 1995. The Psychology of Criminal Conduct and Effective Treatment. In J. McGuire, ed. *What Works: Reducing Criminal Reoffending.* New York: John Wiley.

Andrews, D. A. and P. Bonta. 1995. *The Level of Supervision Inventory—Revised.* Toronto, Ontario: Multi-Health Systems, Inc.

Andrews, D. A., I. R. Zinger, P. Bonta, and F. T. Cullen. 1990. Does Correctional Treatment Work? A Clinically Relevant and Psychologically Informed Meta-analysis. *Criminology.* 28: 369-404.

Bainbridge, William. 1989. The Religious Ecology of Deviance. *American Sociological Review.* 54(2): 288-295.

Catechism of the Catholic Church, Second Edition. 1997. Ft. Collins, Colorado: St. Ignatius Press.

Cesaroni, Carla. 2001. Releasing Sex Offenders into the Community through Circles of Support: A Means of Reintegrating the "Worst of the Worst." *Journal of Offender Rehabilitation.* 34(2): 85-98.

Clear, T., B. Stout, H. Dammer, L. Kelly, P. Hardyman, and C. Shapiro. 1992. *Prisoners, Prisons, and Religion: Final Report.* Newark: New Jersey: School of Criminal Justice, Rutgers University.

Colson, C. W. 1976. *Born Again.* Lincoln, Virginia: Chosen Books.

Colson, C. W. and Van Ness. 1988. *Convicted: New Hope of Ending America's Crime Crisis.* Westchester, Illinois: Crossway Books.

Correctional Service of Canada. 1996. *National Inmate Survey: Final Report.* Ottawa, Ontario: Correctional Service of Canada.

Correctional Service of Canada. 2001. *Community Chaplaincy Report.* Ottawa, Ontario: Correctional Service of Canada.

Colson, C. W. 1979. *Life Sentence.* Lincoln, Virginia: Chosen Books.

Fowler, J. 1981. *Stages of Faith: The Psychology of Human Development and the Quest for Meaning.* San Francisco: Harper and Row.

Gartner, J., T. O'Connor, D. Larson, M. Young, K. Wright, and B. Rosen. 1990. *Rehabilitation, Recidivism and Religion: A Systematic Literature Review.* Baltimore, Maryland: Loyola College in Maryland.

Gartner, J., D. B. Larson and G. Allen. 1991. Religion and Mental Health: A Review of the Empirical Literature. *Journal of Psychology and Theology.* 19(1): 6-25.

Gendreau, P. 1995. The Principles of Effective Intervention with Offenders. In A. T. Harland, ed. *Choosing Correctional Options that Work: Defining the Demand and Evaluating the Supply.* Thousand Oaks, California: Sage Publications.

Johnson, B. R., D. B. Larson, and T. C. Pitts. 1997. Religious Programs, Institutional Adjustment, and Recidivism among Inmates in Prison Fellowship Programs. *Justice Quarterly.* 14(1): 501-521.

Johnson, B. R. 1984. *Hellfire and Corrections: A Quantitative Study of Florida Prison Inmates.* Florida State University.

Lipsey, M. W. 1995. What Do We Learn From 400 Research Studies on the Effectiveness of Treatment with Juvenile Delinquents? In J. McGuire, ed. *What Works: Reducing Criminal Reoffending.* New York: John Wiley.

Losel, F. 1996. Effective Correctional Programming: What Empirical Research Tells Us and What it Doesn't. *Forum on Corrections Research.* 8(3): 33-37.

McGuire, J. 2000. Defining Correctional Programs. *Forum on Corrections Research.* 12(2): 5-9.

McHugh, G. A. 1978. *Christian Faith and Criminal Justice: Toward a Christian Response to Crime and Punishment.* New York: Paulist Press.

McKelvey, Blake. 1977. *American Prisons: A History of Good Intentions.* Montclair, New Jersey: Patterson Smith.

Molzahn, D. 2001. *Circles of Support Accountability Evaluation Report.* Correctional Service of Canada.

O'Connor, T. 1995. The Impact of Religious Programming on Recidivism, the Community and Prisons. *Journal on Community Corrections.* 6(6): 13-19.

O'Connor, T. and C. Parikh. 1998. Best Practices for Ethics and Religion in Community Corrections. *Journal on Community Corrections.* 8(4): 26-32.

O'Connor, T. P., M. Perryclear. 2002. Prison Religion in Action and its Influence on Offender Rehabilitation. *Journal of Offender Rehabilitation.* Spring.

O'Connor, T., P. Ryan, and C. Parikh. 1998. A Model Program for Churches and Ex-offender Reintegration. *Journal of Offender Rehabilitation.* 28:107-126.

O'Connor, T. P., T. Brooks, and M. W. Sprauer. 1999. Spirituality, Religion and What Works—Religious Program Outcomes: This Side of Heaven. Presentation at the American Correctional Association's Congress of Correction, August 11, 1999, Denver, Colorado.

O'Connor, T. P., F. Yang, P. Ryan, K. Wright, and C. Parikh. 1994. *The New York Study of Prison Fellowship Programming: Executive Summary and Final Report.* Silver Spring, Maryland: Center for Social Research, Inc.

Skotnicki, A. 1992. Religion and the Development of the American Penal System. Doctoral Dissertation, Berkely, California: Graduate Theological Union.

Wilson, R. J., L. Sewart, T. Stirpe, M. Barrett, and J. E. Cripps. 2000. Community-based Sex Offender Management: Combining Parole Supervision and Treatment to Reduce Recidivism. *Canadian Journal of Criminology.* 42: 177-188.

Young, M., J. Gartner, T. O'Connor, D. Larson, and K. Wright. 1994. The Impact of a Volunteer Prison Ministry Program on the Long Term Recidivism of Federal Inmates. *Journal of Offender Rehabilitation.* 22(1).

AFTERWORD

Vivian L. Gadsen
Associate Professor, Graduate School of Education
University of Pennsylvania
Philadelphia, Pennsylvania

As the critiques and commentaries of the authors in this volume suggest, concerns related to parental incarceration, reentry, and reintegration, along with the impact they have on families, cross the boundaries that typically divide research and practice and often separate these spheres from policymaking. Addressing these concerns requires collective, collaborative, and strategic efforts that

- reduce risks to children resulting from parental incarceration
- enhance the roles of families and of communities so they can be protective spaces for children
- assist families and communities in addressing the uncertainties arising from parental absence and reentry after incarceration.

Afterword

In addition, correctional institutions, family services, and labor agencies are central to the task of determining what best promotes responsible parenting within both correctional settings and within the prisoners' families and communities of origin. The growing attention to the intersections among incarceration, families, communities, and reintegration make the present a particularly important time for the field of community corrections.

However, the ambivalence that exists among policymakers and society at large toward the impact of incarceration on families and communities—particularly within low-income communities or communities of color—has resulted in the absence of a systematic approach for collecting empirical and ethnographic information about the following things for incarcerated parents and their families:

- basic research and intervention evaluations
- coordinated policies that do not penalize the children and communities of incarcerated parents along with the offender

This lack of concern has led to the erosion of social capital in communities with high rates of incarceration, the development of social policies and services that often advance competing values, and only sporadic success among programs addressing the needs of incarcerated parents. It has also created a climate in the criminal justice system that allows substantial racial disparities in arrests, convictions, and sentencing to continue without question or inspection. The most important consideration that has yet to be addressed is the specific effects that all of these factors have on children whose parents have been incarcerated.

Rather than advancing a single or simple approach, the chapters and the larger literature on corrections and families suggest that the field—researchers and practitioners alike—should take on an inquiry stance: a concept and approach that has been promoted widely in education and has focused on individuals exploring conceptions and enactments of their daily roles and potential sources of knowledge for envisioning and revising their roles (*see* Cochran-Smith and Lytle, 2001). In this field, there simply is not enough information about what works or empirical data on what the long-term implications of seemingly effective strategies are.

If we accept Travis' (2001) position that reintegration is the *end-point* of the process of incarceration, the reality is that we neither fully understand the *process* itself nor the intermediate points that help us connect the set of circumstances and conditions that predate incarceration to those that exist postincarceration. Worse, we have yet to make investments in the knowledge-creating and program-creating enterprises needed to fill this gap in our knowledge and service offerings. Reintegration efforts, for example, often assume that offenders are returning to settings in which they had well-formed, if not meaningful, identities and relationships. A highly valued, highly connected member of a family or community is welcomed back in a way that differs from the reception of a member considered to be more problematic. There is little reason to believe that the person who felt marginalized prior to entering the corrections system feels more empowered and grounded during or after the experience.

The chapters also suggest that there are several issues that should be considered in relationship to the ex-offender and the family, including the following:

- mental health
- substance abuse
- education and schooling
- literacy
- homelessness

These are among the range of problems that are unlikely to be addressed proactively either by the ex-offender or the correctional system during the transition back home. Given the high percentage of inmates who are parents, it is especially unsettling that so little attention is given to care giving—that is, to questions regarding who will provide for the children of the offender during and after incarceration.

Fundamental to any efforts to construct an agenda that helps us determine what works is the creation of policies that recognize the cross-cutting nature of the problems facing offenders and their families—the connections, for example, between and among child welfare, social services, schools and education systems, to name a few. In addition, there is little integration between fatherhood efforts within communities and those within prisons. Moreover, the need for services far exceeds the capacity for prisons to provide such services to fathers or mothers.

For example, of the in-prison fatherhood programs that do exist, most have a very narrow focus—primarily on child support and child-support enforcement—and may undervalue the need for training in education, job skills, and health issues. Program support also needs to be longer term,

Afterword

and, to make the case that these services make a difference. States need access to evaluations of successful models to determine what works.

Practitioners can serve critical roles as translators, conveners, and advocates to help address systemic problems. They can help to *translate* how public policies affect the lives of individuals by articulating the conflicting goals and missions of public and social service agencies and the need for greater interagency communication and coordination. They can serve as *conveners* of efforts within communities that engage their members in determining values and norms and provide new social and economic resources. In addition, they can serve as *advocates* who not only ensure that the concerns of the incarcerated are heard but also identify common ground between the punisher and the punished. However, when considering the various roles of practitioners in serving incarcerated parents and their children, it is essential to acknowledge that they do so in different settings (for example, in social service agencies, in prisons, schools, or communities) and at different levels (at the state level, in local agencies, or in community-based efforts).

How state corrections policies address parenting—fatherhood and motherhood—is emerging as an important issue. Particularly in the case of fatherhood, while a majority of states offer fathering support programs, these efforts tend to be insufficient in scale, episodic rather than ongoing, poorly evaluated, and uncoordinated with fathering efforts in communities (Rethemeyer, Gadsden, Wofford, and Morrison, 2001). The lack of systematic curricula in most cases makes evaluation difficult, which in turn makes it more difficult to prove that fathering support programs have positive impacts on recidivism, reintegration, and child well-being.

In light of this gap, state policymakers must be challenged to ask themselves a number of questions:

- What are some of the best practices for organizing and constructing relationships between state agencies concerned with family support, labor, and child welfare and the criminal justice system?

- Should this coordination be a policy goal?

- If yes, what needs should be addressed and with what indicators of change?

- What are the policy issues that cut across the needs of mothers and fathers around which state agencies might collaborate and operate more effectively?

- How can policymakers think more systematically about the range of existing services and how could they be better coordinated to serve the needs of incarcerated fathers and their families—whether that policy is in welfare reform, child protective services, fatherhood programs, workforce investment, or criminal justice?
- What are the implications of these concepts for Temporary Assistance to Needy Families (TANF) reauthorization?

State policymakers, who determine benchmarks for measuring the outcomes of incarceration and in-prison programs, need to understand incarceration as a life-course event—and to consider its relationship to the ways in which we understand and define notions of parenting. There are many possibilities for paving a pathway. However, among the most promising, as the chapters suggest, are: (1) listening—and paying attention—to the experiences of children of incarcerated parents; (2) paying attention to the experiences of practitioners when designing programs; (3) working to eliminate barriers to parenting while in prison and to reintegrating into one's community upon release; (4) considering issues of abuse and domestic violence; (5) fostering community; (6) refining the notion of outcomes to clarify who is defining them and for whom; (7) helping to articulate the diversity among incarcerated fathers; and (8) understanding practitioners' roles as translators, conveners, and advocates.

Lastly, for research on incarcerated parents and their families to serve practice and policymaking effectively, a number of steps must be taken. Researchers need to find ways to work with practitioners when collecting data to build trust with a population and ask the right questions. They need to develop a broader ecological and conceptual framework for thinking about role transitions surrounding incarceration, within the context of an institution and *vis-à-vis* the family and the community. They need to develop more refined and realistic outcome measures that are tracked over a significant period of time. They also need to incorporate feedback from the community and practitioners into research methodology and design and design data-collection strategies that emerge from everyday settings such as schools, healthcare providers' offices, and public libraries. The objective is to obtain qualitative profiles detailing the experiences of individuals, families, and communities, rather than limiting study to quantitative measures describing a population's demographics and broadly defined outcomes. In particular, information about incarcerated parents and their families must be shared and transferred readily among researchers, practitioners, agencies, funders, and the populations with which they work.

While concerns surrounding incarceration, reintegration, and their impact on communities have drawn considerable attention from policy-makers, practitioners, and researchers over the last decade, it is unclear whether society is willing to view offenders and the impact of incarceration in a more expansive and humane fashion. The pendulum often swings from corrections and punishment to retribution, with the unintended consequence of taking retribution on already vulnerable children and communities. It may be that community corrections generally requires more public outreach and education. The effort to infuse family and community concerns into discussions of incarceration, reentry, reintegration, and criminal justice more broadly defined requires a specific public instructional effort at least as intensive as our research, policy, and programmatic efforts. The key to this public agenda may be to focus on intergenerationality—for example, to invest in children, parents, families, and communities now to effect change over time—and on equity—such as redressing the inequity of sentences meted out to the poor and minorities. Without a greater public appreciation of the costs incarceration imposes on larger society, creating and maintaining a parenting and fathering effort in prisons will be a difficult undertaking at best.

References

Cochran-Smith, M. and S. L. Lytle. 2001. Teacher Learning Communities. In J. Guthrie, ed. *Encyclopedia of Education*. New York: Macmillan.

Rethemeyer, R. K., V. L. Gadsden, J. T. Wofford, and M. Morrison. 2001. State Fathering Efforts in Correctional Settings. Presentation at the Fathers and Families Roundtable Series, *Constructing and Coping with Incarceration and Family Re-Entry: Perspectives from the Field*, National Center on Fathers and Families, University of Pennsylvania.

Travis, J. 2001. Heretical Propositions for Improving Re-Entry. Keynote Address. Fathers and Families Roundtable Series, *Constructing and Coping with Incarceration and Family Re-Entry: Perspectives from the Field*, National Center on Fathers and Families, University of Pennsylvania.

INDEX

A

AA. *See* Alcoholics Anonymous
abolition movement, 244
Aborigines. *See also* ethnicity/race
   community ministries, 8
   criminogenic needs, 262
   culturally sensitive programs, 179, 262
   elders, role of, 180, 262
   family violence training, 180
   federal offenders, 169, 180
   healing lodges, 8, 255, 261-264
   incarcerated population, 261-262
   religious education, 244
   Royal Commission on Aboriginal Peoples, 261
   spousal violence study, 169
abuse predictors, 173-174
abuse, defined, 157. *See also* violence; offenders (violent)
Abusive Beliefs Inventory, 184
Abusive Relationship Inventory, 184
Acquired Immunodeficiency Syndrome (AIDS), 19
active listening, 98
actuarial measures, 164-165. *See also* risk assessment; family violence treatment programs
addictions. *See* substance abuse/use

adjustment disorder, 131
adoption and foster care, 16, 41, 65
Adoptions and Safe Families Act, 141, 142
Adult and Adolescent Parenting Index, 101
African-Americans. *See also* ethnicity/race
   batterer programs, 180
   children of criminal offenders study, 143, 145
   Core Learnings, 61
   culturally sensitive programs, 110, 111, 180-181
   family dynamics, 17
   father, role of, 62, 80
   imprisonment and social identity, 26
   incarceration risk factors and rate, 41, 63
   intergenerational practices, 76
   male marginalization, 62-63
   parent education programs, 105
   war on drugs, 3
Aid to Families with Dependent Children (AFDC), 66
AIDS. *See* Acquired Immunodeficiency Syndrome
Alcoholics Anonymous (AA), 247. *See also* faith-based programming
alcoholism/alcoholics. *See also* substance abuse/use
   alcohol, role in spouse abuse, 173

Index

Alcoholics Anonymous (AA), 247
   inmates, drug and alcohol abuse of, 94
Alpha, 264. *See also* faith-based programming
Alternatives to Violence Program, 265. *See also* faith-based programming
Alvarado, R., 105
Anderson, E., 10
Andrews, D. A., 7, 14-15, 156, 176, 226, 249
Anglican (Episcopal) church, 244
Annie E. Casey Foundation, 29. *See also* family-oriented programs
Antisocial Personality Disorder Checklist, 195
Antisocial Personality Questionnaire, 195
Aquinas, Thomas, 243
Asian-Americans, 105. *See also* ethnicity/race
assessment batteries
   best practices, 185
   program effectiveness, evaluating, 183, 185
attachment, 211-212. *See also* social bond theory
attachment theory, 97. *See also* parent education
Attachments Project. *See* Center for Children of Incarcerated Parents
Attitudes Toward Women Scale, 183-184
autobiographies, 170-171. *See also* family violence treatment programs

B

Babcock, J., 187
Bainbridge, W., 252
Baker, L., 159
Balter, L., 105, 110
Bars None, 265. *See also* faith-based programming
Bates, R., 29
batterers. *See also* offenders (violent)
   antisocial, 169
   individual factors, 173
   profiling, 169
   programs for, 180
   traits, 177
Beck, A. J., 45
Beckett, K., 61
Behavioral Skills Training, 97. *See also* parent education
belief, 211-212. *See also* social bond theory
Big Brothers/Big Sisters, 205, 208, 214, 215
Big Brothers/Big Sisters of the Blue Grass, 224
biophysical model, 160. *See also* violence; offenders (violent)
Bloom, B., 57

Blumenthal, K., 137
Bodnarchuk, M., 184
Boer, D. P., 184
Bonta, J., 7, 156, 176, 249
borderline personality
   batterer profile, 169, 173
   family violence, witness to, 170
Borderline Personality Organization, 195
Bourdouris, J., 96, 29
Boys and Girls Clubs, 205
Braithwaite, J., 31
British Columbia, Grief Recovery Group, 265-266
Bronfenbrenner, U., 91
Brooks, T., 252
Bryson, R., 214, 215
Buddhist, practice in prison, 252. *See also* faith-based programming
Bunston, T., 97
Bureau of Justice Assistance, 29. *See also* family-oriented programs
Bureau of Justice Statistics, 45, 46, 94
Burke, S., 25
Burton, L. M., 76
Bynum, T. S., 47

C

Cadsky, O., 184
Cahn, T. S., 173
California
   foster care studies, 141
   Riverside County Jail, 139
   study bias, 137
California Department of Corrections, 139
Calvin, 243
Canada
   Aboriginal Healing Lodges, 8, 255, 261-264
   chaplain-to-offender ratio, 252
   chaplaincy interventions, 250-251
   church organizations in prison systems, 244
   Circles of Support and Accountability, 255-257
   Commissioner of Corrections, 261
   Community Chaplaincy, 255, 257, 261
   domestic violence survey, 158
   faith groups in offender rehabilitation, 252
   faith-based ministry, 242, 264-265
   Family and Corrections Network, 24
   intimate femicide, 175
   recidivism of male abusers, 172

Statistics Canada, 158
Supreme Court, 261
Canada Correctional Service. *See* Correctional Service of Canada
Canadian Prairie, 262. *See also* Canada; Aborigines
Canon Law, 243
Carr, C., 8
Caspi, A., 173
Catan, L., 125, 129-130
Catholic Church, 244, 245, 246
Center for Children of Incarcerated Parents, 7
  "allo-parent" co-caregiver, 140
  Attachments Project, 139
  children's study, 141-144
  demographics, 140
  guidelines for investigations, 146-147
  intergenerational criminality, 135
  MotherRight Project, 139
  study bias, 137
Center for Social Research, 249
Chaplaincy Division of the Correctional Service of Canada, 254
chaplains. *See* Community Chaplaincy ministries
Charles Mott Foundation, 29. *See also* family-oriented programs
Chase-Lansdale, L., 50
Cheng Gorman, J., 105, 110
child delinquency, 135. *See also* juveniles
child homicide, 159. *See also* family violence
child protective services, 138
Children of Criminal Offenders and Foster Care Study, 141-144, 142t, 143t
children of incarcerated offenders. *See also* incarcerated parents
  academic performance, 128-129, 131
  adoption and foster care, 16, 41, 65
  Attachments Project, 139
  child delinquency, 135
  developmental consequences, 52-53, 56-57
  empirical research, 124-125
  father absence, effect, 40, 42, 56-58, 63
  Great Britain study, 129-130
  isolated offenders, 132-133, 137
  mother-child prison visitation, 131
  MotherRight Project, 139
  parent education programs, 106
  parental incarceration, impact of, 123, 135-136
  preincarceration household patterns, 133-134
  prenatal drug exposure, 130-131
  psychopathology, 131
  reunification with parents, 133-134
  visiting centers, 28
Children of Offenders Study, 125
Christian Council for Reconciliation, 264. *See also* faith-based programming
Christian fundamentalism, practice of, 246
Circles of Support and Accountability (CSA), 255-257. *See also* faith-based programming
Clear, T. R., 41, 52, 253
client-centered theory, 225. *See also* mentors
Clothing Depot, 265. *See also* faith-based programming
cognitive distortions, 173.
cognitive restructuring, 172, 177. *See also* cognitive-behavioral programs
cognitive therapy. *See* cognitive-behavioral programs
cognitive-behavioral programs
  adult offenders, conformity to, 177
  batterers, 177
  criminal recidivism, 175-176
  high-risk offenders, 174
  irrational beliefs, 172
  juvenile clients, 174
  Rational Emotive Behavioral Therapy (REBT), 172
  responsivity principle, 176-177
  risky thinking, 172
  self-talk, 172
  spousal assault, 174
  treatment integrity, 181-182, 186
Cohen, R. S., 69
Cole, K. M., 228
Coleman, J., 3, 4
Colorado, Domestic Violence Screening Instrument (DVSI), 167
commitment, 211-212. *See also* social bond theory
community and restorative justice model, 208. *See also* mentoring programs
Community Chaplaincy ministries. *See also* faith-based programs
  demographics, 258-260
  drop-in centers, 257, 258
  early intervention, 258
  grief, 259
  interventions, 250-251
  mental health, 259
  offender reintegration, 257
  offenders, specialized needs, 258-260

peace bonds, 259
rage interventions, 259
strict release conditions, 259
suicide prevention support, 259
volunteers, 260
community reentry, 24
community-based training programs, 23
comprehensive case management approach, 33
Computerized Lifestyle Assessment Instrument (CLAI), 195
conceptual level matching model, 227. *See also* mentoring programs
Conflict Tactics Scale (CTS2), 185
conjunctive faith, 245. *See also* faith-based programs
control theory, 211. *See also* juveniles; mentoring
Conty, C., 47
cooperative parenting, defined, 68
coparenting, impact of incarceration, 68-69. *See also* incarcerated parents
Core Learnings, 54, 55t, 61
Correctional Service of Canada
    Aboriginal federal offenders, 169, 180
    alcohol, role in spouse abuse, 173
    chaplaincy survey, 251
    Community Chaplaincy, 257
    community ministry, 257, 258
    correctional planning process, 250
    financial support, 260-261
    Offender Intake Assessment, 250
counseling, nondirective, 178
counterconditioning, 179. *See also* offenders (violent); family violence treatment programs
court-mandated programs, 186, 187. *See also* family violence treatment programs
criminal background checks, 21
criminal justice interventions, 187. *See also* offenders (violent); family violence treatment programs
criminal justice populations, 206
criminal recidivism. *See* recidivism
criminogenic needs
    Aborigines, 262
    family violence, 175-176
    intimate violence, 169-170
Cuff, D., 8
Cullen, F. T., 14-15, 213
culturally sensitive programs
    Aborigines, 179, 262
    for African-Americans, 110, 111, 180-181
    in parent education, 105
Cunningham, A., 159

D

Daly, J., 177
Dammer, H., 253
Danger Assessment Scale (DA), 165
Danzinger, S. K., 63
Darity, W. A., 62, 63
Darity-Myers model, 63
Davis, R. C., 188
Delaware, Department of Corrections, 207
delinquent youth. *See* juveniles
depression, 131, 173
desistance, 171, 219
detention and judgment, 65. *See also* offenders (male)
Dick, T., 159
Dickens, C., 214, 215
DiClemente, C. C., 178
Discipleship Seminars, 252. *See also* faith-based programming
Dobash, R. E., 187, 188
Dobash, R. P., 187, 188
domestic homicide, 174. *See also* family violence; domestic violence
Domestic Violence Screening Instrument (DVSI), 167
domestic violence. *See also* family violence; family violence treatment programs
    Canadian survey, 158
    child homicide, 159
    children, as witnesses to, 159-160
    homicide, 174
    incidence, rate of, 158-159, 160
    intimate femicide, 165, 166
    risk assessments, 165
    treatment programs, 156
dominance/isolation, 185
double-quiet dyads, 226. *See also* mentors
Dowden, C., 14-15
Drama (Regional Psychiatric Center-Prairies), 264. *See also* faith-based programming
drop-in centers, 257, 258. *See also* Community Chaplaincy ministries
Drug Abuse Screening Test (DAST), 195. *See also* substance abuse/use
drug use. *See* substance abuse/use; alcoholism/alcoholics

Duluth model, 161, 187. *See also* violence; offenders (violent); family violence treatment programs
Duncan, G., 50
Dutton, D., 160, 162, 165, 184, 187
dynamic risk factors, 249, 250. *See also* faith-based programming
dysthymic disorder, 131

E

Early Childhood Family Education, 91. *See also* parent education
ecological model, 100, 111. *See also* incarcerated parents; parent education
Edin, K., 62
effective correctional intervention, 226. *See also* mentoring programs
egalitarian nonviolent relationship strategies, 161. *See also* family violence
emotional/verbal abuse, 185. *See also* family violence
Emperor Constantine, 243
Emperor Theodosius, 243
Enos, S., 102, 108-109
equality wheel, 161.
Esselstyn, T. C., 128-129
ethnicity/race
  children of offenders' study, 141-144
  cultural sensitivity, 105, 110-111, 262
  intergenerational practices, 76
  La Bodega de la Familia, 33
  parent education programs, 105
  prison population, 110
  risk factors, 41
evolutionary theory, 161. *See also* violence; offenders (violent)
external monitoring, 23-24

F

Fagan, J., 173
faith development, 245. *See also* faith-based programming
faith-based programming
  Aboriginal healing lodges, 8, 255, 261-263
  Alcoholics Anonymous (AA), 247
  chaplain-to-offender ratio, 252
  Christian community influence, 242-243
  Circles of Support and Accountability (CSA), 255-257, 263
  Community Chaplaincy, 255, 263
  culturally sensitive programs, 262
  defined, 246-248
  dynamic risk factors, 249, 250
  faith, significance of, 244-245
  historical perspective, 242-244
  monastic prisons, 243
  offender demographics, 258-260
  program, defined, 248
  Quakers' penitentiaries, 243-244
  recidivism, 252-254, 256, 257
  reductionism, 246, 247
  religiosity, 253
  Salvation Army, 244
  spirituality and health, 251-252
  spirituality and offender rehabilitation, 252
  stages of faith development, 245
  static risk factors, 249
  volunteers, 248, 260
faith-based volunteers, 248. *See also* faith-based programming
family
  advocacy organizations, 24
  African-American, 17
  American, 16
  community reintegration, 65
  conferences, 31
  emotional and social issues, 25-27
  kinscripts, 76
  literacy programs, 95
  male-female relationships, 25
  monitoring of prisoners at home, 23-25
  mother, role of, 16-17
  multigenerational research, 76
  paradigms, 75-76
  reintegration after incarceration, 16-17
  reunification, 18, 19, 20
  role transitions, 71
  social identity after imprisonment, 26
  structural changes, 93
  system, complexity of, 109
  ties during imprisonment, 17-19
Family and Corrections Network, 24, 29
Family Household Study, 49
Family Support Services, 32. *See also* Texas; family-oriented programs
family violence. *See also* violence; offenders (violent); family violence treatment programs
  child homicide, 159
  child protective services, 138
  childhood maltreatment, 170-171
  criminogenic needs, 175-176
  demographic factors, 171-172

INDEX

domestic homicide, 174
drug and alcohol abuse, role of, 94
equality wheel, 161
federal offender, 170
feminist theory, 161, 162
intimate femicide, 175
intimate violence, 157
parent-child attachment, 170
parental attitudes and beliefs, 101
power and control wheel, 161
responsivity principle, 176-179
social and political concerns, 158
spousal violence of Aborigines, 169
family violence perpetrators. *See* offenders (violent)
Family Violence Program description, 191-195
family violence treatment programs
assessment battery, sample, 194t
attrition rate, 177
autobiographies, 170-171
batterer programs, 180
court-mandated programs, 186, 187
diversity, sensitivity to, 179-180
domestic violence, 156, 158, 170
group programs, 186
individual factors, 173-174
mandated treatment programs, 187
meta analyses, 187-188
needs principle, 156, 224
program effectiveness, evaluation of, 183-186, 188
programs, review of, 155-156
responsivity principle, 176-179
substance and alcohol abuse, 172-173
treatment integrity, 181-182
treatment models, 156
victims, needs of, 157-158
family-oriented programs
parent education programs, 89
postincarceration, 28, 31-32
prison-based, 28
Fatherlit Research Database, 54
fathers
employment status, 63
incarcerated. *See* incarcerated fathers; incarcerated parents
indicators for care, 41, 58, 61
noncustodial, 52, 65
nonincarcerated, 64
presence, 56, 61
responsible fathering, 56
risk factors, 41

role transition, 71-74
Fathers and Families Core Learnings, 53-54, 61, 104
fear of abandonment, 169. *See also* offenders (violent); psychopathy
federal prisons. *See also* prisons; state prisons
demographics, 2-3
offenders, 170
parenting education programs, 105
female offenders. *See* offenders (female)
female-headed households, 63
female-on-male violence, 157
feminist model, 161. *See also* violence; offenders (violent)
fictive kin, 17, 79. *See also* African-Americans
filial therapy, 98, 106. *See also* parent education
First Nation, 261. *See also* Canada
Fishel, E., 75
Fisher, J. C., 228
Fishman, L., 25
Florida, prison visits, 18, 19
Fo, W., 214, 219, 223, 225
Forgiveness Group (Regional Psychiatric Center-Prairies), 264, 265. *See also* faith-based programming
foster care
and adoption, 16, 41, 65
multidimensional treatment, 145
Fowler, J., 245
Fragile Families survey, 49, 59
FRAMES approach in family violence treatment/education, 178, 178t
Frankle, S. L., 161, 172
Friedman, S., 128-129
functional family therapy, 145
Furano, K. P., 227

G

Gabora-Roth, N., 7
Gadsden, V. L., xii, 76
Gambling Addiction Reflection Group, 265. *See also* faith-based programming
Gartner, J., 252
gatekeeping, 70
Gelles, R. J., 158, 159
gender correlations
common needs, 107-108
incarcerated parents, 92-94
parent education, 92-94, 107-108
parent programs, designing, 104

280

Gendreau, P., 181, 252
generativity, 58
Georgia, Department of Corrections, 207
Gilgun, J., 95
Glueck, 212
Goal Attainment Scale-Family Violence (GAS-FV), 185. *See also* family violence
Golding, E., 63
Gondolf, E. W., 63, 156, 177, 180, 186, 188
Goodman, G., 214, 225
Goodwin, L., 62
Great Britain study, 129-130
Green, C., 187
Grief Recovery Group, British Columbia, 266. *See also* faith-based programming
grief. *See* Community Chaplaincy ministries
Grossman, F. K., 63

H

Hagan, J., 3, 4, 41, 79, 213
Hairston, C. F.,
  incarceration impact on families, 41, 137
  long-term prisoners, 16
  offender reentry, 5
  parenting education, 94
  parenting programs, 79
  prison-based program objectives, 29
  prisoners' family handbooks, 25
  program effectiveness, 29
Hamberger, L. K., 173
Hanson, K. R., 170, 172, 174, 177
Hardyman, P., 253
Harlow, C. W., 95
Harris, Z., 102
Hart, S. D., 184
Hastings, J. E., 173
Hawkins, D. J., 225
Head Start, 49
healing lodges. *See* Aborigines
hepatitis, 19, 260
Herjanic, B. L., 135
Hickey, E. W., 160
high-risk offenders, 174
Hirschi, T., 211
Hispanics, parent education programs, 105. *See also* ethnicity/race
HIV. *See* Human Immunodeficiency Virus (HIV)
Holston, M. A., 127
home visiting, 145
homosexual relationships, 166. *See also* spousal assault
Hostility Toward Women Scale, 183-184

household patterns, preincarceration, 133-134
Howell, M. J., 170
Human Immunodeficiency Virus (HIV), 260. *See also* Acquired Immunodeficiency Syndrome (AIDS)
Hunt and King, 253
Hunter, S. M., 127, 134

I

Illinois, Safer Foundation, 23
impression management, 184. *See also* offenders (violent); family violence treatment programs
incarcerated fathers. *See also* children of incarcerated parents; incarcerated parents;
  child support, 66
  common needs, 107-108
  employment and joblessness, 61, 63
  father absence, impact of, 40
  father-child relationships, 63, 93-94
  father-mother relationships, 66
  intergenerational learning, 75, 76-77
  noncustodial, 65
  parental differences, 92-94
  primary systemic barriers, 64-65
  prison system barriers, 67
  release and family reentry, 67
  role transitions, 71, 73-74
  statistics, 44
incarcerated mothers. *See also* children of incarcerated parents; incarcerated parents;
  Attachments Project, 139
  common needs, 107-108
  female-headed households, 63
  intergenerational learning, 75
  mother-child bond, 104
  mother-child correctional facilities, 139
  mother-child prison visitation, 131
  MotherRight Project, 139
  parent education experience, 103
  parental differences, 92-94
  prenatal drug exposure, 130-131
  role transitions, 71
incarcerated parents. *See also* children of incarcerated offenders; incarcerated fathers; incarcerated mothers;
  child delinquency, 135
  community issues, 3
  concern for children, 104
  demographics, 89, 94-95

ecological model, 100
education attainment, 95
family violence, 95
impact on children, 89, 269-270
literacy programs, 95
national study, 93
parent education programs, 89
peer facilitators, 98-99
process model, 72
research findings, 126-128, 273
risk factors, 95
social impact, 91
social support systems, 98-99
substance abuse, 94
incarceration
community impact, 1-2
family reintegration, 16-17
intergenerational, 145
societal stigma and impact, 26, 63
statistics, 2-3
systemic barriers, 64, 65-66
Index of Self-Esteem, 101
individuative-reflective faith, 245. *See also* faith-based programs
inmate, second-generation, 75
instrumental provisions, 212
Interfaith Visitation program, 264. *See also* faith-based programming
intergenerational criminality, 135. *See also* incarcerated parents
intergenerational learning, 74-75. *See also* incarcerated parents
International Community Corrections Association (ICCA), x, xi, 4, 244
InterVarsity Press, 265
intimate femicide, 175. *See also* offenders (violent)
intimate violence. *See also* offenders (sexual); offenders (violent)
criminogenic needs, 169-170
demographic factors, 171
intuitive-projective faith, 245. *See also* faith development
Inuit, 261. *See also* Canada; ethnicity/race
Inventory of Beliefs about Wife Beating, 184
involvement, 211-212. *See also* social bond theory
isolated offenders, 132-133, 137

J

Jaffe, P. G., 159
Jeffries, J., 29, 53

Johnson, B. R., 252
Johnston, D., 7, 92, 93, 96, 130
Jones, A., 188
Judaism, practice in prison, 252. *See also* faith-based programming
Juvenile Justice and Delinquency Prevention Act of 1974, 206. *See also* juveniles; mentoring programs
Juvenile Mentoring Program (JUMP), 206
juveniles. *See also* mentoring programs
absent fathers, effect of, 56-58
antisocial peers, 211
cognitive-behavioral interventions, 174
control theory, 211
criminal parents, 211
delinquent youth mentoring programs, 209, 211, 213, 226-227
mentor relationships, 226-227, 228-229, 230
multimodal drug prevention program, 214-215
program resistance, 209
recidivism, reducing rate of, 213, 219
restorative justice model, 31
social skills development, 174
social support, 213

K

Kairos Marathons, 264. *See also* faith-based programming
Kampfner, C., 125, 131
Kantor Kaufman, G., 172
Kass, N., 214, 215
Kelly, L., 253
Kerry, G., 175
kinscripts, 76. *See also* family
Kirby, P., 112
Kling, J., 61
Koban, L. A., 92, 93
Kolman, A. S., 127
Koons, B., 47
Kroner, D. G., 184
Kropp, P. R., 165, 184
Krueger, R. F., 173
Kumpfer, K., 105

L

La Bodega de la Familia, 33. *See also* family-oriented programs; ethnicity/race
Lamb, M. E., 56
Landreth, G., 102
Larson, D., 252

Latinos. *See also* ethnicity/race
    children, study of, 143
    culturally sensitive programs, 110
    father, role of, 62
    incarceration risk factors, 41
Laub, J. H., 212
LeFlore, L., 127
lesbian and gay couples, 157. *See also* offenders (violent)
Level of Service Inventory, Revised (LSI-R), 249, 250
Levesque, D. A., 187
Levine, J. A., 49
Leyton, E., 160
Life Recovery Groups (Stony Mountain Institution), 265. *See also* faith-based programming
Lin, N., 212
Lipsey, M., 189
literacy programs, 95
Lockett, P. W., 79
Los Angeles County,
    Center for Children of Incarcerated Parents, 135, 142
    Children of Criminal Offenders Study, 142-144
low-risk offenders, 174
LSI-R, 249, 250
Luther, 243
Lynch, J. P., 63

M

M2W2, British Columbia, 264. *See also* faith-based programming
Maccoby, E., 224
Maiuro, R. D., 173
male offenders. *See* offenders (male)
Malla, S., 159
mandated treatment programs, 187. *See also* family violence treatment programs
marginalization, 62
marginalized males, 62. *See also* offenders (male); African-Americans
marital therapy, 28
    Mason, P. L., 62
Massachusetts
    Correctional Institution, 208
    Women's Mentoring Program, 208
Massachusetts Department of Corrections, 207
Matthews, B., 8
Mazaheri, N., 159

McBride, B. A., 69
McGowen, B., 137
McGuire, J., 247, 248, 257
McLanahan, S., 59
McLoyd, V. C., 224
Medway, F., 97
Memphis, Tennes*see*, the Work Place, 33-34
men. *See* offenders (male)
Mendoza, S., 16
Menghraj, S., 29
mental health. *See* Community Chaplaincy ministries; psychopathy
mentoring programs
    adult offenders, 218-219
    Big Brothers/Big Sisters, 205, 208, 214, 215, 227
    Big Brothers/Big Sisters of the Blue Grass, 224
    Boys and Girls Clubs, 205
    community and restorative justice model, 208
    conceptual level matching model, 227
    delinquent youth programs, 211, 213, 214-215
    effective correctional intervention, 226
    evaluations, experimental designs, 214, 216t, 217t, 218
    evaluations, nonexperimental designs, 220t, 221t, 222t
    gender, impact on relationships, 224
    importance of, 211, 224
    instrumental and expressive support, 212-213
    justice context, value in, 219, 223, 230
    Juvenile Mentoring Program (JUMP), 206
    limitations of, 229-230
    mentors, role of, 207, 228-229
    modeling theory, 226
    multimodal drug prevention program, 214-215
    National Mentoring Partnership, 208
    needs principle, 224
    offender-focused model, 208
    Oklahoma adult offender program, 209
    Partners Against Crime, 207
    Partners Against Crime Program, 218-219
    Points of Light Foundation, 206
    Positive Role Model Program, 211
    program barriers, 208
    program development, 230-231
    protective factors, 210-211
    recidivism reduction, 213, 219, 230

Index

responsivity principle, 226
restorative justice, 208
social bond theory, 211-212
volunteer recruitment, 209, 227-228
Women's Mentoring Program, 208
YMCA, 205
youth demographics, 223-224
mentors. *See also* mentoring programs
 as advocates, 208
 characteristics, 224-226, 228-229
 client-centered theory, 225
 college students, 215
 developmental relationships, 225, 227-228
 double-quiet dyads, 226
 positive reinforcement, importance of, 225
 prescriptive relationships, 225, 227
 volunteer recruitment, 209, 227-228
 youth, matching with, 226-227, 228-229, 230
meta analyses, 187-188. *See also* family violence treatment programs
Metis, 261. *See also* Canada; ethnicity/race
Mexican-Americans. *See* Latinos; ethnicity/race
Michigan, 36th District Court in Detroit, 207, 218
Michigan Alcoholism Screening Test (MAST), 195
Middle Ages, 243
Miller, W. R., 178
Mincy, R., 69
Minnesota, Early Childhood Family Education, 91
minorities. *See* ethnicity/race
Model Program for Churches and Ex-offenders, 249
modeling theory, 226. *See also* mentoring programs
Moffitt, T. E., 173
Molzahn, D., 8
monastic prisons, 243. *See also* faith-based programming
monitoring, 23-25
Morash, M., 47
Morrow, K. V., 215, 225, 227
Moskos, C., 25
mother-child correctional facilities, 139. *See also* Center for Children of Incarcerated Parents; incarcerated mothers
Mother-Child Correctional Programs (MCCPs), 140
Mother-Child Correctional Programs Symposia, 139, 140

MotherRight Project. *See* Center for Children of Incarcerated Parents
mothers. *See also* incarcerated mothers; offenders (female); offenders (violent)
 careers, 103
 female-headed households, 63
 mother-child bond, 104
 mother-child correctional facilities, 139
 mother-child prison visitation, 131
 MotherRight Project, 139
 role of, 16-17
motivational interviewing, 178, 179
Multi-Health Systems, 167
multidimensional treatment foster care, 145
multimodal drug prevention program, 214-215. *See also* substance use/abuse; mentoring programs
multisystemic therapy, 145
Mumola, C., 48, 93, 94
Muslim, practice in prison, 246, 252. *See also* faith-based programming
Mustin, J., 106
Myers, S. L., 62, 63
mythical-literal faith, 245. *See also* faith-based programs

N

NA. *See* Narcotics Anonymous
narcissistic, 177. *See also* psychopathy; offenders (violent)
Narcotics Anonymous (NA), 259
National Center on Fathers and Families (NCOFF), 54
National Community Chaplaincy, 260
 See also Community Chaplaincy ministries
National Conference of State Legislatures, 66
National Institute of Health, 218-219. *See also* mentoring programs
National Longitudinal Study of Youth (NLSY), 49, 61
National Mentoring Partnership, 220
Native Americans, 105, 110. *See also* ethnicity/race, 110
needs principle, 156, 168-169, 224
negative social capital, 3
Nelson, M., 23
nested ecological model, 162, 163t. *See also* family violence treatment programs
New Testament, 242
New York
 City Jail, 207
 La Bodega de la Familia, 33

noncustodial fathers, 65
nondirective counseling, 178
nonequivalent criminal justice interventions, 187. *See also* offenders (violent)
nonincarcerated fathers, 64. *See also* incarcerated fathers
North American Multidisciplinary Conference on Spirituality, 251
Nurse, A., 17, 25

O

O'Connor, T., 249, 252, 254
O'Donnell, C., 214, 219, 223, 225
Offender Intake Assessment, 250
offender-focused model, 208. *See also* mentoring programs
offenders (female). *See also* incarcerated mothers; offenders (violent)
    community reentry, 20-23
    family process variables, 14-15
    family reunification, 18, 19, 20
    incarcerated fathers, distinction from, 47, 59, 60
    motherhood demographics, 59
    mothers, role of, 16-17
    parenting programs, 79
offenders, high-risk, 174, 189. *See also* offenders (violent)
offenders (juvenile). *See* juveniles
offenders, low-risk, 164. *See also* offenders (violent)
offenders (male). *See also* incarcerated fathers; offenders (sexual); offenders (violent)
    abuse by, 157
    community reentry, 20-23
    distinction from incarcerated mothers, 47, 59, 60
    evaluation of mentoring programs, 218-219
    family reunification, 18, 19, 20
    father absence, impact of, 40
    fatherhood program, 33
    fatherhood roles, 48-50
    marginalized males, 62
    mentoring relationships, 226, 229, 230
    mothers, role of, 16-17
    noncustodial fathers, 52, 65
    prison and community-based programs, 29
    release and family reentry, 67
offenders (sexual)
    intrapsychic features, 162-163
    recidivism studies, 256
    registry, 21
    treatment programs, 156
offenders (violent)
    abuse predictors, 173-174
    avoidant traits, 177
    batterers, 177
    child homicide, 159
    childhood history, 170
    criminal lifestyle factors, 174-175
    family violence perpetrator strategies, 179
    female partner, abuse of, 157
    female-on-male violence, 157
    individual factors, 173-174
    interpersonal violence, 187
    intimate violence, 157
    lesbian and gay couples, 157
    narcissistic, 177
    nonequivalent criminal justice interventions, 170
    relapse prevention plan, 182
    reoffending rate, 184
    same-sex violence, 157
    self-regulation, 174
    sexist roles, 172
    substance and alcohol abuse, 172-173
    theoretical models, 160-163
Office of Juvenile Justice and Delinquency Prevention (OJJDP), 218
Ogbu, J., 79
Ogloff, J. R. P., 184
Oklahoma
    adult offender mentoring program, 209
Oklahoma Department of Corrections, 207
oppositional-deviant disorder, 131
Oregon, Center for Social Research, 249
organized religion, influence, 244. *See also* faith-based programming
outing, 157. *See also* offenders (violent)
Overcomers Twelve Step Program, 266. *See also* faith-based programming
Overnight Family Accommodation (Grand Cache Institution), 265. *See also* faith-based programming
overnight family visits, 28. *See also* prison-based programs

P

Palm, G., 6, 104
Paradise, L., 112
parent education. *See also* incarcerated fathers incarcerated mothers; incarcerated parents

Index

Behavioral Skills Training, 97
beliefs and attitudes, 99, 101
child development, 101-102
cultural values, 105, 262
defined, 90-91
developmental stages, child and parent, 106
family literacy programs, 95
filial therapy, 106
Parent Effectiveness Training (PET), 97-98
peer parent educator, 108
program intensity, 110
racial/ethnic diversity, 105
research, 101-103
self-development, 98
self-esteem, 98, 101
statistics, 96
STEP, 97-98
studies on fathers, 113t, 115t
studies on mothers, 113t, 114t
Parent Effectiveness Training (PET), 97-98. *See also* parent education
parent-child contact. *See also* children of incarcerated parents, 57
parenthood, process model, 72
parenting alliance, 69
Parenting Group (Regional Psychiatric Center-Prairies), 265. *See also* faith-based programming; Canada
Parenting Stress Index (PSI), 101
parents, incarcerated. *See* incarcerated parents
Parikh, C., 249, 254
Partners Against Crime Program, 207, 218. *See also* mentoring programs
paternal care giving, 58. *See also* children of incarcerated parents
patriarchal societies, 161. *See also* family violence
Paul Deception Scale, 195
PCL-R. *See* Psychopathy Checklist-Revised
peace bonds, 259
Pearson, J., 66
peer parent educator, 108
Perpetrator Assessment Handbook, 165
perpetrator's intrapsychic features, 162-163. *See also* offenders (sexual); offenders (violent)
Perryclear, M., 254
Person to Person, 264. *See also* faith-based programming; Canada

Personal Responsibility and Work Opportunity Reconciliation Act (PRWORA), 43, 50, 65, 66
Philadelphia, "What Works" ICCA Research Conference, xi
Pitt, E., 49
Planning Process, 250
Points of Light Foundation, 206
Poisson, S., 159
Pollack, W. S., 63
Porter Parental Acceptance Scale, 101
Positive Role Model Program, 211. *See also* mentoring programs
postrelease success. *See* recidivism
power and control wheel, 161. *See also* family violence
Power, T., 177
prayer support, 260. *See also* faith-based programming
predictors, abuse, 173-174
preincarceration household patterns, 133-134
prenatal drug exposure, 130-131. *See also*; children of incarcerated offenders; substance abuse/use
prescriptive relationships, 225, 227. *See also* mentoring programs; mentors
President Bush, 244
primal faith, 245. *See also* faith-based programs
Prison Fellowship, 264. *See also* faith-based programming
Prison Fellowship Ministries, 252
Prison Pause, 265. *See also* faith-based programming
prison system
    abolition movement, 244
    ethnic minority populations, 110
    faith programs, commitment, 253-254
    long-term prisoners, 16
    monastic, 243
    mother-child prison visitation, 131
    populations increases, 206
    programs, 28
    release rules, 67
    religious practices, 252
    role transitions, 73
    system barriers, 67
    visitation, 18
prisoners, long-term, 16. *See also* Hairston, C. F.
process model of parenthood, 72

Prochaska, J. O., 178
procriminal peers, 174, 175
Project Art Lab, 265. *See also* faith-based programming
Project RIO, 23
Propensity for Abuse Scale (PAS), 167
psychological abuse, 185. *See also* violence
psychopathy
    adjustment disorder, 131
    bipolar disorders, 259
    borderline personality, 170
    depression, 131, 259
    dysthymic disorder, 131
    in children, 131
    narcissistic, 177
    oppositional-deviant disorder, 131
    schizophrenia, 259
    suicide prevention support, 259
    traumatic stress reactions, 131
Psychopathy Checklist-Revised, 165, 195
public housing, 21
Puerto Ricans, 76. *See also* ethnicity/race
Pugliesi, K. L., 170

Q

Quakers
    penitentiaries, 243-244
    prison abolition movement, 244
quasi-experimental evaluations, 186, 188. *See also* family violence treatment programs

R

race/ethnicity. *See* ethnicity/race
racial/ethnic diversity, 105
Radin, N., 63
rage interventions, 259
Raine, A., 126, 133, 135
Ranes, T. R., 69
Rappaport, R., 74
Rational Emotive Behavioral Therapy (REBT), 172
recidivism.
    adult offenders, 218-219
    batterers, males, 163
    cognitive behavioral treatment, 175
    demographic factors, 171
    faith programs, impact, 252-254, 256, 257
    family impact, 14-15
    family violence, treatment effect of, 162
    posttreatment, 175
    re-arrest, 3
    risk assessment, 164
    sex offenders study, 256
    spousal assault, 172
    treatment integrity, 182, 184, 188
    youth, 213, 219
reductionism, 246, 247. *See also* faith-based programming
reflective practice, 112. *See also* parent education
Reformation period, 243
Regional Psychiatric Center-Prairies, 264-266. *See also* faith-based programming
reintegration. *See also* mentoring programs
    community issues, 3
    housing, 21
    incarceration, end point of, 271
    program models, 30-34
Reiss, D., 75-76
relapse prevention plan, 182. *See also* offenders (violent)
Relationship Style Questionnaire, 195
religiosity, 253. *See also* faith-based programming
reoffending rate, 184
responsivity principle, 226. *See also* mentoring programs
restorative justice, 208. *See also* mentoring programs
restorative justice models. *See also* family-oriented programs
    delinquent act/crime, 31
    juveniles, 30
Rethemeyer, R., 5
reunification, 133-134
Rhode Island, Positive Role Model Program, 211
risk assessment
    clinical judgment, 164
    spousal assault, 165
risk principle, 156, 164. *See also* family violence treatment programs
Robie, C., 187
Robins, L. N., 135
Robinson, D., 160, 170, 173, 174
Rogers, Carl, 225
role play, 172
Rollnick, S., 178
Roman Empire, 243
Rooney, J., 177
Rose, D. R., 41, 52
Rosen, B., 252
Rosenfeld, B. D., 187

INDEX

Royal Commission on Aboriginal Peoples, 261. *See also* Canada; Aborigines
Russia, incarceration rate, 2
Ryan, P., 249, 254

S

Sabol, W. J., 63
Safer Foundation, 23
Salvation Army, 244
same-sex violence, 157
Sampson, R. J., 212
Saskatoon Christian Centre, 264. *See also* faith-based programming
Saunders, D. G., 159
Scotland, recidivism prevention in, 15
second-generation inmate, 175
self-development, 98. *See also* parent education
self-esteem, 98. *See also* parent education
self-report attitudinal measures, 183-186
sex offender registries, 21. *See also* offenders (sexual); offenders (violent)
sexual offender. *See* offenders (sexual)
sexually transmitted diseases, 260
Seymour, C., 46
Shapiro, C., 253
Sharp, S., 16
Sherman, L. W., 215
Shipley Institute of Living Scale, 195
Showers, J., 100, 102
Sikh, practice in prison, 252. *See also* faith-based programming
social bond theory, 211-212. *See also* mentoring programs
social learning strategies, 211
social learning theory, 160. *See also* violence
social support systems, 98-99. *See also* incarcerated parents
social work models, 31. *See also* reintegration; family-oriented programs
Solicitor General, 262. *See also* Canada
Sonkin, D. G., 165
Sounding the Depths, 266. *See also* faith-based programming
South Carolina Department of Probation, Parole, and Pardon Services, 25
spirituality and health, 251-252. *See also* faith-based programming
spousal assault. *See also* domestic violence
 abuse predictors, 173-174
 criminal lifestyle factors, 174-175
 homosexual relationships, 166
 risk assessment, 166-167, 170
 self-regulation, 174
 sexist roles, 166
 substance and alcohol abuse, 172-173
Spousal Assault Relationship Assessment (SARA). *See also* spousal assault; domestic violence
 DVSI, comparison to, 167
 PCL-R comparison to, 167
 risk factors, 166-167
Spousal Assault Risk Assessment (guide), 166, 167, 195
spousal homicide, 165-166. *See also* domestic violence; offenders (violent)
Sprauer, M. W., 252
Spring, J. B., 102
St. Luke's Renewal Center, Nova Scotia, 264. *See also* faith-based programming
Stack, C. B., 76, 79
Stanton, A., 127, 129, 137
state prisons
 demographics, 2-3
 parent education programs, 105
static risk factors, 249. *See also* faith-based programming
Statistics Canada, 158, 173. *See also* Canada
Steinmetz, S. K., 159
Steps to Security (Drumheller Institution), 266. *See also* faith-based programming
Stewart, L., 7
Stony Mountain Institution, 265-266. *See also* faith-based programming
Stout, B., 253
Straus, M. A., 158, 159, 172
strict release conditions. *See* Community Chaplaincy ministries
Styles, M. B., 215, 225, 227
subsidized housing rules, 21
substance abuse/use. *See also* alcoholism/alcoholics
 chaplaincy interventions, 250-251
 drugs, war on, 3
 inmates, drug and alcohol abuse, 94
 multimodal drug prevention program, 214-215
 prenatal exposure, 130-131
 spousal abuse, role in, 172-173
 treatment, 156
Suderman, M., 159
Sugarman, D. B., 161, 172
suicide prevention support, 259. *See also* Community Chaplaincy ministries

Sullivan, M. L., 213
Supreme Court of Canada, 261. *See also* Canada
synthetic-conventional faith, 245. *See also* faith-based programs
Systematic Training for Effective Parenting (STEP)
    culturally sensitive programs, 110
    parenting skills training, 97-98

T

Taylor, B. G., 188
Taylor, J., 160, 170, 173, 174
Taylor, V., 25
team parenting, 68
Temporary Assistance to Needy Families (TANF), 43, 273
Terry, C. W. III., 207
Texas
    Family Support Services, 32
    Project RIO, 23
    University of Texas at Austin School of Social Work, 32
Texas Department of Criminal Justice, 32
theoretical treatment model, 162. *See also* family violence treatment programs
Thoennes, N., 66
Todres, R., 97
Tolman's Psychological Maltreatment of Women Scale, 185
traumatic stress reactions, 131
Travis, J., 3, 271
treatment programs
    domestic violence, 156
    feminist-focused, 162
    foster care, multidimensional, 145
    integrity, 181-182
    sex offender, 156
    substance abuse, 156
Trone, J., 23
tuberculosis, 19

U

United (Methodists) church, 244
United Nations, 252
United States
    Department of Justice, 45
    domestic violence, 158, 172
    faith groups in offender rehabilitation, 252
    Family and Corrections Network, 24, 29
    incarceration rate, 2
    mentoring programs, 210

sex offender registries, 21
universalizing faith, 245. *See also* faith-based programs
University of Calgary Faculty of Medicine, 251
University of Illinois, community-based programs, 29
University of Maryland, mentoring evaluations, 214
University of Pennsylvania, 54

V

Vera Institute of Justice study, 29. *See also* family-oriented programs
verbal/emotional abuse, 185. *See also* family violence
victim mediation, 31. *See also* restorative justice model; family-oriented programs
victims. *See* offenders (violent); family treatment programs.
violence. *See also* family violence treatment programs; intimate violence; offender (violent)
    psychological abuse, 185
violent offenders. *See* offenders (violent)
visitation in prison, 18
visiting centers, 28. *See also* prison-based programs
Vitaliano, P. P., 173
voluntary paternity acknowledgment form, 66
volunteer recruitment, 209, 227-228. *See also* mentors

W

Wallace-Capretta, S., 170, 172, 174
war on drugs, 3. *See also* substance use/abuse
warrant expiry date offenders (WED), 258
WED offenders. *See* warrant expiry date offenders
Weissman, S. H., 69
West, P. A., 135
Western, B., 59, 61
Wiccan, practice in prison, 252. *See also* faith-based programming
Williams, O., 180
Women's Mentoring Program, 208. *See also* mentoring programs; offenders (female)
women, abuse of. *See* spousal assault
women. *See also* gender correlations; incarcerated mothers; offenders (female)
    community reentry, 20-23

    demographics, 59
    female-headed households, 63
    intergenerational learning, 75
Wong, S., 184
Work Place, 33.
Wright Adjustment Scale, 253
Wright, J. P., 14-15
Wright, K., 252, 254

Y
Yang, F., 254
Yllo, K. A., 172
YMCA, 205
Young, M., 252
Youth Authority, 127

Z
Zalba, S., 127, 133, 134, 137, 138

About the Authors

Contributors

Dr. Vivian L. Gadsden, the editor of this volume, is director of the National Center on Fathers and Families, graduate group chair, and associate professor in the Graduate School of Education at the University of Pennsylvania. Throughout her career, Dr. Gadsden has been committed to improving the well-being of children and their families. Her research focuses on intergenerational family development, learning, and literacy, and the implications of fathers' and mothers' interactions with children across the life-course within diverse cultural and ethnic groups and for families living in poverty. A significant area of her work explores the nature and development of responsible fathering, particularly among low-income, minority fathers, and the effects on children, families, and communities. In 1994, Dr. Gadsden became the director of the National Center on Fathers and Families, an interdisciplinary policy research center committed to deepening research and practice on fathers and families. From then until now, she has been at the forefront of moving this critical topic into the national limelight and of bringing together the voices and efforts of researchers and practitioners to improve policy affecting children, families, and communities. Under her leadership, the National Center on Fathers and Families has conducted a variety of research studies; initiated a national roundtable series, the Fathers and Families Roundtable; and created a nationally renowned database, the FatherLit Database. The National Center on Fathers and Families also has been a part of efforts, ranging from the White House's and federal government's initiatives on fathers and families to local initiatives on fathers,

About the Authors

children, and families. Dr. Gadsden is a nationally known researcher with numerous publications on issues related to families and parents, children's learning, race, and culture. Her current research projects include a four-generation study on African-American families, focusing on the transfer of knowledge and beliefs from mothers and fathers to children; a parent-child Head Start project with African-American and Puerto Rican families; a project with young, urban fathers; and a policy study on state fatherhood initiatives within state correctional systems.

Reverend Chris Carr recently retired as the director general of the chaplaincy division of Correctional Service of Canada in Ottawa, Ontario. He was the principal negotiator with the Interfaith Committee on Chaplaincy, and he developed the Code of Professional Conduct for Chaplains. Reverend Carr promoted different forms of program evaluation in chaplaincy, including prison-marriage research and a religious education program for prisoners with substance abuse problems. In addition, he promoted the development of community chaplaincy with a comprehensive report, standards, and Circles of Support and Accountability. He also edited a history of chaplaincy in Canadian penitentiaries, *A Living History*.

Dr. Dwight Cuff is the senior project officer for performance assurance in the chaplaincy division of Correctional Service of Canada in Abbotsford, British Columbia. He has worked for the Correctional Service of Canada for more than eleven years. For seven years, he was a contract chaplain at Kent Institution, a maximum-security institution in British Columbia. After that, he was co-regional chaplain in the Pacific Region, where he supervised chaplaincy services in British Columbia. He is currently piloting a research project designed to evaluate and measure the impact of chaplaincy on offenders, offender families, ex-offenders, staff, and the community. Dr. Cuff has a Master of Theological Studies from the Atlantic School of Theology and a Doctor of Ministry from Bethel Theological Seminary. His doctoral research was in the area of male spirituality. He is an active member of the Salvation Army.

Natalie Gabora-Roth is a project officer for the Family Violence Prevention Programs in the Canadian Federal Correctional System.

Creasie Finney Hairston, Ph.D., is professor and dean of the Jane Addams School of Social Work at the University of Illinois-Chicago and a program development and research consultant on programs and services for poor children and families. She received her MSSA and Ph.D. degrees from Case Western Reserve University. Prior to her current position, she served as associate dean of the Indiana University School of Social Work and served on the faculties of the University of Tennessee, West Virginia University, and the State University of New York at Albany. Dr. Hairston is recognized nationally for her leadership in promoting family-oriented correctional policies and programs and institutional and community partnerships that address broad social services and criminal justice goals. Her articles have appeared in leading academic journals and textbooks and in publications for practitioners and the general public. Her recent works include a co-edited volume of the journal *Child Welfare*, focusing on incarcerated parents and their children, and a co-edited book of research, *Kinship Care: Improving Practice through Research*, published by the Child Welfare League of America.

Denise Johnston, M.D., is cofounder, along with Katherine Gabel, of the Center for Children of Incarcerated Parents in Eagle Rock, California and director of the Childhood Trauma Project, a program of research and development services for children in foster care, conducted jointly by the Center for Children of Incarcerated Parents and The Casey Family Program. Dr. Johnston is a founding member of the board of directors of the Girls in Gangs Task Force, a coalition of professionals and community organizations addressing the needs of incarcerated female juveniles in Los Angeles County. She is also a founding member of Justice Partners, the first advocacy organization in Los Angeles County addressing the issues of women in the criminal justice system. Dr. Johnston is a consultant to both the Task Force on Drug-Endangered Children, providing curriculum development and training to California's Office of Criminal Justice Planning, and the California Department of Corrections' Community Prisoner Mother Program, providing staff training on childhood trauma, child development assessments, and evaluation of attachment among prisoners and their children. She received her M.D. from the Stanford University School of Medicine. Dr. Johnston's recent works include a coauthored book, *Children of Incarcerated Parents* (1995), published by Lexington Books, and a forthcoming book, *Working with Criminal Offenders and their Children*.

Betsy A. Matthews is assistant professor in the Department of Correctional and Juvenile Justice Studies at Eastern Kentucky University. She earned her Master of Arts in applied behavioral science from Wright

About the Authors

State University in Dayton, Ohio. She is currently pursuing a doctoral degree in criminal justice from the University of Cincinnati. Ms. Matthews has worked as a probation officer in Greene County, Ohio, and as a research associate with the American Probation and Parole Association in Lexington, Kentucky. In 1999, she joined the faculty in the Department of Correctional and Juvenile Justice Studies at Eastern Kentucky University. Her primary areas of interest are community corrections and correctional rehabilitation. She has been involved in the evaluations of two intensive supervision programs, a drug court program, and three residential substance abuse treatment programs. Ms. Matthews has also conducted more than forty assessments of adult and juvenile corrections programs using the Correctional Program Assessment Inventory (CPAI). She is currently conducting a study of Big Brothers/Big Sisters of the Bluegrass to examine the characteristics that contribute to the development of a strong social bond between youths and mentors and to explore how the strength of that social bond affects youths' involvement in delinquency.

Reverend David David Molzahn, Ph.D., is special advisor to the director general (Community Ministries) in the chaplaincy division of Correctional Service of Canada in Ottawa, Ontario. His areas of responsibility include community chaplaincy corrections, Circles of Support and Accountability, and volunteer development. He earned his Master of Theological Studies in counseling and a Ph.D. in religion and society. For the past fifteen years, Rev. Molzahn has been involved in various community ministries in different parts of Canada, including delivery of treatment programs for family violence, sex offenders, and grief and loss. In addition, he has provided public presentations on various topics relating to community corrections and grief and loss.

Glen F. Palm, Ph.D., is professor of child and family studies at St. Cloud State University and senior research scientist at the National Center on Fathers and Families. He developed the parent education licensure program at St. Cloud State University and teaches courses in child development, family studies, and parent education. Dr. Palm also coordinates The Dad Project, a local initiative of the Early Childhood Family Education program that focuses on supporting male involvement in the lives of young children. As a researcher/practitioner, he has studied ethics in parent and family education, fathers' perceptions of attachment, the parent education needs of incarcerated fathers, and the role of fatherhood in influencing men's values and moral and religious beliefs. He has also served as a local program evaluator for Early Head Start, Even Start Family Literacy, and Early Childhood Family Education programs. Dr. Palm was co-editor of the book *Working with Fathers: Methods and Perspectives* (1993), and has contributed chapters on fatherhood to a number of books including a recent chapter on parent education for incarcerated fathers in *Clinical and Educational Interventions with Fathers* (2001).

Dr. Lynn Stewart is the manager of Living Skills, Counter-Point and Family Violence Prevention Programs for the Correctional Service of Canada. She has worked as a correctional psychologist in several different capacities and settings, including an institution with federally sentenced male offenders and in a facility for women in England. She spent ten years as a regional community psychologist coordinating psychological services for male and female offenders on conditional release. Recently, she developed the high- and moderate-intensity family violence prevention programs and post-program maintenance manuals for federal offenders with histories of violence against intimate partners and oversaw their national implementation. These programs were accredited by an international accreditation panel in march 2001 as programs likely to be effective in reducing criminal recidivism. Dr. Stewart is involved in research on program effectiveness, motivating offenders for change, and family violence intervention.

Dr. R. Karl Rethemeyer is assistant professor of public administration at the Rockefeller College of Public Affairs and Policy at the State University of New York-Albany and senior research scientist at the National Center on Fathers and Families at the University of Pennsylvania. Dr. Rethemeyer, a recent graduate of the Kennedy School of Government at Harvard University, has worked on several National Center on Fathers and Families projects related to fathering and families, including the Urban Fathers Project (which focuses on the experiences of young urban fathers), the BAyFIDS project (which explores the nature and scope of public and private fathering support efforts in the San Francisco Bay Area), and the Incarcerated Fathers Project (which surveyed state-led efforts to provide fathering support in prisons). Dr. Rethemeyer has also conducted research on the nature and degree of integration between public and private social service efforts and the use of technology for adult literacy instruction. He is author and coauthor of several published and forthcoming works on fathers and families.